A central theme of Jonathan Andr
from the Middle East is the for
minorities who have been hunte(
genocide that had its origins in t
breaking for communities that hav
wrenched from the soil and the homes that they love. But violent
disruption also has consequences for majority communities that lose
diversity and become monochrome and less tolerant places. Anyone
wanting to understand why, despite all of their suffering, these ancient
communities want to stay in their homelands, should read Jonathan
Andrews' book.

Lord David Alton, Professor the Lord Alton of Liverpool

In this excellent book, Jonathan Andrews takes us on a difficult journey
with the refugees, the displaced, the oppressed and the asylum seekers.
In this journey we see their tears, hear their groans and touch their
wounds. When I finished reading this book I could not stop thinking of,
"how can we stop this misery?"

**Mouneer Anis, Anglican Bishop of Egypt with N.Africa and the
Horn of Africa**

This timely book addresses one of the key presenting challenges of our
time and manages to do so in a succinct and readable format. This is all
the more remarkable in view of the complexity of the subject and the
fact that Andrews has tackled all the various forms of regional migration,
not just the ones that make the headlines. He also succeeds in
maintaining nuance and rigour as he leads us through the subject, while
using documented individual case histories to illustrate his points and
add colour to the analysis.

There are 21 million refugees in the world today, according to the
UN. In addition to these 21 million people, another 44 million people
are displaced within their own countries. Yet we discover, as Andrews
documents, the hazardous migrant routes across the Sahara and
Mediterranean, that at least as many migrants from Africa are fleeing the
effect of climate change on agriculture as are those fleeing conflict or
religious persecution.

The latter topic is dear to Andrews' heart and he covers well such
issues as why Middle East church leaders are asking outsiders to help
enable believers to stay rather than helping them to emigrate. This
requires changes to the prevailing governance and culture to be
welcoming, respectful and inclusive of all, to regard diversity as an asset
that enriches the whole for the benefit of all. One prominent call in the
book is for indigenous people of goodwill, including Christians, to
contribute to creating such environments wherever they are. And amidst

all the suffering, Andrews helps us to see that there are already positive signs of various sorts—and indeed that God is at work in the Middle East.

David Taylor, Editor of Lausanne Global Analysis, chair of trustees, Christian Solidarity Worldwide (CSW)

Last Resort is a vital resource for the global church as it responds to the massive people movements of today. Jonathan's analysis is important in highlighting the complexity of migration and displacement, teasing out specific dynamics, trends and impacts among various communities of the Middle East, and raising nuanced questions about how the body of Christ should engage in regions of origin, transit locations and arrival points. As we better understand the distinctives of categories such as religious persecution, economic migration and conflict displacement, we are better equipped to respond with appropriate sensitivity and strategy. Crucially, Jonathan's assessment is grounded in the human dimension. The rich case studies, drawn from his long engagement in the Middle East, are vital reminders that this is about the lives and dignity of children, women and men made in the image of God. As global phenomena, migration and displacement have a worldwide human impact—so *Last Resort* is for us all!

Daniel Hoffman, Executive Director, Middle East Concern

We're indebted to Jonathan for a thorough, wide-ranging and sympathetic survey of the realities displaced people face. *Last Resort* will help you understand their challenges, welcome and serve them, engage with the wider global issues that constrain them, and support Middle East Christians and Churches as they respond and minister to so many people on the move.

Canon Mike Parker, Middle East Director SIM

One of the novelties of this book lies in connecting migration with issues of religious freedom or belief. It distinguishes itself from other books on migration and the Middle East by considering what role religion plays in migration to and from the Middle East and North Africa and beyond. In particular it recognises violations of religious freedom, outright persecution and genocidal acts as a major source of migration. From other books on freedom of religion and belief or on religious persecution it differs by looking at the issues from the angle of migration in its multitude and complexity of aspects. It is backed by years of experience and research. It is a unique and very commendable resource that is a must read for practitioners in the field of migration, the Middle East and freedom of religion or belief.

Prof. Dr. Christof Sauer, Evangelische Theologische Faculteit Leuven, Belgium

Last Resort

Migration and the

Middle East

*To Peter and Christine
with heart felt thanks for your
encouragement and prayer over many years.*

Jonathan Andrews

Jonathan

Oct 2017

GILEAD
B O O K S
PUBLISHING

First published in Great Britain, October 2017
by Gilead Books Publishing

2 4 6 8 10 9 7 5 3 1

British Library Cataloguing-in-Publication Data:
A catalogue record for this book is available from the British
Library.

ISBN-13: 978-1-9997224-0-1

Cover design: Nathan Ward

Dedication

To those of any faith or none who are
involved in giving the forcibly displaced
and other vulnerable migrants a sense of
home and hope.

Also by Jonathan Andrews:

Identity Crisis: Religious Registration in the Middle East
(2016, Gilead Books Publishing)

CONTENTS

Acknowledgements

Specific thanks to those who have read drafts of this book in whole or in part, and whose comments and suggestions have invariably been helpful – including Stephen Carter, Malcolm Catto, Rob Cook, Gordon Grüneberg, Barbara Hall, Daniel Hoffman, David Hunt, Martin Leonard, David Meakin, Alison Pascoe, Nik Ripken and Robert Sutton as well as the staff of Church Response for Refugees.[1] The final text is improved because of the time and insights offered by each contributor.

Appendix 1 is included with the kind permission of the facilitator and chairperson of the Religious Liberty Partnership (RLP).[2]

My sincere thanks and appreciation to Caro McIntosh for generating the maps which she did using QGIS and includes data from http://www.gadm.org

I remain appreciative of the numerous people over many years who have shared part of their journey through life with me, especially those which involve

---

[1] www.forrefugees.uk (accessed 3rd March 2017)
[2] www.rlpartnership.org (accessed 19th May 2017)

an element of migration. Some are summarised in this book, but more generally they have enriched my understanding of how migration affects the lives of those involved, and how it shapes the context for succeeding generations. I am also indebted to the many people from across the Middle East and North Africa who have shared their stories and insights into this rich and diverse part of the planet we share, and similarly grateful to those of many nationalities and backgrounds who have shared their experiences of travelling, observing, working and connecting with this region. Perspectives and observations by people from different continents are always instructive.

My thanks also to Chris Hayes at Gilead Books Publishing, whose expertise in publishing I have greatly appreciated. Finally, and perhaps most importantly, thanks are due to my wife, Wendy, for her support throughout the trials and tribulations of condensing this vast topic into what I trust is a manageable and presentable contribution.

Introduction

This book examines the patterns of migration within, through and from the Middle East, a region which has been at the crossroads of continents and on major trade routes throughout recorded history, as it is today. The Middle East continues to be significant in global trade and migration, with literally millions of people moving to the region as migrant workers, especially to the countries of the Arabian Peninsula.

The Middle East has been fought over by major powers for many centuries. Violence continues to reshape society in some places, notably Iraq (since 1990) and Syria (since 2011), prompting mass displacement of peoples within their own countries as well as to neighbouring lands and beyond. In Iraq's case, we ask whether sectarian conflict or a 'brain drain' has had the greater impact. In Syria's case, we note that conflict has brought people to the region as fighters, suppliers, support staff and humanitarian workers. In the wider Arab world, forcible displacement arises from conflict in parts of Yemen (notably since 2015), Libya (since 2011), and Sudan, as well as parts of other countries.

At one level, migration is the story of humanity. Some people have always been on the move, seeking adventure, exploration, new opportunities,, an escape from natural disasters, to avoid oppression and persecution, to reduce pressure on limited resources, or simply to find a better life. It's important to note this variety of motivations, the fact that some choose to migrate while others feel obliged to do so, and that the distinctions are not always clear. Some choose to remain and endure what others regard as too oppressive and believe forces them to leave. We can say that some are pushed to leave while others are pulled to go elsewhere. For many who migrate there are both *push* and *pull* factors; reasons to leave the place they are – *push* factors – and an assortment of aspirations, knowledge and desires that make a certain destination attractive – what *pulls* people towards somewhere else. Different people faced with the same circumstances make different decisions.

Forced displacement is experienced by all too many people, a consequence of natural disasters, violent conflicts, or oppression and persecution. The latter can have political, ethnic, linguistic, cultural or religious roots; in many cases trying to be definitive is less than helpful, since a variety of motivations combine to form a potent cocktail of marginalisation, ostracism, oppression and physical violence that causes some people to flee.

The Middle East is no exception to the global trends for short, medium and long-term migration. Increasing urbanisation is reshaping parts of the Middle East and the wider Arab world. Poor governance causes oppression and marginalisation of certain people in some places. The twentieth century saw several examples of forced mass migrations within the Middle East; the region continues to live with the consequences of the dispersal of Armenians and Palestinians, as well as Jewish migration within and to the region.

Migration is not always clear-cut. For example, a friend arrived in a foreign country legally, was exploited by the system in general and marginalised by those of his own nationality, and lost his legal status before finding work with employers who treated him well. He came as a student and completed his first year of study but was unable to register for the second year. This story, which we shall look at in more detail in Chapter 4, introduces us to the idea of 'irregular' as well as 'regular' migration (terminology that is, importantly, gentler than 'illegal' and 'legal'). It also gives us an example of the movement of people of limited means, as distinct from the movement of highly paid senior executives and high profile sports stars. In 2013 Mark Carney, a Canadian, became Governor of the Bank of England. David Beckham was a soccer player who worked in Spain, the USA, Italy and France as well as his native England during his playing career. By contrast, people who are fleeing natural disasters or man-made conflict typically enter a neighbouring country by irregular means in search of safety; in many situations, they move across borders where normal border protocols based on passports and visas have been suspended. They seek either a temporary stay until they are able to return to rebuild their lives, or the opportunity to build a new life in a new location. What happens when and if they are able to return? Who decides whether it is safe and viable to return, and for whom? If they have been displaced for a period of years, then in what sense is their original location home? Different generations of the same family often give different answers.

This book explores the various types of migration, looking into the causes and the experiences of some who relocate. It concentrates on the Middle East, although it includes the Arabian Peninsula and North Africa. A major theme is religiously motivated migration, noting that discrimination on religious grounds is counter to international conventions and invariably problematic in practice. A crucial factor when considering religiously motivated migration is the fact that, according to descriptive research, up to 90% of converts to Christianity who leave the region stop practising Christianity within ten years of arriving in a Western country. Enabling converts to leave the region must be seen as the option of last resort, applied only where there are no viable and local alternatives.

This book keeps the global, historical, socio-economic and political contexts of migration in view, a reflection of the interconnected world in which we all participate and to which we all contribute. For the forcibly displaced, who are all too often labelled as 'refugees', it asks why the international systems for migration are the way they are, noting what works well and what, typically and often tragically and unjustly, does not. Burden sharing amongst nations has never worked as intended; nations close to the source of forced migration have always carried a disproportionate share of the consequences. This tendency continues to affect the Middle East profoundly, where some people who face desperate situations resort to desperate methods.

Christians have been present throughout the Middle East since the first century – and the constant, consistent and public appeal of church leaders throughout the Middle East this century has been for people to be enabled to stay. Along with this commonly comes the acknowledgement that "We understand why some people choose to leave, and we do not stand in their way," but crucially they add, "Please recognise that mass emigration does not help the Church." Therefore, "If they cannot stay in their city or country, then at least enable them to stay in the region." King Abdullah of Jordan, President Sisi of Egypt and other political leaders in the region have also called on Christians to remain because they are essential to the continued existence of healthy, dynamic, pluralistic societies that enrich everyone. Several commentators note that a Middle East without an overt Christian presence should be a frightening prospect.

The call on people to remain is a reflection of the Middle East's predominantly collective culture. Western readers may well object, urging that the choices of individuals should be respected – and in this we immediately see one of the tensions of migration: the balance of individual and communal rights, responsibilities and relationships, and the effects on communities of decisions made by individuals and families.

Another distinction between typical Western and Middle Eastern cultures is that the former are guilt-based whereas the latter are based on an honour-shame dynamic. Guilt-based societies emphasise fact, and adherence to legal norms, and a constant danger is that they sink into a rigid legalism where everything is decided within formal structures and processes. Under an honour-shame dynamic, the actions of one person profoundly affect the social groups of which they are a part. The equivalent danger here is a descent into an endless cycle of revenge. There is a strong element of justice in both cultural systems, although it is expressed in different ways, and has different effects on society. Each needs the insights of the other.

Migration within, from and to the Middle East is not limited to Christians; some people of other faiths choose to move. What is frequently termed the 'brain drain' has been a significant, if rarely acknowledged, feature of the region that has profoundly affected its business, cultural, social, political and religious leadership – Iraq being but one example from the

Middle East. A typical motivation for this is the desire to seek a better future for the next generation.

It's easy to talk about the importance of enabling people to stay, but what might it look like in practice? One big-picture answer is adjusting governance and culture to be welcoming, respectful and inclusive of all, and regarding diversity as an asset that enriches the whole for the benefit of all. Such approaches need to be lived out locally. One theme of this book is for indigenous people of goodwill, including Christians, to contribute to creating such environments wherever they are. One feature of societies throughout the Middle East is segregation along religious lines, a symptom of, and a key contributor to, a deficiency of pluralism (see Glossary). One manifestation of this is discrimination on religious lines, which is a fault line throughout the region, and is one reason why Christian leaders across the Middle East typically strongly resent actions or calls for action by those from *outside* the region which include any element of religious discrimination, especially if it is ostensibly in their favour. Whatever the short-term, superficial attractions of such approaches, they reinforce a source of marginalisation and mistreatment, to the long-term detriment of all Middle Easterners, as well as being a contravention of international law.

Undermining the consistent rule of law applied equally to all further reinforces a root cause of the challenges seen in much of the region.

Chapter 1 is a case study on Lebanon, a country that illustrates many aspects of migration. It welcomes students, migrant workers and business links from its region and beyond, and some of its people choose to study and work abroad. It hosts forcibly displaced people from three conflicts – and each of these groups is treated differently within Lebanon. Chapter 2 gives an overview of the history of migration and a summary of forced migration in the Middle East during the twentieth century. It adds a summary of what the displaced need; crucially, it notes that being able to worship aids the recovery of adherents of all faiths. Chapter 3 looks at terminology, and introduces us to the international mechanisms for assisting the forcibly displaced. Terminology on migration is problematic and can be pejorative. The word 'refugee' has a legal definition and a different meaning in common usage. Other significant terms are migrant worker, economic migrant, asylum seeker, internally displaced person (IDP), foreign student and tourist visa holder, and many people who migrate do not fit into neat categories. Throughout this book, the term 'migrant' is used as a collective term for all those who are moving from one location to another.

Chapter 4 examines migrant workers, and includes a focus on the countries of the Arabian Peninsula. Several of these states are endeavouring to adjust the balance of migrant and indigenous workers. Chapter 5 examines migration for religious reasons, including pilgrimage, study, involvement in humanitarian work, proclamation of the faith and responding to religiously motivated injustice, harassment and marginalisation. This leads into Chapter 6, which summarises displacement within and from Syria, and its effects on the neighbouring countries of Iraq, Israel, Jordan, Lebanon and Turkey. The section on Iraq discusses the displacement of Iraqis following invasions in 1990 and 2003, where of particular note is the fact that since 1990, a brain drain has profoundly affected all aspects of society, perhaps more than forced displacement arising from sectarian violence.

Chapters 7 and 8 look at migration routes taken by some Syrians, as well as people of many other nationalities as they endeavour to move further. Crossing oceans and deserts leaves those who are moving by irregular means vulnerable to the forces of nature and exploitation by unscrupulous agents. These chapters examine some of the mechanisms that are used to manage such movements, including arrangements that European countries have made with Turkey, Sudan, Afghanistan and others. These appear to combine erecting barriers to disturb the flows of migration with initiatives to address *push* factors and improve burden sharing.

Chapter 9 examines the history and development of the international mechanisms for assisting the forcibly displaced. It assesses what works well and what does not, and describes some efforts at improving the mechanisms. It praises grass-roots efforts by many people of goodwill, and notes that high-level rhetoric, whilst commendable, appears unlikely to lead to broad-based change to international mechanisms.

Finally, Chapter 10 addresses the question of how God is working amidst current events. This chapter is included at the request of several Middle Eastern Christian leaders. It is my personal view, which I trust they and others will find helpful. Some Christians migrate away from the region – more by regular migration than irregular, a trend that has been present for decades. Yet to say that the region is being denuded of Christians overlooks the trend that many in the region are converting to the Christian faith. These two phenomena are changing the nature of the Christian presence in some, perhaps many, parts of the Middle East.

One recurring theme of this book is the effect of events on Christian communities across the Middle East. What challenges and opportunities have arisen and how, individually and collectively, have Christians responded? Why do some choose to leave? Why do some of those who leave later choose to return? How are other communities affected by changing patterns of migration?

Incidentally, in this book I refer to people who convert to Christianity as *Christians*. Chapter 10 discusses groups of converts who do not identify themselves using the term Christian. I understand their reasons and respect their opinion. I believe that my approach for this book provides a clear, succinct and consistent description of who is part of the Church in the sense of the totality of the followers of Jesus Christ.

Appendix 1 is the Religious Liberty Partnership's (RLP) Policy Statement on Relocation as a Response to Persecution. It explains the context of and rationale for the policy of regarding relocation outside the country or region of origin as the option of last resort, to be used only where there are no viable alternatives.

Appendices 2 and 3 look at two areas where some ask for positive discrimination in favour of Christians. Discrimination on religious grounds is invariably problematic in the Middle East. It militates against the pluralistic societies which are essential for creative dynamics that nurture, nourish and enrich the lives of all. These appendices look at two specific areas, showing that in each case the discrimination fails to address the real issue. Affirming and perpetuating a root cause of the Middle East's struggles can hardly be expected to be part of solving its problems.

A Glossary is included to provide a succinct and comprehensive summary of key terms and concepts.

The arrangement of the material might be surprising to some readers. The aspects of migration that receive the most media coverage are the forcible displacements of people from Syria, Iraq and other places of crisis and conflict; yet it is the slower paced, less dramatic but much more continuous and constant changes – those due to urbanisation within the region and a brain drain of well-qualified people – that are having the greater effect. It is also the case that regular and irregular migration combine and overlap in significant ways. For this reason, the issues of regular migration are covered first, although even in Chapter 4 there is material relevant to forcible displacement.

The following pages include powerful examples of what some people will do *for* and *to* others. Sacrifice and service contrast with cruelty and oppression; good news can be found amidst the bad if one seeks it. It is not my intention to gloss over or in any way minimise the trauma experienced by the forcibly displaced, or to ignore the agonising over life-changing decisions experienced by many who migrate. It is my aim, with as much sensitivity as possible, to cover the positive developments that I have seen – and continue to see – emerge from migration. There are always opportunities in disruption, and some people of goodwill are able to grasp them for the benefit of many others. It is also my intention to urge anyone considering migrating or working with the forcibly displaced to prepare themselves well for the inevitable distress and disruptions to life – their own and that of others – that they will encounter. One type of tragedy that I have seen too often is well-intentioned people who seek to assist migrants but who, in the end, aggravate the situation because of their limited knowledge, experience and understanding. The consequences of this are borne by migrants who already have more than enough difficulties. To a lesser extent the others affected are the staff of organisations who really do know how to support migrants. There is scope for more people to be involved – but please prepare well. Just as migration is a long-term undertaking, so is supporting migrants.

Onward into our journey with migration. Let us take a detailed look at the country of Lebanon, which will reveal migration from as well as to and within the country, illustrate how economic migration operates alongside forced displacement, and show honourable as well as deeply exploitative practices.

Chapter 1
Lebanon – a microcosm of migration

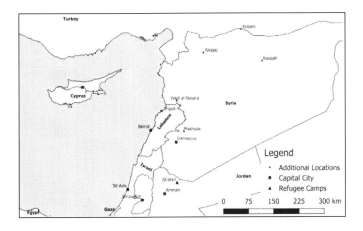

Lebanon is well acquainted with migration issues. It has been profoundly affected by forced displacement of others, providing sanctuary to Palestinians, Iraqis and Syrians in particular over several years. As well as being a receiving country for the forcibly displaced, Lebanon also welcomes many who are come for business, study and leisure. Numerous residents of countries in the Arabian Peninsula own apartments in Beirut, the capital, or villas in nearby hills. Property prices, especially for anything with a good view, are high. Many come to study at universities in Beirut, several of which are well-accredited institutions.

Migrant workers are welcomed, in a sense, to work in a variety of roles. For many years, most of the staff employed by the companies who run rubbish collection were Syrians. This is a classic example of the global norm that migrant workers do the dirty, dangerous or degrading work – 'the 3 D's' – that nationals do not want to undertake.

Domestic workers – cherished or confined?

Many Lebanese employ domestic workers. Some of these workers are well-treated, while others are less fortunate. One day I met with a Catholic priest whose work included assisting abused domestic workers. He told me about a meeting led and facilitated by Lebanese women that discussed women's rights. The priest realised that most participants were restricting the conversation to nationals. What, he asked gently, did those present think were the rights of Sri Lankan and other Asian women resident in Lebanon? This question had not occurred to some! The colloquial term for a domestic worker is 'a Lankee'. This reflects where many, but by no means all, domestic workers come from, and it has an element of being dehumanising – a trend that is all too common when people on the move are being exploited by others.

In October 2012 Amnesty International issued a report describing poor treatment of some migrant workers, including excessive work hours, withholding of wages, effective imprisonment, and physical and sexual abuse. It also documented a case of physical abuse by police officers.[3] In October 2009, eight domestic workers were reported to have died as a result of abuse. In January 2009, the Ministry of Labour introduced a standard employment contract that clarified certain conditions of employment, together with new regulation of employment agencies. Amnesty noted that there remained a lack of effective enforcement at that time. Many migrants effectively had no rights, and the legal system either ignored their complaints or supported their employers. Contracts were often only issued in Arabic, which most migrant workers cannot read, and specify entitlement to a day *off* per week when the crucial issue is whether the migrant can leave the premises and have a day *out*.

---

[3] Amnesty International; *Human Rights organisations demand the Lebanese authorities to put an end to the security agencies' violations against foreigners*; 18th October 2012; www.amnesty.org/en/documents/mde18/001/2012/en/ (accessed 11th November 2016)

Some desperate domestic workers resort to desperate measures, including leaving their place of work by jumping off the balcony. For some, this is catastrophic: they die from the injuries sustained. An alternative action is drinking harmful substances, leading to a day in hospital – one way of spending a day out of their place of work, or should we say confinement?

In June 2013, the Association of Owners of Recruitment Agencies in Lebanon adopted a self-regulating code of conduct to protect the rights of migrant domestic workers, who were not protected under the Lebanese labour law. This is a positive initiative, although its impact appears to have been limited due to the absence of enforcement mechanisms. The government appears to have taken no action to reduce the risk of exploitation and abuse of workers. A report issued in May 2017 substantiated these concerns.[4]

Such issues are by no means limited to Lebanon; domestic workers in numerous countries face similar issues. Knowing who to trust is far from easy – a

[4] IRIN News; *Slave labour? Death rate doubles for migrant domestic workers in Lebanon*; 15th May 2017; http://www.irinnews.org/feature/2017/05/15/slave-labour-death-rate-doubles-migrant-domestic-workers-lebanon (accessed 30th May 2017)

challenge that numerous migrants face. In general, the lower the pay range and the more options the employers have, then the greater the risk of a migrant worker being exploited. Other industries in which abuse is rife in some countries are construction and clothing manufacture.

One type of nightclub – a form of modern slavery?

Another area where migrants coming to Lebanon are abused is in the 'sex industry'. Lebanon has a set of nightclubs identified as Super 8 Nightclubs, and they are venues for a sophisticated form of prostitution. Each evening at these clubs a number of women, invariably young, attractive and foreign, dance on a stage. Clients of the club may ask to speak with one of the girls, and if they wish to proceed they call a manager to their table. The client and the manager than agree a price and meeting place. The client collects the woman, returning her some hours later. When not dancing or with a client, the women are kept in a hotel, confined to one floor with all exits locked and the lifts programmed not to stop. Food and other supplies are provided by what would be called room service for regular hotel guests. These women are effectively enslaved, with all their movements carefully controlled. Failure to comply with the instructions of the operators typically results in physical abuse. Without doubt, similar systems exist in all too many other countries.

Some Lebanese Christians are deeply concerned about this system and actively seek to do something about it. One aspect of what they do is to seek to rescue the entrapped women, providing those able to escape from this situation with alternative accommodation, employment and assistance to recover and leave the country. Others are endeavouring to challenge the demand side of this business by raising awareness amongst men about the gross injustices involved in Super 8 Nightclubs. Such actions are an example of people seeking to address injustice and bring good news and hope to the victims. It would not surprise me if other people of goodwill were involved in such action; moral uprightness and social action are not restricted to Christians.

Education and employment at home and abroad

The flow of people is far from being one way. Many Lebanese have moved abroad to study or work. One frequent location is the small states along the northern coast of the Arabian Peninsula, such as Bahrain, Kuwait, Qatar and the United Arab Emirates

(UAE). It used to be the case that many people left their families in Lebanon and visited them regularly; they did this for financial reasons and because of the high standard of education in Lebanon which they desire for their children. In recent years more people have taken their families with them, not least because high quality education is now widely available in the Gulf States.

Lebanon has an extensive system of private schools as well as a public system, and the private system has a number of high quality institutions, several of which have achieved accreditation to international standards – enabling pupils to apply directly to Western universities. A crucial question is whether these schools are preparing people to live in Lebanon or the West. Ideally, the answer should be that they prepare pupils to be citizens of an interconnected and interdependent world.

One family that I know is illustrative of this point. Several of the younger members of the family chose to study in the West. One met and married a Westerner, and has remained abroad. Others have completed their studies and then worked in the West for a number of years. They then returned to Lebanon, where they were able to take managerial-level jobs.

There is a widespread expectation amongst young graduates in many Middle Eastern countries that they will get senior or middle management roles immediately. To work abroad for a few years and then return allows them to undertake entry-level jobs in a different cultural context where the expectation that children of the better off will get supervisory roles immediately does not apply.

It is also the case that some non-Lebanese people choose to study in Lebanon. It has a range of universities, and has several Christian theological colleges, some of which attract students from the Middle East, the wider Arab world and beyond.

Migrant workers and international students are examples of migration by choice. Lebanon also has much forced displacement of people to, within, and through the country. As we consider forced displacement, we will look at internal displacement before examining the arrival of people forcibly displaced from elsewhere.

Internal forcible displacement – the civil war and its legacy

The central element to this context is the Lebanese Civil War, typically dated as having run from 1975 to

1991. This is described in detail in various sources[5] – for our purposes we need to note that at its height there were at least 40 armed groups fighting one another in various parts of the country. One consequence was that the country became segregated on ethnic and religious lines, with individual communities comprising people of the same ethnicity and religion, and with terms of identification being used in a very specific way. This means there were not just Christian and Muslim, but Maronite Catholic, Sunni, Shi'a, Alawite and many more. A description and history of the origins of this diversity is given in my previous book, *Identity Crisis*, which describes how the segregation of society on religious lines adversely affects the whole of society to the long-term detriment of all.

Numerous countries became involved in this conflict. One such country was Lebanon's southern neighbour, Israel, which invaded parts of the country in 1978 and 1982. Ostensibly, this was to secure its own northern border, and Israel maintained a presence in southern Lebanon until 2000. Israel's withdrawal allowed

[5] See for example Robert Fisk's book *Pity the Nation*, third edition (2001, Oxford University Press) and/or David Hirst's *Beware of Small States* (2010, Faber and Faber)

former residents to return and rebuild their communities. In contrast, at the same time a number of people felt obliged to leave Lebanon – they feared reprisals because of their perceived support for, or collaboration with, the Israelis. Some were welcomed into Israel, while others had to leave the vicinity. One person moved himself, his family and his organisation to Cyprus. He commented that the Israelis were supportive of his activities – a satellite TV channel proclaiming Christianity and broadcasting in Arabic – but he thought that the returning local officials would be less sympathetic. This is an example of religious activities being perceived as having political connotations.

Israel may have withdrawn, but it continued to exert its influence and military might on Lebanon, and serious conflict occurred in the summer of 2006. This is often referred to internationally as 'The Hezbollah–Israel War', although many Lebanese know it as 'The July War' and Israelis as 'The Second Lebanon War.' One effect in Lebanon was a pattern of displacement not seen before or since – the war had a profound, if not widely recognised, effect on Lebanon's Christian communities.

There had been clashes across the border prior to 12th July 2006, but on this occasion, the incident was a serious one: five Israeli soldiers were killed and two captured. Israel's response included a military invasion of parts of southern Lebanon, and airstrikes throughout much of the country. Hezbollah's response to this included rockets fired into northern Israel, as well as attacks on Israel's ground forces that had entered Lebanese territory. The conflict ended when a UN-brokered ceasefire came into effect on 14th August; although Israel continued to maintain a naval blockade until mid-September. The ceasefire was part of UN Security Council Resolution 1701, which was adopted on 11th August. The terms of this resolution were formally accepted by the Israeli and Lebanese governments, although neither fully implemented its terms. For example, Lebanon did not attempt to disarm Hezbollah, and Israel continued to violate Lebanese airspace.

The two soldiers who were captured on 12th July died of injuries they sustained while being kidnapped. Their bodies were returned as part of a prisoner exchange that took place on 16th July 2008. Cross-border prisoner exchanges are a rare form of migration.

What effect did the conflict have on Lebanon, in particular on migration issues? One high-profile effect was that many expatriate residents left the country. Amongst this flow of people, some domestic workers who had become trapped in the country were able to leave. The authorities who were handling departures understood that some workers would not have their passports available because they were being held by employers who were out of the country at the time. This understanding also allowed those whose passports had expired to leave.

Many Lebanese who were living in the south of the country moved north. These journeys became progressively more difficult due to damage to roads, especially bridges, and most found shelter with friends or in communal buildings, including schools. Support was provided by host communities. One consequence of this was a disturbance of the segregation that took place during the civil war. Most of the displaced were Shi'a Muslims, and many of the hosts were Christians and Sunni Muslims. Communities were forced to meet one another. In this case, most of the internally displaced were able to return home relatively quickly; the infrastructure was rebuilt and much of life returned to a semblance of normality.

At deeper levels, this conflict profoundly affected Lebanese society. For example, many Christians were obliged to interact with Shi'ite Muslims, and for many people of all faiths, the conflict forced them to consider their future in the country. I visited Lebanon in February 2007. One evening in a café my host asked the waitress whether she would leave if she were given the opportunity to do so. Without hesitation, she said 'yes,' and said that all her friends would do likewise. My host remarked that this was typical of their society – all that many people could see was uncertainty, instability and the prospect of living with the constant awareness that the future was unknown. The alternatives abroad looked much more attractive.

There is always opportunity in disruption. This war was an opportunity for those Christians who wanted to express their faith in practical action to those of other religions. These Christians had to address the legacy of the Lebanese Civil War, when those who were different had to be presumed to be enemies, and which set the context for what was to follow from 2011 onwards.

Receiving forcibly displaced people is a constant in Lebanese history. We will look at the causes of these many displacements in the following chapter. Suffice here to say that following independence in 1943, the first wave of Palestinians arrived during 1947 and 1948, before further waves occurred in 1967 and 1970. The continuing presence of Palestinians has influenced the government's response to subsequent arrivals: of Iraqis, starting in 2003, and Syrians in 2011.

Palestinians – residents or citizens?

Lebanon remains host to numerous Palestinians. Some have integrated into society, some have inter-married with Lebanese, and others have migrated outside the Middle East. Many, though, remain classified as Palestinian refugees with limited legal status within Lebanon, including no rights to own property (though they may rent property anywhere in the country). One motivation for these rules is that giving them Lebanese citizenship would affect the religious demographics of the country; which would have far-reaching political implications, due to the use of religious affiliation within the political system.[6]

The number of Palestinians resident in Lebanon is disputed, but is growing in accordance with the

[6] See Jonathan Andrews' *Identity Crisis* (2016, Gilead Books Publishing) Chapter 6, especially pages 85-88

general demographic trend. In December 2010, a UN official stated there were 350,000 to 400,000. Some commentators regard this figure as too high, since people remain registered even if they leave the country, and suggest figures of between 200,000 and 250,000.[7] In addition there were between 10,000 and 40,000 registered with the Lebanese government but not the UN, plus an estimated 3,000 to 4,000 who were not registered anywhere. Many Palestinians in Lebanon live in the 12 officially recognised camps which were established in 1948 to accommodate around 100,000 people. Many of them feel trapped in these camps by economic circumstances, and growing populations are accommodated by adding additional rooms and storeys to existing buildings in the camps.

One Beirut freeway passes by the Shabra and Shatila camps. To an outsider like myself, the distinction between what is the camp and what is not is hard to discern; the high-rise architecture is very similar, as is the style of shops and the business frontages at street

[7] For example, International Crisis Group; *Nurturing Instability: Lebanon's Palestinian Refugee Camps;* 19th February 2009; www.crisisgroup.org/middle-east-north-africa/eastern-mediterranean/lebanon/nurturing-instability-lebanon-s-palestinian-refugee-camps (accessed 9th December 2016)

level. To those who live in the area, it is very clear which streets are in and which are outside the camp, and, at the edge, which side of the street is inside and which is not. Who has authority, and where, is very clear to residents and local officials; the Palestinian camps organise their own affairs.

There are tensions within some of the camps amongst supporters of different political parties and/or armed groups, notably those loyal to Fatah and Hamas, the two principal entities in the West Bank and the Gaza Strip, each of which have political, social service and military wings. The dynamics appear to be changing, partly in reflection of events in the West Bank and the Gaza Strip.

The tensions in Nahr al-Bared camp near Tripoli, a coastal town in northern Lebanon, exploded into overt violence in 2007, with clashes involving the army and members of an armed group. The violence started on 20th May when police raided an apartment in Tripoli to arrest people suspected of committing an armed bank robbery the previous day. Militants loyal to the Fatah al-Islam armed group resisted arrest, and started gun battles that spread to surrounding streets. The army surrounded the camp and ordered the militants to surrender. They refused, and a violent siege lasted until 2nd September. The Defence Minister reported that 202 militants were arrested, 222 had been killed and a further unknown number had been buried inside the camp. 163 army personnel were killed. The 40,000 residents of Nahr al-Bared were displaced to other Palestinian camps and to temporary accommodation in schools. Some residents were able to return during 2008; however, the process of rebuilding continued to proceed slowly, and often only to poor standards.

Historically, the Palestinian situation that affects the whole of the Middle East was significant in the establishment of the international legal framework for refugees. We will look more closely at this in Chapter 9. For our current focus on Lebanon, we need to note that the UN's refugee agency, more formally known as the United Nations High Commission for Refugees (UNHCR), operates under an agreement with the government, the terms of which can be adjusted by the government whenever it chooses. This has had limited impact on support for Iraqis in Lebanon but has, I believe, had major consequences for Syrians. It also has consequences for those who flee to Lebanon to escape religious persecution in their own countries, typically because they have converted from Islam to Christianity. We will return to this in Chapter 5.

Iraqis and Syrians – 'guests', but for how long?

Most Iraqis proved to be temporary visitors, with many staying only for short periods before moving on to other countries, mostly in the West. As such, they were not regarded as a burden; they came, rented property and were economically active, and then departed. Few needed or asked for assistance.

The situation was very different for the Syrians who started fleeing into Lebanon as the Syrian crisis erupted in 2011. Our focus here is on the effects of this on Lebanon; we will look at the impacts on Syria itself, as well as on other neighbouring countries and beyond, in Chapter 6. The government forbade use of terminology that applies to the Palestinians; so the word 'guest' was to be used, not 'refugee', and the word 'camp' was banned, with 'tented community' applied instead. The government did not want another long-running and apparently never-ending situation wherein a large community of displaced people would become a permanent, distinct community within Lebanese society.

The Syrians who came were different from the Iraqis. First, they came in vastly higher numbers. Second, they were more varied in their wealth and their ability to support themselves.

Those who arrived early in the Syrian crisis were, in general, from the rich and middle classes; they came with resources. Most found places to live in Lebanese society. Later waves were (in general) from poorer backgrounds. Some found makeshift accommodation in abandoned or partly constructed buildings. They made what adjustments they could, especially for the winter months. The supply of such 'accommodation' was soon fully utilised.

One response to the demand for more accommodation was the establishment of hundreds of small 'tented communities' throughout the country. Each has a Syrian manager who rents the land from a Lebanese landowner. The manager then sublets the plots to fellow Syrians. In many cases, all residents of a tented community are from the same area of Syria. Some dwellings have concrete bases, while others do not; building materials are scavenged, with old advertising billboards one notable source. I found it somewhat ironic to see dwellings for displaced people whose exterior walls seemed to advertise holidays in plush Mediterranean resorts or luxury goods that were portrayed using technologically glamorous Formula One cars. Most dwellings have mains electricity, albeit a limited supply. The manager often provides work-parties to local farmers and other businesses, for which he receives the wages and then distributes to those involved. (The legal status of such work is debatable). The manager is a very significant person in each tented community.

In May 2015 the Lebanese government instructed the UNHCR to cease registering Syrians. At this point there were 1,078,338 registered Syrian refugees, plus an estimated 500,000 to 600,000 who were unregistered.[8] There are several reasons why some choose not to register: some have sufficient financial means and the contacts necessary to be self-supporting, whilst others fear reprisals against them or their family if it becomes known to the Syrian authorities that they have left the country.

Public opinion in Lebanon changed over time. Initially, there was widespread sympathy towards Syrians, and the observation that most were self-supporting; but as the numbers of Syrians continued to grow, so resentment started to rise amongst some Lebanese. The economic impact of hosting forcibly displaced people is complex. There is always

[8] Sourced from: http://data.unhcr.org/syrianrefugees/regional.php on 6th November 2015 (accessed 11th November 2016). The estimated figure was commonly cited by Lebanese people involved in humanitarian support of displaced Syrians.

opportunity in disruption for those willing and able to respond to the changed circumstances. The Lebanese are very entrepreneurial, and some sought to take advantage of the situation; for example, those who were able leased land for tented communities, and there was a construction boom in Tripoli and elsewhere based on using Syrians as cheap labour – many of whom were willing to work for lower wages than had been offered prior to the crisis. Alongside this, Lebanon, like many host countries, received humanitarian assistance from the international community through UN bodies and NGOs – this money was coming into the country from abroad, much of it being spent within the country, particularly when humanitarian organisations used it to employ national staff.

The historical context created a huge opportunity for those Lebanese Christians who were willing and able to embrace the challenge. Many organisations and churches have become involved, providing humanitarian aid, small-scale schools, and pastoral and other forms of support. Many cooperate and coordinate their activities with the UNHCR and other organisations. One challenge that was reported to me by a church leader was that some humanitarian organisations providing financial donations to churches were making no provision for administrative overheads. To do so is normal practice in financial support, and is the means by which NGOs finance the operational overheads that underpin their humanitarian services. Presumably, the assumption was that the churches were using existing facilities and all staff are volunteers; but such assumptions were not always true.

One key message I heard at a gathering that I attended in 2015 was that Christians need to be trendsetters in responding to this situation. The need for compassionate support is clear, with some arguing that leaving Syrians unsupported would create the conditions for another civil war. There are two parts to this argument, the first being the historical precedent that the arrival of a large number of Palestinians in 1970 destabilised the ethno-religious balance and was a contributory cause of the Lebanese civil war, and the second that desperate people with no means of supporting themselves and their families will become recruitment targets for armed groups which are able to offer salaried jobs.

This argument also confronts the long-standing enmity of many Lebanese towards Syrians. This enmity is a legacy of the Lebanese Civil War, and the overt presence and involvement of Syria in Lebanon from 1991 to 2005. This situation changed as a result of the assassination of the former Lebanese Prime Minister Rafik Hariri on 14th February 2005, when public protests (in which it is commonly estimated that at least one quarter of the population participated) prompted the withdrawal of the Syrian army from Lebanon. Opinions were divided about what covert Syrian presence continued after this; however, what clearly did continue was the long-standing presence of many Syrians in Lebanon as labourers.

One implication of this is that some of those in Lebanon who would seek to assist Syrians face opposition from elements within their own community – as seen on the occasion when local officials refused permission for new schools, partly due to vociferous complaints by neighbours.

It was noted at the time that the Christian response combined high professionalism in aid distribution with a consistent, caring and personal service. The contrast here is with major aid organisations, who tend to simply deposit large amounts of physical material with little if any personal contact with the people they want to help. It also contrasts with those mosques that are providing aid which is conditional upon recipients being aligned politically, theologically and denominationally (to use the Christian term) with the givers.

Christian organisations are all clear that Jesus is at the heart of everything they do, and make this clear to those they are supporting. Those that ask about Christianity are informed where their enquiries can be fulfilled. The response of recipients is their choice and does not affect whether humanitarian support will continue being provided to them. This practice is counter to the prevailing culture that people should look after their own, but not those who are different.

Most Syrians in Lebanon want to return home. Consequently, the focus needs to remain on supporting them where they are and working for an end to the crisis; the focus should not be on helping them to leave the region.

Various challenges have arisen to prevent support being given to the Syrians in Lebanon. One challenge concerns children born to Syrian families in Lebanon – some people are unable to register births, and the children become legally stateless, a topic that we will return to in Chapter 9.

Provision of education has been problematic. The scale of the need is huge, and I have been pleased to see informal schools being established in some tented communities. One model for doing this is for a wooden structure to be erected as a school building, often also being used as a community centre outside of school hours. Residents of the community itself are then employed as teachers, and the morale boost to the whole community is profound, and a pleasure to see. This approach does, however, require external financial support to cover the construction and the salaries. International aid money has been provided to Lebanon to enable more Syrian children to attend school, but alas, not all of it is spent as intended. One story that shows the kind of problem that Syrian schoolchildren can face is the experience of a group of children who were taken to a state school after the national children had gone home for the day. However, rather than being educated, they were being used as cleaning staff. One trusts that those providing the aid money that financed this are checking not only that Syrian children are in school but, crucially, that they are being educated when they are there.

A further story is the one of a group of children who were attending an informal school in their tented community, and were instructed to attend an official school. One week after transferring they returned to the informal school, stating that they much preferred the informal setting and had learnt nothing at the official school.

One serious legal restriction is that the Lebanese government does not allow education for Syrian 'guests' beyond Grade 6; meaning that children receive primary but not secondary education. Most Lebanese that I know regard this as a short-sighted policy.

One aspect that certainly needs addressing is the official recognition of what education children have had. Education is valuable regardless of the status of the certificates that are awarded on completion; yet in our interconnected world, paper qualifications are significant, especially if students are looking for further study or to work abroad.

Lebanon illustrates many aspects of migration, both the migration of those who move by choice, and those who migrate to escape violence. We have noted the issues faced by migrant workers – a topic that we will return to in Chapter 4. We will now broaden our attention to reflect on migration throughout human history and survey some of the events and forced displacements that have shaped Lebanon and the rest of the Middle East.

Chapter 2
Migration – is displacement the story of humanity?

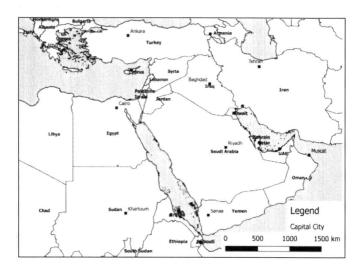

In *The Ascent of Man*, Jacob Bronowski notes that mankind originated in equatorial Africa, and that civilisation first occurred in the ancient Near East, a region roughly corresponding to the modern Middle East. From such origins mankind spread throughout the world.[9] Bronowski is himself an example of someone who migrated: he was born in Poland,

[9] Jacob Bronowski; *The Ascent of Man* (1973, BBC)

moved to the UK with his family, and in later life worked in the USA.

Similarly, Alice Roberts' later work *The Incredible Human Journey* traces the spread across the earth of our species, *Homo sapiens*, from its emergence in Africa. It notes the challenges to migration caused by oceans, mountains, deserts, other geographic features, climate, and notes other animals, including intelligent species in Asia and Europe, that failed to survive.[10]

Academic research into the spread of mankind appears to be in a rich phase, with new tools leading to additional insights. The field of genetics, aided by the recently developed ability to extract and sequence DNA from very old bones, is adding to what can be known from historical, anthropological and other disciplines – Alex Rutherford's book *A Brief History of Everyone Who Ever Lived* gives a good description of these developments.[11] The general idea that mankind emerged in Africa and has migrated worldwide from there remains widely accepted. Migration measured

[10] Alice Roberts; *The Incredible Human Journey* (2009, Bloomsbury)
[11] Alex Rutherford; *A Brief History of Everyone Who Ever Lived* (2016, Weidenfeld & Nicolson)

over long time periods is indeed the story of humanity.

There have been periods of greater and lesser levels of migration. In *The Lexus and the Olive Tree*, Thomas Friedman remarks that 10% of the world's population moved continent – not just country – in the three decades prior to the First World War (1914-18).[12] Friedman's concern here is setting the context for his focus on the wave of globalisation unfolding at the start of the twenty-first century. One aspect of this globalisation is greater migration, primarily driven by economic and educational considerations. We will look at economically motivated migration in Chapter 4.

Not all migration has been voluntary. The trans-Atlantic slave trade of the seventeenth and eighteenth centuries provided labourers for sugar plantations in the West Indies, and in Chapter 1 we encountered a modern form of entrapment, confinement and complete control of some people by fellow human beings who exploit their labour as an integral part of

---

[12] Thomas Friedman; *The Lexus and the Olive Tree,* second edition (2000, Harper Collins)

enriching themselves and those who invest in their businesses.

Other examples of forced migration arise from colonisation, which occurred reasonably peacefully in some places but involved violent confrontation elsewhere. In some cases, native populations were forcibly displaced. Another category of forced migration is penal colonies, with people forcibly, albeit legally, transported as a form of punishment. Such places typically had very skewed demographics, with far more male residents than female. The journey was arduous, and high death rates occurred. The British government addressed this by using private companies to transport convicts to Australia with payment based on those who were assessed as able-bodied on arrival. This practice led to dramatic reductions in the death rate during transportation.

Another long-running aspect of human migration is urbanisation. The earliest humans lived in small rural contexts. The emergence of cities and the infrastructure to support them took time; but urbanisation is a continuing global trend, with an ever-increasing proportion of human beings living in urban settings. We will observe the changing social patterns arising from this in Chapter 8.

The Middle East during the twentieth century – displacement and dispersal

Narrowing our focus to the Middle East, we need to be aware that during the twentieth century, people were on the move for a variety of reasons. There was a general, slow flow of people moving within the region, of people leaving the region and of others moving in. Urbanisation was one aspect of this.

A number of events have prompted surges of migration, all of them controversial in the Middle East. Our purpose here is to provide a context of mass migration. I do not wish to give an assessment of the rights and wrongs of the political and military events that caused these displacements. Typically, I will use the UN terms for states and geographic areas. This should not be taken as recognition or otherwise of the legitimacy of borders and demarcations, some of which are disputed and most of which were devised by Western colonial powers. The text endeavours to reflect the different positions taken by concerned parties, notably the diversity of Israeli and Palestinian views of what is known by the UN as the West Bank and the Gaza Strip. I am aware that the term West Bank is used in different ways by different sources; the UN designation is the Israel-Jordan border that had de facto acceptance and recognition from 1949 to

June 1967. This includes East Jerusalem, which some sources treat as a separate geographical area.

Two further clarifications on terminology will be helpful. I avoid the word 'terrorist', since one person's terrorist can be another person's freedom fighter. There is no internationally agreed definition of the word 'terrorist'. One factor in this uncertainty is the recognition of the right to resist occupation, with the situation of the Palestinians in the West Bank a commonly cited example. I use the term 'armed group' for what others may label as a terrorist entity or a militia. It is worth noting that several organisations have political, social service and armed wings; Hezbollah in Lebanon and Fatah and Hamas in the Palestinian areas are examples of this. We need to be aware that labelling such entities as 'armed groups' can overlook their other areas of activity, many of which are well-respected by the recipients of the public services provided. I do wish to be clear that I regard gratuitous violence as evil, and believe that all such criminal activity should be met with the full force of the law; likewise for crimes of conspiracy to commit acts of violence. I commend the honourable expression of political, social and other grievances and regard it as a shortcoming of our age that extremism typically gets more headlines than constructive contributions to society and public debate do.

I have included anecdotes as a reminder that the events listed affected people with names, lives and feelings; they are not just about numbers of nameless and faceless objects. The descendants of those involved live with the consequences of what happened to previous generations. One senses the raw emotions of some of those affected.

Two ethnic groups feature prominently: Armenians and Palestinians, who have both become widely dispersed due to forced migrations.

Armenians – displaced and settled

Numerous Armenians were displaced during the events of 1915, which are referred to in many circles under the term 'Armenian Genocide'. I have met numerous Armenian people, several of whom have recounted that their grandparents were affected by being forced to make a long and hazardous journey, mostly on foot. They are aware that if their grandparents had not survived and become established somewhere else, then they would not have been born.

The Armenian Genocide has been a sensitive topic in Turkey for many years. In 2005 officials acknowledged that "pain occurred on both sides" and in September 2006 a conference on this subject was held in Istanbul, despite protests and a court-enforced change of venue. In November 2013, a conference in Istanbul provided the first open forum for academics and Turkish communities to discuss these sensitive issues inside Turkey. It was co-sponsored by the Hirant Dink Foundation and Boğaziçi University, and was streamed on-line. In December 2013, the then-Foreign Minister of Turkey, Ahmet Davutoğlu, declared the Ottoman deportation of Armenians in 1915 to have been "wrong" and "inhumane."

In general, Armenians desire the large number of deaths of their people in 1915 to be officially acknowledged as *genocide*, a term that is defined in international law and carries significant consequences, including the necessity for reparations and compensation. The applicable international law, the Convention on the Prevention and Punishment of the Crime of Genocide, was adopted by the United Nations General Assembly on 9th December 1948, and entered into force in 1951.[13] It cannot be applied retroactively, and therefore does not apply to the events of 1915. This convention does, however, create a sense of expectation that compensation is due. The Turkish government seeks to avoid any appearance of liability and so rejects officially using or recognising the term genocide. It does acknowledge that there were casualties on both sides. The scale of these events makes compensation a very expensive and time-consuming proposition, and this is our first example of a situation where righting the wrongs of the past would be problematic even if there were the political will to do so.

There have been attempts to improve relations between Turkey and Armenia. On 4th September 2008, then-President Gül visited Armenia, and on 6th September he and the President of Armenia watched as their countries played a soccer match. Both presidents attended the return fixture, which was played in Bursa, Turkey. In December of that year a group of more than 200 Turkish academics and

[13] Available from the UN; www.un.org/en/genocideprevention/ documents/atrocity-crimes/Doc.1_Convention%20on%20the%20 Prevention%20and%20Punishment%20of%20the%20Crime%20of%2 0Genocide.pdf (accessed 23rd February 2017)

newspaper columnists launched an online campaign entitled *I apologise*. In January 2009, the state prosecutor opened an investigation into whether the authors had "insulted the Turkish nation," a criminal offence under the controversial and problematic Article 301 of Turkey's Penal Code. Also that month, police arrested several people on suspicion of planning attacks against the leading authors. One of the Turks involved remarked that he was passionate about restoring damaged relationships, notably between Turkey and Armenia as states, as well as between their peoples. He longed for the border to be opened for trade and mutual visits. He was only too aware of his government's position on the term genocide, and he was not surprised when some fellow Turks reacted angrily. The events of a century ago remain deeply emotive.

The Armenians were scattered by these events, and significant communities can be found in Iran, Lebanon and other Middle Eastern countries. Some remain resident in Turkey, where they have citizenship.

Turkey – a nation of migrants?
In 1923 the modern state of Turkey emerged from the remnants of the Ottoman Empire. The country's formation included an exchange of population with

Greece, as ethnic Greeks and Turks moved, some by choice and others by force, to become resident in the country ostensibly of their ethnicity.[14] Fifty-one years later there was a second example of the exchange of ethnic Greeks and Turks, this time in Cyprus.

On 20th July 1974, Turkey invaded Cyprus at the culmination of a period of political and ethnic strife. The invasion led to the division of the island, a situation that persists. Victoria Hislop's novel *The Sunrise* illustrates the loss and violence experienced by some at this time, as well as the ability of individuals to live together despite ethnic differences.[15] One Cypriot told me about the home that her family lost when they were compelled to flee south, and said that she had long since stopped expecting anyone to provide compensation.

The ethnic origins of Turkish citizens are instructive. The Turkic people originate in Central Asia; Turkmenistan is much closer to their place of origin than is Turkey. Their current location is an enduring legacy of the mass migrations prompted by the

[14] Louis de Bernieres' novel *Birds Without Wings* (2004, Secker and Warburg), and Victoria Hislop's novel *The Thread* (2011, Headline Review), both portray this forced exchange of peoples.

[15] Victoria Hislop; *The Sunrise* (2014, Headline Review)

actions of Genghis Khan. There are also Turkish citizens of Caucasian origin: the descendants of people who migrated to avoid massacres and other abuses during the nineteenth century. In 1913 a number of ethnic Turks were displaced into Turkey from Bulgaria due to conflict in the Balkans.

Israel – born with displacement

Another issue where events in the twentieth century continue to resonate to this day stems from the declaration on 14th May 1948 of the establishment of the modern state of Israel.[16] This is a complex, and frequently divisive, subject. Here we need to give a brief account of it, keeping our focus on migrations in the twentieth century that affect the context of the Middle East. One such migration was the arrival in what became the state of Israel of Jewish people, mostly from Europe – a flow of arrivals which increased significantly in the aftermath of the Second World War. The motivations of these migrants varied, including some who wanted to escape ethnic persecution, and others with an ideological

[16] See the note at the start of this sub-section about my use of the international terms for countries and territories, which is not to be taken as endorsement or otherwise of the legitimacy of these entities and their recognised or assumed borders.

motivation to create a Jewish homeland in a location to which they believed they had a long-standing historical and religious claim.

There had been a series of uprisings and violent clashes involving Jews and Palestinians in the period between the two World Wars, and any semblance of normality broke down in 1947, with harassment, violence, and massacres perpetrated by various parties, leading to the forcible displacement of numerous people of several ethnicities.[17] Palestinians typically use the term Nakba, meaning literally 'catastrophe', for these events.

One Palestinian lady proudly showed me the key of the house in Haifa that she was forced to leave, together with her then-young family, in 1947. The family was one of those evacuated by horse and cart under British supervision, and went first to Jordan and then to Lebanon. In the 1980s, several of her children moved to the UK and they were able to

[17] See, for example, Colin Chapman's book *Whose Promised Land?*, fifth edition (2015, Lion Hudson)

secure residency and subsequently British citizenship for their mother.[18]

The events surrounding the declaration of the state of Israel prompted further migrations; numerous Jewish people were forced to leave the countries of their birth, and citizenship, where their families had lived peacefully for generations. On one of my visits to Israel, the two men operating the shared taxi service from Tel Aviv airport to Jerusalem had been born in Russia and Morocco. The one of Moroccan origin had been forced to leave with his family because of violence against Jewish communities in 1947-48 and 1967. A friend in the UK spoke of an ancestor who had been forced from Egypt, and whose family was arrested and detained before being told that they were free to leave the country. They left taking one suitcase each. Their home – a mansion – and everything else they owned had to be left behind, and was effectively confiscated by the government and handed to others. People from Egypt, Iraq, Morocco, Tunisia and other Arab countries were granted citizenship in Israel, although many were treated with

[18] This story is told in Siham Musallam Brown's book *Yesterday, Today and Forever* (2007, Ritchie)

suspicion.[19] We will return to the story of some of them in Chapter 9.

Two other countries, Iran and Sudan, need to be mentioned here, before we return to the continuing saga of the central Middle East.

Iran and Sudan – sources and hosts of the displaced

Iran had revolutions in 1953 and 1979. The first saw the return of the Pahlavi dynasty of Shahs in a coup orchestrated by the USA and the UK. This was by no means the first and, alas, not the last example of such imperialist meddling in the Middle East. In this case, these Western powers removed a democracy and replaced it with a monarchy. Some Iranians left the country, some permanently and others for a period of exile. Some left immediately, others left during the years that followed as the oppressive nature of the Shah's style of governance became clear. The Islamic Revolution of 1979 saw Ayatollah Ruhollah Khomeini return from exile in France to assume the newly created position of Supreme Leader, a post that

---

[19] Elizabeth Kendal gives some statistics in her book *After Saturday Comes Sunday* (2016, Resource Publications); for example, 119,788 Jews migrated from Iraq to Israel in 1950 and 1951 (page 5).

combines the roles of head of state and head of the state religion. Strictly speaking, the head of government is the President – currently Hassan Rouhani – although in many respects the real authority lies with the Supreme Leader. This revolution prompted a fresh wave of Iranians to leave.

At the end of the twentieth century Iran was host to approximately four million people who had been displaced from two of its neighbours – an estimated half a million Iraqis, and three and a half million Afghans. Of the Afghans, one and half million were working legally as migrant workers, one million were registered as refugees and one million were present with no legal status. Migration took place to as well as from Iran.

Sudan gained independence in 1956. It has been beset by internal conflict ever since, causing vast amounts of displacement, mostly within the country, though some Sudanese have moved to Egypt and Libya in particular, and several other countries have received migrants. Many people have gone as migrant workers, notably to Libya, and others have become irregular migrants in Egypt, Israel, Jordan, Yemen and elsewhere. One problematic area of conflict has been western Sudan – the provinces of Northern, Western and Southern Darfur. During the 2000s, some Sudanese fled westwards into Chad. At the same time, internal conflict in Chad forced some Chadians to move eastwards into Sudan. Both groups found some degree of safety in the other's country, despite neither considering themselves safe in their own.

Let us return to the wider Levant (literally meaning the lands around Damascus), which in our context includes Israel, the West Bank and the Gaza Strip, as well as Iraq, Jordan, Lebanon and Syria.

The Levant – displacements in 1967, 1970 and 1975

The Six Day War of June 1967 led to further forced displacements. Israel took control of large parts of the Golan Heights (from Syria), the West Bank (from Jordan) and the Gaza Strip and Sinai Peninsula (from Egypt). In 1985 a Palestinian man remarked to me that he happened to be in Jordan in 1967, and had been unable to return to his home in the West Bank ever since. There were family members that he had not seen during the intervening years. In 1985, I, a tourist, was able to cross from Jordan to the West Bank but he, a tour guide, was not. One hopes that subsequent developments affecting the status and governance of the West Bank will have allowed this man to visit his relatives.

September 1970 witnessed several developments that forced some people to migrate, including the hijacking of three airliners, which were taken to Dawson's Field in Jordan. The passengers and crews were released unharmed but the aircraft were destroyed. It was one of the first high-profile acts of violence by some Palestinians, a desperate cry for their situation to be acknowledged, recognised and addressed. Fearing unrest amongst the Palestinians in Jordan, King Hussein ordered his army to forcibly eject some Palestinians from the country. Many of those affected relocated to Lebanon; others went to Syria. The events became known as Black September.

The attack on Israeli athletes at the 1972 Munich Olympics came two years later; on that occasion 11 Israelis were killed, together with those who attacked and attempted to kidnap them. Sadly, amongst desperate people with few options, some will resort to desperate courses of action and means of expression.

We noted in Chapter 1 that the arrival of Palestinians in Lebanon in 1970 was one cause of the Lebanese civil war. Patricia St John's novel *Nothing Else Matters* is based on these events, putting human faces to raw facts. The book portrays a family faced with the choice between leaving – and quickly – or being massacred. They escaped with very few of their possessions.[20]

In 1979 Israel and Egypt signed The Egypt-Israel Peace Treaty, which formalised the Camp David Accords that had been agreed the previous year. One provision was the return of the Sinai Peninsula to Egypt, which required the eviction of a number of Israeli citizens living in towns or settlements that had been built in Sinai. Then in 2005 Israel closed the settlements that it had built in the Gaza Strip. Seven thousand Israelis were obliged to relocate, albeit with due compensation and assistance provided by their government. Many left voluntarily; the actual process of forcibly removing those who chose to resist was handled much more diplomatically and sensitively than had been the case in Sinai in 1979.

Iraq – invasions and displacements in 1980, 1990-91 and 2003

In September 1980, Saddam Hussein, then President of Iraq, launched an attack on Iran, starting a war that

[20] Patricia St John; *Nothing Else Matters* (republished 2007, Scripture Union)

lasted eight years. During this conflict, Saddam Hussein was supported by a number of Western and Middle Eastern states. This changed dramatically in August 1990, when Iraq invaded Kuwait. Some Kuwaitis fled to Saudi Arabia, driving across the desert rather than along roads, many of which had been blocked by the Iraqi army.

The forced removal of Iraqi military forces from Kuwait in 1991 was followed by internal conflict within Iraq. The Iraqi military conducted operations in the south and north that prompted the flight of many Iraqis. The international response to this was the establishment of no-fly zones in the north and south of Iraq. The three predominantly Kurdish provinces established de-facto autonomy, a status that was formalised in 2005 – the position of this particular ethnic group is summed up in the traditional phrase that 'The Kurds have no friends except the mountains': a recognition that this group is distrusted by its neighbours and has been exploited at various times in history.[21] When they are attacked, there is likely to be shelter and safety in the

[21] One historic exception is the empire of the Medes and Persians, with the term Medes usually being taken to mean the Kurds.

mountains, a location which marching armies find difficult to assault, at least when using large numbers of troops, although the use of air power makes this less true than it once was.

The 1990s saw Iraq subjected to sanctions as the international community sought to ensure that Iraq would not threaten its neighbours again. One consequence of this was serious damage to the health system, causing (amongst other things) a rise in child mortality rates. One wonders how many Iraqis, especially professionals, chose to emigrate during this period. In what sense, if any, was this forced migration? Clearly not in the sense of fleeing imminent danger; yet many felt obliged to leave in the sense that they were restricted or unable to exercise their professional skills in Iraq, and had a reduced or lost sense of hope in the future for themselves and their families if they stayed. Defining forced migration is not always straightforward.

In 2003 the USA led an invasion that removed the government of President Saddam Hussein. This led to a period of intense instability in parts of the country, prompting high levels of internal migration, as well as seeing large numbers of people moving abroad, notably to Jordan and Syria. Arguably the problem was not so much the invasion but the manner in which the country was administered by the invaders. Any gratitude for the removal of former President Saddam Hussein soon dissipated – amongst the problems was that the Iraqis advising the administrators were mostly people who had returned from exile and consequently had little credibility with most of the populace.

Iraq was not the only country to endure significant levels of internal migration during this decade. There was significant displacement within Lebanon during the summer of 2006 as we discussed in the previous chapter, and in the following decade, the 2010s, both Iraq and Lebanon experienced further mass migrations, albeit this time due to events elsewhere in the Middle East.

The Arab Spring – 2011, including the emergence of Daesh

The events of what was originally termed the Arab Spring, from 2011 onwards, have included several occurrences of displacement in Egypt, Libya, Syria and Yemen in particular. Displacements in Egypt have typically been low-key and localised, with many people forced from the northern parts of the Sinai Peninsula by the actions of armed groups. In Libya, the events that followed the removal of Colonel Qaddafi in October 2011 included some Libyans fleeing into Tunisia as well as many expatriates who were living and working in Libya returning home. Bread was in short supply, not from a lack of ingredients but because most of the bakers were Egyptians who had left. The Libyans who remained did not have the skills to do the work. We will explore the issues around expatriate workers in Chapter 4.

The most widely reported situation of forced displacement is Syria, and we will cover the details of this in Chapter 6. It is sufficient here to note that the countries most affected by this migration were the neighbouring ones of Iraq, Jordan, Lebanon and Turkey. There were onward issues for Europe, and the Syrian situation was a contributor – but by no means the only one – to what is all too often described as 'Europe's refugee crisis'. We will look at the numerous issues raised in Chapters 7 and 9. Sharing the burden of refugees globally is always problematic in practice, despite it being the stated objective of the relevant international law and institutions. Much less reported is the situation in Yemen, which was, on many humanitarian indicators at the start of 2017, a more serious situation than in Syria. Conflict erupted here in 2015, and patterns similar to those seen in

Syria, with numerous armed groups controlling parts of the country, rapidly emerged.

One armed group that came to prominence was the one that renamed itself the Islamic State in 2014. I refer to this group as Daesh for reasons that will be explained in Chapter 6. Having taken control of some areas of Syria, in August 2014 Daesh brushed aside part of the Syria-Iraq border and seized control of part of Iraq, and their takeover of the city of Mosul led to much displacement. Christians and adherents of other non-Muslim religions were, typically, given the choice to leave, pay 'protection money', convert to Islam, or be killed. Shi'a Muslims were given fewer options, with all too many murdered on the spot. Many of the victims of Daesh's atrocities are Muslims.

The group issued a global call for migration, urging Muslims everywhere to move to 'their state'. Those who responded represent a tiny fraction of the global Muslim population. One wonders how many Muslims worldwide lived with the fear of waking to a text or email from a child saying that they had joined Daesh. We must also note that Daesh uses the term 'Muslim' to mean 'Muslims who think like we do'. Certainly they exclude Shi'ite Muslims from their definition.

This survey of conflict and forced migration shows that migration is all too common, and that for some of those affected there is no quick recovery. Some displaced people remain displaced for generations. In the long term, a new *normal* needs to be established. The term 'resilience' is often used to speak about the ability to recover from a setback and return to *normal*. Across the Middle East there are many situations where 'resilience' is not applicable; there is no return to what was regarded as *normal* prior to a particular displacement. So, what is needed for the displaced? What does a typical forced migration look like, and what support is required from those who are willing and able to become involved in addressing it?

What do the forcibly displaced need most? The roles of UNHCR and FBOs

We might define a disaster as an interruption to normal life. This includes disruption from natural as well as man-made causes. The term 'disaster' is applied to events on a scale that means they affect a large or significant number of people, but similar principles apply to small-scale incidents such as house fires or religiously motivated persecution of individuals or families.

The initial emergency response is to meet the basic needs for water, shelter, food, medical care and security in the first place of safety reached by people leaving disaster. By security here we mean a sense of being safe, of protection from danger. The initial objectives are focused on stabilising the situation. The next stage is to begin recovery work that creates a new *normal*. After natural disasters this is often achieved by rebuilding damaged or destroyed homes, businesses and infrastructure. The idea of 'resilience' is often applicable in such situations, since a return to 'normal life' as it was prior to the crisis is a realistic goal.

What about situations where resilience is less applicable – those situations where returning home is unlikely for a significant period of time? Here, people need to settle in the first safe location reached or move on elsewhere in a controlled and supported manner. Alas, all too many become stuck in instability for years.

In December 2012 António Guterres, then head of the UNHCR, invited more than 400 leaders of faith-based organisations (FBOs) to discuss better support for the displaced.[22] The two-day meeting held in Geneva had the title *Faith and Protection*, and included people from several religions. It was one of a series of High Commissioner's dialogues under the umbrella term of *Protection Challenges*.[23] We will look at the principles that emerged from this consultation; but first, we need to introduce the role of the UNHCR and FBOs in disaster contexts.

The UNHCR is the UN agency responsible for the international refugee system. It was established in the 1940s, replacing several earlier organisations. Its mandate is to operate systems that support forcibly displaced people until they are able to return home or are able to establish a new life elsewhere. As part of the UN's apparatus, it is obliged to respect the primacy of national governments; wherever it operates, it is obliged to work in accordance with the wishes of the government of that country.

FBOs are typically non-governmental organisations (NGOs) with an overt religious basis to their mandate

[22] António Guterres led the UNHCR from 2005 to 2015. In January 2017 he became Secretary General of the United Nations.
[23] See for example UNHCR; *Background Document*; 29th November 2012; www.unhcr.org/uk/protection/hcdialogue/50aa5b879/background-document.htm; (accessed 2nd May 2017)

and operations. Many FBOs have charitable status, although some choose not to for a variety of reasons. We need to acknowledge that FBOs are controversial in some circles. Much of this controversy is rooted in concerns over respect for gender equality. Various branches of several major religions are perceived to give women lower status than men in some areas of life, and one of the first principles of humanitarian work is that it is conducted without discrimination. Many FBOs which are active in providing humanitarian support are well able to demonstrate that they fulfil the principle of providing aid without discrimination on gender or other lines. Some organisations are founded and largely staffed by people with a religious conviction while the organisation does not include reference to this in its core documents. Such entities are NGOs but not officially FBOs, despite their founding being rooted in the practical expression of a religious belief.

Five principles emerged from the December 2012 consultation between UNHCR and FBOs. First, that being able to express their religious faith is essential to enable displaced persons to recover. Conversely, denial of religious expression works to keep people trapped in instability. Religious beliefs enable many adherents to put their situation into a broader context, allow them to start expressing what has happened to them and their community, and provide a starting point for coming to terms with their radically changed circumstances.

Second, that the displaced need to be welcomed by host communities. What is at stake here is addressing the sense of isolation, of being alone. Conversely, a lack of welcome exacerbates the sense of rejection that was experienced when they were forced to migrate in the first place. Host communities are often limited in their welcome, although, on a more positive note, some are very welcoming and willing to adapt, and to assist the displaced to settle, establish themselves and become integrated.

Third, that the emotional capacity of the displaced needs rebuilding. Physical healing, where required, is part of recovery. Equally important is psychological healing. Awareness and provision of post-trauma support emerged in the 1980s, though one might argue that it provided a researched, academic and professional basis for the practices that had been employed by generations of those affected by traumatic events. This professionalization, which established and propagated best practice, began in the West. One trend over recent years amongst organisations who are involved in supporting those who have faced persecution for being or becoming a Christian has been to provide post-trauma support to victims. More significant has been the encouragement and enabling of some Middle Eastern people to become qualified in the field, and to provide such a service amongst their own communities.

Fourth, that displaced persons need the capacity to become part of a community that values them for what they contribute as well as who they are. One indication that initial recovery is underway is when the displaced realise that a new *normal* must be established, and that they need to participate actively in making this happen. It requires the host community to create the space for this, which often entails providing education for children, local language learning for all, and opportunities for employment and trade to those who can work.

This leads to the final point, which is that the vast majority of displaced people are willing and able to participate in meeting their own needs. They seek opportunities to help themselves, not to simply be recipients of aid provided by others. For many human beings, being able to work – to provide for oneself and one's dependents – affirms dignity and nourishes a sense of self-worth; meaning, for example, that if construction is needed, then the displaced should be involved in the work. In the next chapter we will describe an informal school that was established with displaced people with teaching skills being employed as the teachers.

An illustration of the latter idea is provided by Victoria Hislop in her novel *The Island*, which focuses on a leper colony in the mid-twentieth century. The inhabitants of the island had been forced to migrate because of an illness which at the time was incurable and (falsely) thought to be easily communicable to others. Chapters 5 and 6 of this novel discuss the desire of some members of this colony to improve the lot of themselves and of the community which they had been obliged to join.[24]

Amongst the issues and factors that need to be kept in mind is the fact that the displaced need a sense of hope in the future. If that is restricted or denied where they are, then those who are able will seek to move again, searching for a location where they can be self-supporting and contribute to society.

[24] Victoria Hislop; *The Island* (2005, Headline Review)

What also needs to be kept in mind is the place of religion within society. In their book *God is Back*, John Micklethwait and Adrian Wooldridge, two prominent journalists, note that religion is playing an increasingly significant role in the lives of more people.[25] It is a recognition that religious factors in events need to be taken into account when understanding and responding to events, and that religions can provide a positive contribution to societies which are willing to welcome their contribution to a pluralistic society.

This chapter has focussed on irregular migration. The previous chapter noted the issues of migrant workers – a topic to which we will return in Chapter 4. Before that, we will pause to examine the terminology surrounding various categories of migrants. Who is a 'refugee' in the legal sense of the word? Who is one in the usually broader sense in common usage? Are

[25] John Micklethwait and Adrian Wooldridge; *God is Back* (2009, Penguin); in 2009 John Micklethwait was Editor-in-Chief of *The Economist* (he moved to Bloomberg in 2015) and Adrian Wooldridge was *The Economist's* Washington Bureau chief.

some economic migrants? When do students become economic migrants? For some of those who have moved to other countries the answers to such questions are not clear; their experience defies neat categorisation. Finally, it is worth keeping in mind that we are all the descendants of those who migrated. Many of us have come to belong somewhere; others of us are in the process of making somewhere new our home.

Chapter 3
Terminology – refugee, migrant worker, etc.

The terminology around migration has become increasingly mixed. Crucial to our understanding is that most usages of the word 'refugee' do not apply the word according to the legal definition of 'a refugee'. In this chapter we will define our terms, and use some stories that illustrate why neat categorisation does not, and cannot, work. Reducing issues to neat, flat 'a versus b' generalities might provide a useful starting point when first encountering the topic, but these inherent oversimplifications will need to be expanded whenever depth of awareness, understanding and insight are required. We will look at the terms for the forcibly displaced before looking at those for people who migrate for leisure, study or work.

The legal definition of the word refugee is important, and we need to keep applying it. It is in the United Nations Convention Relating to the Status of Refugees, known as the 1951 Refugee Convention, as well as in the Additional Protocol added in 1967.[26] We will describe the derivation of this in Chapter 9, when we explore the extent to which the international system is fit-for-purpose in the twenty-first century. Suffice to say here that the 1951 Convention restricted the term 'refugee' to those fleeing their country prior to 1st January 1951, and the 1967 Protocol removed this restriction. UN member states are encouraged to become 'state parties' to the Convention, meaning that they undertake to include the provisions in domestic law.

The international norm is to encourage countries to establish national systems for handling forcibly displaced people. Almost all Western countries have such systems, which use the term 'asylum.' The international system, which is overseen by the UNHCR, covers countries without a national system. We will look at the international system first and then describe the similarities and differences commonly seen between national systems.

[26] Available at www.unhcr.org/uk/1951-refugee-convention.html (accessed 16th August 2016)

The legal definition of the term **refugee** which is given in Article 1 of the Convention applies to a person who:

> "owing to well-founded fear of being persecuted for reasons of race, religion, nationality, membership of a particular social group or political opinion, is outside the country of his nationality and is unable or, owing to such fear, is unwilling to avail himself of the protection of that country; or who, not having a nationality and being outside the country of his former habitual residence as a result of such events, is unable or, owing to such fear, is unwilling to return to it."

We will note in passing here that this definition includes a recognition that some people are *stateless* – defined as someone "who is not considered as a national by any State under the operation of its law."[27] We will return to this topic in Chapters 6 and 9.

---

[27] UNHCR; "Introductory Note" to the *1954 Convention relating to the Status of Stateless Person*; page 3; www.unhcr.org/ibelong/wp-content/uploads/1954-Convention-relating-to-the-Status-of-Stateless-Persons_ENG.pdf; (accessed 1st May 2017)

In legal terminology, one cannot be a refugee in one's own country. A person who is displaced within their own country is referred to as an *internally displaced person*, **IDP** for short, with the plural being *internally displaced persons*, IDPs. In some usages the word 'people' is used instead of persons. This definition is clear in legal terminology, but in Chapters 6 and 8 we will see situations in which it is problematic in practice, in parts of Iraq and Somalia.

Those who cross a state border into another country to escape conflict or persecution need to apply for some form of status in the country they have reached. Typically, they apply to be recognised as refugees. At this point they are **applicants for refugee status**. Whilst their claim is being evaluated and assessed they cannot be forced to return to their own country. If their claim is accepted, they have 'refugee status', and the term 'refugee' is applicable in the legal sense. People with refugee status cannot be compelled under normal circumstances to return to their country. This is known as the principle of **non-refoulement**. Exceptions can be made if the refugee is convicted of a serious crime, or if their presence threatens the national security of the host country.[28] This is the theory; but alas there are examples of it being broken, two of which are described in Appendix 4.

Most people are careful to discern two forms of refoulement. The first is where someone is directly rejected or expelled, and thereby forcibly returned to a location where they face serious threats to their life or liberty. A second form is the use of indirect pressure that is so intense that it leads individuals to believe that they have no practical options other than to return to a location where they face a serious risk of persecution or threats to their life or liberty.

Those who have, or who are seeking, refugee status always have the option of making a **voluntary return** – that is, choosing to return to their own country. Doing so automatically invalidates any refugee status or application. There are positive reasons for a voluntary return, such as positive changes in the home country, and we will see an example in Chapter 6. A more subtle reason for voluntary return is when people fail to settle in the country they have moved to, and decide to face the challenges that might arise back home. We will see an example of this in Chapter 5.

[28] Refoulement is covered by Article 33 of the Refugee Convention.

In practice, the criteria to be granted refugee status are threefold. First, applicants must describe why they are unwilling to return to their own country. There are typically two ways to achieve this. One is to show that the applicant has been the victim of serious injustice or harm, and that this is likely to happen again should the applicant return. A common method of demonstrating this is photographs of the injuries. This is colloquially referred to as 'show me the scars'. The alternative approach is to present documentary evidence that somebody with a very similar situation to the applicant's has suffered, or is suffering, serious mistreatment. Either way, something amounting to serious abuse has to have occurred to someone.

Second, it must be shown that what the applicant fears is a substantial fear. In practice, this means that there is a credible threat to either their life or their liberty.

Third, it must be shown that the applicant's own country is either unable or unwilling to provide due protection. There is a subtle challenge here; those granting refugee status are making a statement about the government of the applicant's country of nationality. In situations of violent conflict and crisis – such as Syria – or substantial natural disaster, then this is obvious. In Chapter 5 we will see examples of situations where this can be problematic.

One subtle point is that in many contexts, 'threat to life' means being killed, murdered or executed after an unjust trial; it does not include starving because of exclusion from society, discrimination in employment or the absence of a social welfare safety net that is applicable to everyone. If the definition is harshly applied, then it can become a source of abuse for some. We will return to this in Chapter 9.

Being granted **refugee status** is a significant step since it guarantees – at least in theory – safety and some level of support. The person or family concerned moves into the next stage of the process, which is a **resettlement** programme. This process looks for a country willing to offer the refugee a permanent home. Many refugees spend years awaiting resettlement.

If and when someone is accepted for resettlement, they are obliged to move to a third country. There are very occasional exceptions when the country in which they are residing agrees to their remaining permanently. If the resettlement process has taken a long time then this second move can be as traumatic as the original flight from the danger in their own country.

An alternative to refugee status is **protected status**. This means that it has been accepted that the person cannot return home at this time, but that those in authority expect that they will be able to return safely at some point, and the situation will be kept under review. Those with protected status can stay where they are, although they cannot settle on a permanent basis; they must expect to be obliged to leave their new home for their former one at some point.

The final possible outcome of an application for refugee status is rejection. This gives the applicant no legal status where they are. They are being told that those making the decision believe that they can return safely to their own country. In some cases this means the authorities think they will be safe somewhere in their own country even if they would not be safe in the place that they used to call home. People whose applications are rejected are expected to make a voluntary return, move to a third country willing to let them enter, or face deportation. Deportation is a complex and potentially expensive process for the reasons described in Appendix 4; it is the option of last resort for many host countries.

Those countries that operate their own **asylum systems** typically apply similar criteria and processes. So, formally, someone who applies is referred to as an 'asylum applicant' or 'asylum seeker'. Colloquially, the term refugee is often used. Those whose applications are accepted are granted the right to remain – some on a permanent basis, which usually leads to citizenship in due course, and others on a temporary basis under 'protected status'.

Of note is the fact that people can only apply for asylum after they have entered a country. One subtle but significant change in recent years was that several countries changed the law and procedures at airports so that those in transit were not allowed to go to the immigration desks and apply for asylum. Some years ago, a mother and her children used such a practice to apply for asylum in Germany. She and her husband were suffering intense religiously-motivated persecution. She had been able to go on holiday to an African country, and was transiting through a German airport on the way home. She followed signs for arrivals, ignoring the signs for flight transfers, and at the immigration desk she applied for asylum. At that time, this was a legally valid procedure. Her application was duly accepted, and she was allowed into the country, where she could remain while her case was evaluated. This procedure is no longer valid. Anyone attempting to do this today would be informed that they had not yet entered Germany, and so were not eligible to apply for asylum. They would then be escorted to the transfer desk and on to their connecting flight. Germany is by no means the only country to have changed their law and procedures in this way to reduce the number of applicants for asylum.

The extent to which countries allow asylum seekers to work varies. This is also the case with refugee systems – some countries allow applicants and those in resettlement programmes only limited opportunities for employment. We will look at the advantages and disadvantages of this in Chapter 9.

The accepted international norm is that people should apply for refugee/asylum status in the first safe location that they reach. Within the EU, this is enacted as the 'Dublin Principle', which we will explore in Chapter 7. In practice, this norm inhibits equitable burden sharing amongst countries, an issue that we will examine in Chapter 9.

The principle of **family reunification** is recognised in the immigration laws of many countries. This principle allows those legally resident in a country to sponsor the arrival of close family members. In most cases, the law stipulates criteria for this, which can include the person or persons already resident having sufficient financial income or resources to provide for their relatives.

For many applicants, the refugee and asylum processes are traumatic. The many people who are denied the opportunity to work often find the way they are treated to be dehumanising. We must remember that these processes commonly take years.

I tend to use the term **displaced persons** to cover all people forcibly displaced from their homes; it is an umbrella term for IDPs, refugees, applicants for refugee status and asylum seekers.

Having looked at forced migration, we must now turn our attention to those who choose to migrate. Typically, they fall into three broad categories: workers, students and tourists, plus a number of less commonly-used and more specialised types. As with other terminology, neat categorisation rarely works well here.

We look at the broad categories, beginning with tourism, the means by which many travel abroad.

Tourism is a global industry, with numerous countries seeking to attract visitors from elsewhere. For some it is simply a vacation on a beach or beside a pool, for others it is adventure in strange and different places; for many, tourism broadens the mind by exposure to different peoples and cultures.

We can define tourism as visiting another country for a short period of time, during which one does not undertake either paid employment or formal academic study. Many people visit other countries as part of their work, for example to attend conferences, participate in meetings, conduct research, or to meet with associates, suppliers and customers. Their entry into the countries visited is typically on a 'tourist' visa, whether it is one applied for in advance or received upon arrival. This also applies to those travelling to undertake short-term voluntary work. This is a minor example of neat categorisation being overly simple.

Likewise, higher education is a global industry, both for students and academic staff. The UK is one of many countries that actively seeks students from other countries. Such people add to the number of potential applicants to universities, and add to the pluralistic dynamics of classrooms, seminars and student communities, all of which enrich the student experience and broaden the learning of all. It is noteworthy that many universities globally are offering courses taught in English precisely in order to attract expatriate students.

Most countries allow foreign students to work. Usually this is restricted to part time work during term, with more weekly hours permitted during vacations. As we have said, neat categorisation rarely works; people in this category are part-time migrant workers as well as foreign students.

Student visas are typically valid for one academic year, and the initial application requires an acceptance letter from the institution where they will be studying. Those on multi-year courses can renew their visa upon successful completion of each academic year.

Some countries offer foreign students a post-study work visa for one or two years. The intention here is to give them work experience that complements their academic study. It can also be viewed as a long-term investment in them, trusting that they will look favourably on the country where they studied, and seek increased business links with that country throughout their careers, to mutual benefit.

This leads us to the third category of those visiting other countries, namely those with formal employment. Simplistically, they fall into two categories: those who arrive in a country with a job already arranged, and those who enter and then start looking for suitable employment. One might use the terms **migrant worker** for the former and **economic migrant** for the latter. A rather specialised category is those people who are establishing their own business as an expatriate.

Many migrant workers send some of their income to family members in their country of origin. These payments are typically referred to as **foreign remittances**. For some countries, such money is a large source of money from abroad, and in some – for example Lebanon – such remittances both come in and go out from the country. I recall one Lebanese friend lamenting the significant outflow of funds to neighbouring Syria. "If there are one million Syrians here and they each send just US$10 per month home, that is a ten million dollar a month drain on our economy." He was not in the mood for a discussion on this, so I chose not to mention the inflow of capital from numerous other countries sent by Lebanese people working abroad. Nor did I mention that most migrant workers spend most of their income in covering their accommodation and living costs, and so their money is circulating in the local economy. Those with executive and other highly-paid positions are an exception to this.

A visitor to a South-East Asian country observed that approximately every third house in several streets had been substantially improved. In reply, a national explained that those were the homes where the family had a member working abroad. Foreign remittances are a form of wealth redistribution on a global, cross-national basis.

Some migrant workers bring some close relatives with them, typically their spouse and children. Obtaining visas for other relatives can be problematic, even for a visit. For example, a Jordanian family in one of the small Gulf States applied for the husband's elderly mother to come for a four-month visit. The husband's siblings were seeking to share the care of their elderly mother amongst themselves, including the one working abroad. The application was refused, much to the disappointment of the wider family, although a second was successful.

Some of the smaller categories are for diplomats and humanitarian visas. We will look at an example of the latter in Chapter 5. I regard diplomats as those who do migration the easy way, at least in terms of the formal processes of entry to and residency in foreign countries; like other migrant workers, they have a job to do, with all that that entails.

In Chapter 2 we described Ayatollah Khomeini's time in France from the 1960s to 1979 as **exile**. This term is applied to people who leave their country for political reasons, often related to having challenged an autocrat who responds with threats of imprisonment or other serious consequences.

As noted in the Introduction, I am using the term *migrant* as a collective term for all those moving away from home by choice or force. I also use the terms **regular migration** and **irregular migration**, usually to distinguish between migration that is fully legal, following all due border-crossing procedures, and that which is illegal. This terminology is intended to be gentler and non-judgemental, recognising that there are situations in which people believe that they have no good, legal options available.

Most migrants can be asked to leave the countries in which they are resident. The exception is those who have refugee status, or who have an application for such status. Those whose applications are rejected can be deported. Regular migrants can be expelled, meaning that their visa is cancelled and they are obliged to leave the country within a defined, and usually short, timeframe.

One story illustrates why neat categorisation breaks down. Someone who had worked in Afghanistan explained how Afghans were able to finance travelling to Europe using irregular means. "Several families get together and choose which of their young adults to send, and they pool their resources to pay for the travel. They pick the person most likely to handle the journey and then find employment. When the person is successful, he will send money back that repays the investment made by all contributors. In due course they hope that the person who was sent will facilitate others being able to migrate." So, how should we categorise the person sent? He is travelling in search of work, so the term economic migrant would be applicable. He becomes a migrant worker should he be successful. The migrant frequently presents himself as a 'refugee' who has been forced to leave his country. He makes his story fit whatever is most likely to secure him entry.

This illustrates the term ***transit country***. In this case, Iran and Turkey are transited as the migrant makes his way towards Europe. He will probably regard Greece and the Balkan states as transit countries on his route to his preferred destination in Western Europe.

Some people who undertaking such journeys by irregular means use the services of a **people smuggler**, often shortened to smuggler. The definition of a smuggler is someone receiving financial payment or other material gain for assisting someone in crossing international borders illegally. Such arrangements are consensual; the migrant voluntarily enters into what is a commercial transaction. International law on this criminalises the smuggler but not the client/migrant. There is a contrast here with **people traffickers**, who move others across borders without their consent. People-smuggling has become a very lucrative global business whose financial value is considerably higher than that of the trade in illegal drugs or weapons. One exposition of this 'industry' is given by Peter Tinti and Tuesday

Reitano in their book *Migrant, Refugee, Smuggler, Saviour*.[29]

Our next three chapters consider different reasons why some people migrate. In Chapter 6 we look at forced displacement due to armed conflict. This follows a chapter looking at those who migrate for one of a variety of religious reasons. First, though, it is worth reflecting further on people who migrate for work or study. In these three chapters we will observe that simplistic distinctions and categorisation frequently break down. We will also notice that some migrate for short periods, others for decades and a few permanently. Some do very well, finding fulfilment, purpose and quality of life; others suffer abuse and heartbreak. There are always risks in migration.

[29] Peter Tinti and Tuesday Reitano; *Migrant, Refugee, Smuggler, Saviour* (2016, Hurst Publishers)

Chapter 4
Migrant Workers – cherished or exploited?

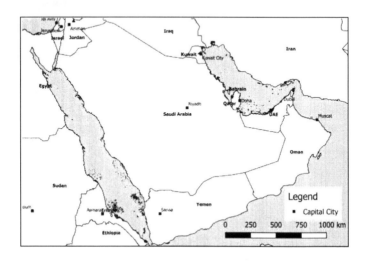

In this chapter we will explore further some aspects of the situation of migrant workers. The chapter begins with a story and reflections from migrants in the UK, before returning to our focus on the Middle East region.

Some migrant workers live and work in another country for many years; others go for short periods. One example of this is in the medical profession. Part of many training programmes is to do an 'elective' abroad. Typically, the exact nature of what is done is secondary to the general learning aim of broadening experience by participating in the medical system in a different context to one's own. Continuing professional development for some doctors is sometimes achieved by their working in another country for a period of time. Some years ago I heard about several doctors coming to the UK for a one-year placement. Each brought their wife and children with them. (I record the story here as told, aware that there is an inherent element of gender stereotyping). On arrival their plan was to stay for a year and then return home: the doctor was committed to serving his community. However, as the families settled into life in the UK their attitudes and plans started to change. For most families, it was the wife who first stated her wish to stay. In the UK she was treated by society as a person in her own right, not as a chattel of her husband. It is noteworthy here that the wives responded to the *pull* factor of the treatment of women.

Literally millions of people migrate to the Arabian Peninsula countries to work. Qatar and the UAE have very high numbers of migrant workers. During 2016 I was told that just 15% of Qatar's population had Qatari nationality, with the remaining 85% being expatriates. Some of the nationals, reportedly, do not feel like citizens; they have no say in how the country is governed and hence struggle to regard it as theirs, and this is rooted in the governance of the country. They are living as *subjects* of the Emir, grateful for the stability and prosperity, but they do not regard themselves as *citizens* of a state or nation.

In 2010 the UAE's National Bureau of Statistics reported that 18.6% of the total population were nationals, with the other 81.4% being migrant workers. Some estimate that the population of Dubai, one of the seven Emirates that comprise the UAE, was doubling every two years prior to 2008. The financial crisis caused a two-year interruption to the pattern of increasing numbers of migrant workers, and in October 2010 a net immigration rate of 7% per year was reported. Anecdotal evidence suggests that population growth has continued since then.

Many migrants in the Arabian Peninsula are from Asian countries, including Bangladesh, India, Pakistan, Sri Lanka and the Philippines. A rising trend is Chinese people working abroad, although their patterns of employment are different. There are also many Africans, notably Nigerians. A few statistics give us an idea of the scale of migration involved. The Indian Foreign Ministry reported that 781,000

Indians emigrated during 2015, and 817,000 during 2014. During the 2000s, a Filipino Christian leader told me that his country had "tithed its population." A 'tithe' is 10%. Given that the population was estimated at 101 million in 2015, the implication is that approximately ten million Filipinos are migrant workers abroad.

Not all migrants are treated well, as we noted in Chapter 1. In the Arabian Peninsula, attention has been drawn particularly to the conditions for construction workers in Qatar, Dubai and elsewhere. The award of the 2022 soccer World Cup to Qatar has led to an increase in such attention, albeit an interest that is easily distracted by more dramatic developments in the Middle East and around the world.

Migrant workers are very vulnerable to economic peaks and troughs. One story from August 2016 illustrates some of the issues here. The reduction in the price of crude oil from June 2014 onwards led to an estimated 10,000 Indians becoming trapped in Saudi Arabia. They had been working for an oil company which reduced its workforce in response to lower income. The Indians lost their jobs, and had not been paid for the last few months of their employment. Consequently, they were unable to afford flight tickets home. Some, but not all, were being provided with food and drink by their former employer. The Indian government was working with the Saudi Arabian authorities to resolve the situation.[30]

The six Gulf Cooperation Council (GCC) countries of Bahrain, Kuwait, Oman, Qatar, Saudi Arabia and the UAE have collectively come under pressure to address the abuse of some migrant domestic workers, and to reform the 'kafala' sponsorship system so that it meets the standards recommended by the International Labour Organisation's Domestic Workers' Convention. Under the 'kafala' system, employers sponsor the employees' work and residency permits, and hold the employees' passport, thereby tying the worker to one employer. The changes being sought are for the worker to deal directly with the host government, and retain possession of their passport. Such a system would

[30] Asia News; *Foreign Minister: We will bring home 10 thousand Indian workers laid off in Saudi Arabia*; 2nd August 2016; www.asianews.it/news-en/Foreign-Minister:-We-will-bring-home-10-thousand-Indian-workers-laid-off-in-Saudi-Arabia-38204.html (accessed 31st January 2017)

allow the migrant to change employers, thereby enabling them to escape from situations that they found abusive. There has been some commitment to reform, including the drafting of a GCC standard contract, though during 2013 the proposed reforms were assessed as inadequate by many human rights organisations.[31] Kuwait and Qatar have made subsequent changes, addressing many of the concerns raised.

The governments of Oman and Saudi Arabia have policies and programmes to reduce their dependence on migrant workers and boost the rates of employment for their nationals. These programmes are straightforward in theory but far less so in practice.

Saudi Arabia – Vision2030 challenges patronage and other current norms

There are an estimated five million migrant workers in Saudi Arabia. The policy of 'Saudi-isation' (mentioned above), began around the turn of the millennium. Progress remains limited despite a

[31] Human Rights Watch; *Proposed domestic workers contract falls short*; 17th November 2013; www.hrw.org/news/2013/11/16/proposed-domestic-workers-contract-falls-short (accessed 31st January 2017)

number of specific initiatives. The government imposed a fee on employers of 2,500 Riyals (approximately US$650) for each expatriate worker, changed the working week for expatriates to be five days per week rather than six, and raised the minimum wage for Saudis. One effect was that many employers did not officially renew migrants' contracts, meaning that they became illegal residents, and the new laws on working hours were not applied to them. During 2013, the government introduced several measures aimed at reducing the number of migrants working illegally. The measures included making employers liable for the deportation costs of any illegal migrants they were employing, and granted amnesty until 4th November 2013, allowing time for employers and migrants either to regularise their status or to leave. On 4th November, the government initiated a crackdown on those whose residency permits had expired. The crackdown led to violent protests, during which at least five people were killed.

On 25th April 2016 Saudi Arabia announced an economic plan entitled Vision 2030, with the stated aim of confirming the country's status at "the heart of the Arab and Islamic worlds, the investment power house, and the hub connecting three continents." In essence Vision 2030 is an economic diversification programme aimed at reducing the country's dependence on oil exports, which also included an initiative to offer, for the first time, shares in Saudi Aramco, the state-owned oil company. It implied a more open society, at least concerning employment, and will require changes to the education system.

Several factors make Vision 2030 and Saudi-isation difficult. First, many nationals are either unable or unwilling to do certain jobs. For instance, a national would not be hired to work as a family driver, resulting in there being a few hundred thousand foreign men with a job title of 'family driver'. There are many other positions that Saudi nationals would not typically take, such as shopkeepers, street sweepers or garbage collectors. The latter two government services are contracted to Saudi companies who in turn hire mostly Bangladeshi staff. Many nationals want a senior or middle management job immediately (as we saw in Chapter 1), and have a poor work ethic. In February 2010 it was reported that 30 Saudi women were employed as domestic workers in Qatar. The *Saudi Gazette*, an official government publication, commented that citizens being employed in menial work abroad brought shame on the nation.

Second, the service sector pays wages for many jobs, notably in construction and menial tasks, that would not support a local family but which will support a migrant worker who is willing to live in communal accommodation and has no family to support. Changing this would cause a serious period of inflation. Some have noted that the expulsion of many illegal migrants during 2013 caused price rises for some goods and services, reflecting the reliance on migrant workers within many sectors.

Third, the prevalence of corruption and patronage stifles economic development. The concept of patronage is prevalent within many Middle Eastern societies.[32] It is rooted in the assumption that there are limited resources and few opportunities for individuals and groups, leading people to seek a champion or provider – a patron – who will provide them with resources and opportunities in return for loyalty. In many cases, people seek to imitate their patron. Typically, people look to their father or tribal elder as their patron; some look to their government;

[32] One Arab writer who draws attention to the effects of patronage is Marwan Muasher in his book *The Second Arab Awakening and the Battle for Pluralism* (2014, Yale University Press), e.g. pages 31-32, using the term 'rentier system'.

others to non-state actors including armed groups. Nepotism and corruption are significant factors underpinning patronage in many places.

In addition, there are concerns that the education system does not adequately prepare many students for professional employment, which is one reason why many Saudis study abroad. One measure to address this was the opening of the King Abdullah University of Science and Technology (KAUST) in September 2009. This institution is outside the control of the Ministry of Education, thereby allowing it to be co-educational, and removing the requirement for Islamic study in all degree programmes.

The under-employment or unemployment of Saudis that has resulted from this combination of factors has been a serious and growing problem. A concern in many countries is that unemployed youth are susceptible to recruitment by extremist groups. A specific factor that is relevant in Saudi Arabia is that decreasing oil reserves will mean that the country is likely to hit an economic crisis at some point, with some commentators suggesting this may occur within the next 20 years. Analysts note that continued lack of diversification, coupled with corruption, poor work-ethic, rising population, the proliferation of social media, and other factors, could be considered a 'time bomb' with the potential for significant social unrest. Vision 2030 is one aspect of the government's response to such concerns.

So what issues are pertinent to our study of migrant workers? The number of people looking to migrate to work globally is large; there is no shortage of willing workers. In many Arabian Peninsula contexts, there is a wide variety of jobs which nationals are unwilling to take. This arises from social expectations of what is acceptable for whom, as well as issues around work ethic and expectations, educational level and unwillingness to work one's way up the career ladder. Efforts to reduce dependence on migrant workers can be problematic, with consequences for wage rates and consequently the costs of services and goods in the economy.

Oman – education and professionalisation

Oman also has policies and programmes concerning migrant workers. In Oman these workers comprise approximately 23% of the population, rising to around half the population in some places. Meanwhile, the indigenous population is growing, and to ensure that there are jobs for this expanding national workforce, the state has an effective programme of Omanisation, whereby expatriate workers are removed, usually by non-renewal of their contract and/or residency permits, and the jobs they held are made available to nationals. The government actively promotes the adoption of work that is currently undertaken by expatriates as being suitable for locals. For example, during the 2000s the government decreed that all bus drivers must be Omanis, though by contrast, not many Omanis are motorcycle mechanics. Omanis may work as motorcycle mechanics, but until there is a sizeable and growing number, the government will not set an Omanisation target date for this profession.

Oman has a long-standing economic development programme, underpinned by a constantly improving education system. These initiatives were introduced by Sultan Qabous Bin Sa'id Al Sa'id, who has been the monarch since 1970. He has also encouraged many Omanis living in East Africa to return and contribute to the modernisation and economic development of the country. He is widely respected, and the development he has overseen is much appreciated by the majority of Omanis.

The country continues to experience several social transitions as well. One is urbanisation, as many people switch from an agrarian/nomadic lifestyle to an urban lifestyle. This shift is causing significant social disruption. For some families, it is only the men who move to the cities to work, returning to their families periodically. Nomadic peoples use vehicles rather than camels (even if they own camels), and some are nomadic for part of the year and urban for the rest. Another change is that economic development and global media are transforming the attitudes and behaviour of the younger generations, notably in how they dress. This is causing some tensions between older and younger generations.

Intertwining regular and irregular migration

The GCC countries welcome migrant workers but they do not welcome refugees. Iraqis and Syrians are treated in the same way as those of any other nationality; they may enter as migrant workers if they can secure suitable employment.

One situation that has confronted Saudi Arabia and Oman with the issue of irregular migration has been the proximity of Yemen. Yemen is a state party to the Refugee Convention, and the UNHCR operates in the country supporting people who have moved there from the Horn of Africa. Most of these irregular migrants regard Yemen as a transit country en route to GCC members. One suspects that few actually succeed in reaching GCC destinations, because the terrain is difficult and the authorities alert. Saudi Arabia has constructed a fence along parts of its border with Yemen.

Urbanisation is another form of migration, with people moving from rural to urban settings. The UN estimates that the world population living in urban settings passed 50% for the first time at the end of 2008, and such migration often causes social tensions. One reason for this is that typically it is younger people who move, giving skewed demographics in both the rural and urban locations. Some young migrant men look for a bride from their home area once they have established themselves in the urban context, and a practice in parts of Africa is that a man will have a village wife and a city wife, a form of polygamy with some degree of social acceptance. Such trends break down long-standing patterns of care for the elderly, because they mean that younger, usually female, people are not available to provide care in the home.

Migration is *from* the Arabian Peninsula as well as *to* it. We noted in passing that many Saudis choose to study abroad. Many nationals also holiday abroad, and many go elsewhere to escape the intense summer weather. One revealing anecdote illustrates why some want to ensure that they always have the option of migrating elsewhere.

In conversation, one national mentioned to me that he was planning to trade in his yacht for a larger one. He explained that it would have a greater range, which would give him more options, especially if he needed to leave this part of the world. Here is a wealthy, highly able person whose life choices include being alert to the possible need to relocate at short notice. It emerged that the same man owned properties, but not in his own country. At home he was content to rent; his ownership was restricted to the West. Why? Because in London, New York and other Western cities, property ownership was respected and protected by law. In his country, and many like it, there was always the risk that an autocrat might just seize property. The current ruler might be respected as trustworthy in such matters; however, the future was unknown, because his successors might act differently.

What strikes me here is this man's awareness of the situation in his own country and the difference between his country and the Western value and practice that the clear rule of law should be applied equally to all. One suspects that he longs for his country to operate in a similar manner, with due respect for its history and culture. What power or influence does he have to seek change? Is he willing and able to engage constructively, albeit whilst being aware of the risks involved in seeming to challenge the status quo? It seems that the option of being a migrant is more appealing to him; and he has the resources to be confident of being able to migrate well. He is thinking as a *subject* not as a *citizen* of his country.

The question of who precisely is a migrant worker is not always clear. Some years ago I got to know Stephen (not his real name). Stephen arrived in a foreign country (European, but not the UK) as a student. He had a place at a college, and a student visa. He came with a certain set of expectations based on the recruitment literature provided, and suffice it to say that the reality was very different. For example, he had been promised that accommodation would be provided for him, whereas the reality was that he was given a bed for the first night and told to find somewhere to live on his first full day in the country. Another mismatch between promise and reality was the promise that a work placement would be provided. This proved problematic.

Stephen successfully completed the first year of his course, but was unable to pay the fees for the second year. The first year had to be paid in advance. His family had made significant sacrifices to finance their son studying abroad. What was he to do? Could he go home without the qualification? Could he stay, endeavour to earn some money and pay his way through college?

The student visa was valid for a year. It could be renewed – quite easily – provided he had the paperwork to say that he had successfully completed the previous year and paid the fees for the second year. He only had half of the funds required, and so the visa was going to expire. Like all too many in that country, he decided to stay and work, acknowledging that he would become an irregular migrant. For him, like many in similar situations, returning home is the option of last resort when one has not accomplished what one was sent by one's family to achieve.

Stephen found a job in a restaurant that provided board and lodging plus a small salary. Later he found a job with a construction firm. In both cases he was fortunate with his employers; both honoured their commitments to him. He was paid in cash because he could not operate a bank account without a valid visa. Occasionally the construction firm manager phoned him in the morning and asked him not to come to work that day, as he was expecting a visit from the inspectors and did not want an illegal migrant worker on site at the time. The employers were accepting some degree of risk – they would be fined if they were found to be employing an illegal migrant. Equally, they had businesses to operate and needed staff, and the jobs being done were not attractive to most nationals. The economy was well known to, if not rely on, certainly to benefit from the presence of migrant workers doing jobs the nationals considered beneath them. Accepting that some would be working illegally was a price the country accepted as worthwhile.

Stephen never did get back to college, although he did learn a lot. One evening he started listing what he had accomplished and learnt during his time in that country. The list included learning much about life, how to look after and provide for himself, how to handle employers and landlords. He had passed a driving test and bought a car, since registering a car did not require a check of his passport. I realised that he was thinking of going home and preparing what to say to his family. He would not have the paper qualification he set out to acquire, and for which his family had provided the initial finance; but he did have a long list of other 'qualifications' – albeit none with a paper verification.

Shortly after this conversation, he decided to return home. He simply bought a one-way flight ticket, sold his car and gave notice to his employer and landlord. At the airport, the passport official stated the obvious, "You do not have a visa," and asked the obvious, "Have you been working?" Stephen gently replied that he was leaving now and would not be coming back. When pressed, he acknowledged that he had been working – how else had he supported himself for several years? He was allowed to proceed and returned safely to his own country. Why would the officials incur the inconvenience, trouble and costs for themselves and their government of doing anything else?

This same country demonstrates several elements of the issue of migrants acquiring citizenship in the country to which they have moved. The international norm is that one can apply after five years' residency, although various governments adopt laws and procedures with different qualification periods. I have met several people who took the local nationality of the country to which they had moved, in one case because it allowed access to the medical system, saving her considerable amounts of money for regular prescription medication. A Sri Lankan man was not so fortunate. He, and others from many Asian countries, were allowed work permits for a maximum of four years – the intention of which was to remove the possibility of their being able to apply for citizenship. This Sri Lankan duly left, but returned a few months later and resumed working for the same employer. He had changed his passport and was using a different name. Acquiring passports with a different name is a common practice in several countries.

The host government in these cases is not naïve, and knows what is happening. In this case, everyone is content: the employer retains a faithful employee, the country retains the services of an honest, upright, hardworking man, and this Sri Lankan continues to appreciate living and working in a European country. Personally, I am pleased for him, but lament the racism in this European government's policies and practices concerning who can acquire citizenship. At one point the country's national soccer team had more players in its starting 11 who had acquired the nationality than who had had been born with it. This is by no means the only country to grant citizenship to sports stars. Indeed, the practice of this country appears much less dubious than the practice of Bahrain concerning athletes born in Kenya and other African nations. Will Qatar 'recruit' a team for when it hosts the soccer World Cup in 2022?

In this chapter we have examined some examples of people migrating for work reasons, and have observed how regular and irregular migration can intertwine. In the next chapter we look into migration for religious reasons, including pilgrimage, study, fulfilling a sense of mission, and escaping religiously motivated persecution.

Chapter 5
Religiously Motivated Migration – to flee or not to flee?

In this chapter we focus on those who migrate for religious reasons. Several aspects will quickly emerge, including varied motivations, durations of stay, and means of entry to foreign countries. One important point is that being definitive about what is religiously motivated migration, and what is economic migration, is not always easy.

Religiously motivated migrations vary considerably in duration and distance travelled. Some are short term; pilgrimage, for example, can be described as tourism with a focus on religious sites, rituals, experiences and historical study. Some are for a few years; one example is participation in religious education, such as enrolling in theological colleges. Another example is that of people who move to other countries to be proactive participants in religious proclamation, or as staff of an FBO. Such migrations happen for periods ranging from a few weeks to several decades. Some people migrate on a long-term or even permanent basis. This category includes some – but by no means all – of those who migrate to escape religious persecution.

Religious tourism is big business for some locations. Within Christian circles, many visit Israel to see the historical sites associated with Christianity. Some pilgrims choose to face the current political and social realities, actively seeking to meet with local Christians of Jewish, Palestinian and other ethnicities; others prefer to focus exclusively on the past. For all, the sites described in their sacred texts are meaningful places to visit. More broadly, Jerusalem's Old City area is a World Heritage Site which people of many religions or none wish to visit. I find it tragic that access to the area that is known as Temple Mount to most Jews, and as Noble Sanctuary to most Palestinians, is restricted. Prior to 2000, access was available to anyone willing to pay the small fee, with entry to the places of worship on the condition that the applicable dress code was respected and adhered to, hardly an onerous requirement.

Since 2003, pilgrimages have resumed to Karbala and Najaf, two cities of southern Iraq that were significant in the development of the Shi'a strand of Islam. Many of the first visitors were Iranians, including numerous religious scholars keen to see the historic sites and participate in theological discussions.

Returning to Israel and the West Bank, but switching religions, some Jews seek to visit the tomb of Joseph, which is located close to the Palestinian city of Nablus in the West Bank. (We will summarise Joseph's story at the start of Chapter 10). The Israeli authorities conduct elaborate security operations to ensure the safety of these Jewish pilgrims. For example, one night during October 2016 the security operation included helicopters, drones and snipers positioned on high points. This enabled several coach-loads of devout worshippers to visit and pray at the small tomb from eleven at night until dawn. Such pilgrimages, and their associated security operations, occur on a regular basis.[33]

The largest annual pilgrimage is the Hajj. The tenets of Islam encourage all Muslims to participate in the pilgrimage to Mecca at least once during their lifetimes if they are able to do so. At present, approximately two million people attend each year.

---

[33] Al-Monitor; *Why Israelis flock to small tomb in Nablus at night*; 19th October 2016; www.al-monitor.com/pulse/originals/2016/10/nablus-joseph-tomb-jews-night-idf-forces-intifada.html (accessed 29th May 2017)

The event sees vast crowds all doing the same activities on the same day. The resulting crowd pressures are immense, and it is hardly surprising that fatal accidents occur. The religious authorities assert that one activity, the stoning of Satan, should start at noon on the fourth day. The political authorities have requested that the underlying religious reasons for this be re-evaluated and re-interpreted to permit an earlier start time. The motivation for this is the benefit to public health and safety of giving more time for a large crowd to pass through a confined space, and it is an example of the (often delicate) balance of power between political and religious bodies and needs.

Religious tourism is big business. The numbers of pilgrims to Karbala and Jerusalem are significant. The income for the hotel, restaurant and souvenir outlets is a major part of the local economy in places such as Bethlehem and Nazareth. In contrast, facilitating Jewish pilgrimage to Nablus is expensive for the Israeli authorities, and intrusive to local residents, who see negligible benefits for their community.

Pilgrimage is one area of migration for religious reasons, almost always one that lasts for a short period of time. Many pilgrims enter another country using tourist visas. Those on the Hajj are an exception, arriving on a Hajj or Umrah visa, since Saudi Arabia does not issue tourist visas to anyone. In contrast, religiously motivated migrations that involve fleeing persecution last for varying periods of time: some are of a short duration, while others are permanent.

As we noted in the Introduction, the consistent, persistent and overwhelming call of Christian leaders in the Middle East is for Christians to stay, though they recognise why some choose to leave, especially from situations of marginalisation, exploitation and conflict; but an important part of this is often overlooked.

One feature of Middle Eastern society that is crucial to understanding religious issues is the prevalence of the religious registration system. This identifies all people as belonging to one of a defined list of religious communities, and being under the jurisdiction of that community's system of personal status law. This covers marriage, divorce, custody, burial and inheritance. There is no complementary civil system for such matters. My earlier book, *Identity Crisis,* examines the effects of this system, arguing that this segregation on religious lines underpins discrimination, undermines the rule of law, and fuels violence.

Religious demographics have changed significantly during the past 50 years. The effects vary from country to country but similar patterns are present. One consequence is that the nature of the Christian church is changing; there is an increasingly significant number of people who have chosen to become Christians having been born into a non-Christian religious community. Such people have converted from one faith to another, and many of these religious converts are unable to change their religious registration to match their chosen belief; they are obliged to live with the 'identity crisis' of living as adherents of one faith while being treated by the state as belonging to a different religious community.

Iran – forcing Christians to leave?

Iran is an example of changing religious demographics. There are legally recognised Churches serving the Armenian and Assyrian (Chaldean) ethnic minority communities which preserve their own linguistic and cultural traditions. These are very long-standing ethno-religious communities. The Armenian Catholic churches are the largest community, with an estimated membership of between 100,000 and

250,000, and are located mainly in Tehran and the north-western areas of Iran – in fact here there are some predominantly Christian villages, with several church buildings. This distribution reflects the history of Christianity in the country. Unofficial estimates state that there were between 10,000 and 15,000 Assyrians in Iran in 2013. There were an estimated 100,000 Armenians in 1979, but the figure dropped to 20,000 during the 1980s, a fall of 80%.

The attitude of the Iranian authorities towards the long-standing Christian presence in the country changed from 2009 onwards. Prior to this, Christians of several traditions had been a respected and well-accepted presence (though the Assemblies of God Church was one exception, facing many problems including the murder or execution of senior leaders in 1990 and 1994). For many groups, however, the government contributed towards the maintenance of church buildings, in sharp contrast with most Arab-majority countries where equally long-established churches were at best tolerated, treated in some respects as second class and receiving no government finance.

The story of one family illustrates what has become all too common: almost all family members are now living in the USA. Two of the children migrated some years previously, one to the UK and the other to the USA. They initially travelled as students, but found employment and acquired residency, with the one in the UK marrying a British citizen and gaining UK citizenship. The parents were active members of their church in Iran, taking senior non-clerical roles. Their church was one of many that came under increasing pressure from the authorities. The minister was pressured and chose to leave; consequently, the mother assumed a more significant role, although she avoided publicity. When the church was closed by the authorities, the family considered their options. They had been able to visit their children in the UK and USA regularly in the past, and they decided to emigrate, securing residence in the USA on family reunification grounds.

The other main category of Christians consists of converts from Muslim backgrounds, many of whom are ethnically Persian. According to many accounts, the number of such converts continues to rise, although obtaining accurate estimates is very difficult. One reason for the pressure that was placed by the government on long-standing churches was that some of these converts were attending their church services. Many converts participated in less formal forms of worship held in homes, a practice often referred to as 'house fellowships' or 'house churches'. Iranian church leaders supporting these groups report that not all who would like to participate are able to do so. Indeed, some house fellowships have disbanded in recent years because of the heightened security risks following the arrests of some of the leaders. This leaves many of this category of Christian largely isolated, relying on media sources for Christian input.

There are also significant rates of emigration due to the actions and attitude of the government. One trend is for those who are imprisoned and released to leave the country because of the extent of the pressure or level of trauma they have experienced. In addition, they are considered 'toxic' by other believers because of the unrelenting surveillance to which they are subjected. In many cases, the authorities seem content to allow even those who are awaiting trial after being released on bail to leave the country.

The historical trend of emigration from Iran is not limited to Christians; those of other faiths have also migrated, and there is a significant Iranian diaspora in many countries. In recent years, the community in Turkey has increased in size. Amongst all these diaspora communities there are groups of Christians meeting together. It is generally assumed that many such groups in Turkey are monitored by the Iranian authorities.

How does the situation in Iran fit in with the calls of many church leaders in the Middle East that Christians should stay? We will return to this after moving from thinking about Iran and Persians to thinking about the central Middle East and Arabs.

Arabs – changing religious demographics

Egypt is the largest Arab-majority country by population. Estimates for the number of Christians in Egypt vary. I have seen claims for 6%, 20%, and many other figures in between. There are social, political and economic reasons why some Egyptians – and other Arab peoples – over- or under-state such figures. Adhering to strict factual accuracy takes lower priority than acting to further the perceived best interests of a particular group within society. All commentators agree that the percentage is decreasing due to a lower birth rate amongst Christian families compared to others, and a higher emigration rate for Christians. A further complication is religious conversion, since conversion to Islam from Christianity is legally recognised, whilst the reverse is not. Prior to 2011 it was estimated that several thousand Christians officially changed their religion to Muslim each year, mostly motivated by employment and marriage – whether they converted in the true sense of changing their religious belief system is another matter.

Emigration of Christians from Egypt remains a serious problem. I was visiting a Christian organisation in Cairo on the day they were saying farewell to a colleague who was leaving. Those saying farewell commented that their colleague was leaving to go and work in "the land of milk and money." This is a reference to the USA derived by adapting the Bible's use of the phrase 'milk and honey' to describe the land promised to Abraham's descendants. It was a sad day for them. Conversely, on the same visit to Cairo I met several Egyptian Christians who had worked or studied abroad for several years and then returned to Egypt when they felt God asking them to work amongst their own people within their own country. In Chapter 1 we noted that some Lebanese Christians follow a similar pattern.

In the next chapter, we will look at the situation in Iraq and Syria, two countries where the Christian community has declined numerically in recent years.

One factor common to both of these contexts is that accurate demographic data is not available. Consequently, there are many claims and counter-claims which can't be confirmed. For example, in the mid-2000s the then Nuncio,[34] Cardinal Fernando Filoni, remarked that the Chaldean Church was the largest in Iraq, and it had at most 120,000 adherents. In his view, this implied that there were no more than 250,000 Christians in the country; but this number is considerably lower than the most commonly-stated estimates at that time, which ranged from 400,000 to 1.4 million.

For Syria, one demographic study on the city of Aleppo which was published in 2012 reported a figure for the Christian population of under 4%, in contrast to the widely-quoted figure of 12% for this city and 10% nationally.[35] Syria's Christian community was disproportionately affected by agricultural land reforms in 1958 and 1970, when the consolidation of small farms into larger ones left many Christians

[34] The Nuncio is an Ambassador of the Holy See – colloquially, the Vatican.
[35] Joshua Landis; *Fewer Christians live in Aleppo than is commonly thought*; 18th February 2012; www.joshualandis.com/blog/the-poor-plight-of-the-christian-minority-in-aleppo-syria-by-ehsani (accessed 17th February 2017)

unemployed. Typically, they moved to cities and many subsequently emigrated, part of a brain drain from the country.

One area with clear demographic data that documents the declining number of Christians is the number of Christians in Palestinian communities across the West Bank and the Gaza Strip. In 1967 the Christian community was 12% of the Palestinian population. Today, this figure has dropped to less than 2%.[36] This reduction results from a higher birth rate in the Muslim population and from a higher emigration rate for Christians.

Changing religious demographics affect other religious communities. In Chapter 2 we remarked that many ethnically Jewish people were forced to leave the places where they and their ancestors had lived for generations, with Tunisia being one of the affected countries. Despite this, there is still an important synagogue in Djerba, and many Jews visit it on pilgrimage. In the following chapter we will see examples of some Muslims being forcibly displaced by other Muslims because they are adherents of a

[36] One source stated that there are approximately 45,000 Christians in a population of just over 4 million, approximately 1.1%.

different strand of Islam; Sunni-Shi'a tensions which result in violent suppression of one group by the other are an increasingly frequent occurrence. The *Arab Youth Survey* of 2016 notes the revulsion that many young Muslims feel about this development.[37]

The atrocities perpetrated in the name of Islam sicken many Muslims. Groups such as the Pakistan Taliban, Boko Haram, the al-Qaeda network and Daesh are notorious. Daesh is notable for its overt justification of everything from Islamic sources. Amongst Muslims I am aware of a variety of reactions to this; many are profoundly troubled.

The extremist view is by no means the only expression of Islam, and we need to be careful that we do not define a whole, large, diverse group (in this case Muslims), based on the actions of a few. No religion is a monolith, and there is diversity within all major faiths. In much modern media, bad news sells and good news does not. As one journalist said to me, "If it bleeds, it leads." In this context, 'leads' means comes first in the paper or broadcast. There is so

[37] ASDA'A Burson-Marsteller; *8th Annual Arab Youth Survey*; 3rd May 2017; www.arabyouthsurvey.com/en/home (accessed 21st November 2016); finding number 3. NB – this link may change when the next such survey is released.

much good news around us if only we keep alert to look for it.

What effect is extremism having on religious demographics? One is the rise of those who refer to themselves as atheists. This is an overt challenge to the religious segregation of society, and historically, many atheists have faced persecution for their views.[38] Another is the rise in the number of people choosing to become Christians. The same dynamic that we noted in the case of Iran holds true elsewhere; religious demographics are changing. We will return to this topic in Chapter 10.

Our focus in the rest of this chapter is on individuals, rather than on the communities of which they are a part.

Converts to Christianity

Many who have been born into Muslim families and choose to become Christians experience an adverse reaction from their family, their community or their employer. Rejection by family is common, forcing some to move to another suburb or city. Within

---

[38] See, for example, Tom Whitmarsh's book *Battling the Gods – Atheism in the Ancient World* (2016, Faber & Faber)

collective cultures, such moves are a major disruption to typical patterns of family and extended family living. Urbanisation and other patterns of migration help some to handle the effects of this. Others move abroad, frequently within the region as migrant workers. Moving outside the region is not always successful, as illustrated by the story of a man we will call Abdullah.

In the 1990s Abdullah, a Christian from a Muslim background, decided to flee from an Arab country due to intense pressure. A church in Scandinavia offered to sponsor him, arranged a temporary visa and paid for his flight. On his arrival they welcomed him, helped him apply for asylum and provided for all his physical needs. Six months later Abdullah walked into an immigration office and said, "Everything in my asylum application is true. However, life is worse here than it was back home. What do I need to do to return?" He was on a plane within three days.

What happened? The cultural adjustment was too great for him, and the church was unable to provide effective long-term support. This is an example of a voluntary return, and it illustrates the fact that relocating to a Western country does not work well in all cases. What factors affect the likelihood of it working well? How can these factors be addressed? Do the same factors apply to the same degree if people relocate to sub-Saharan Africa, Asia or Latin America?

Since 2009 I have worked closely with others to address such questions. The *RLP Policy Statement on Relocation as a Response to Persecution*, reproduced in Appendix 1, is one result of this collaboration. There are numerous aspects to assisting people to integrate into a new situation, many of which frequently require support over many months and years. One decision we made was not to draw undue attention or publicity to the development of better support mechanisms. We did not want the existence of such mechanisms to act as an incentive for more people to seek to use such services.

Deciding who genuinely needs to relocate or migrate because of religious persecution can be problematic. A case study provides a poignant illustration of the potential dangers. The main facts of Samer's (not his real name) story were agreed by all observers. However, there were variations in describing his motives. The version given me by one Jordanian Christian went as follows. Samer chose to become a Christian some years previously and lived normally close to where he grew up. He conscientiously practised and studied his Christian faith, and became widely accepted amongst fellow converts and amongst recognised Christians. Then he took a job with a Western Christian organisation, and received a relatively high salary. His attitude started to change, becoming less humble and more arrogant. He then decided to relocate to the West. His strategy was to provoke persecution by the authorities, flee to a neighbouring country and gain access to the West by applying for refugee status and subsequent resettlement. The Jordanian authorities duly responded to his provocative behaviour, notably by opening a case against him in an Islamic Shari'a court. Jordan, like other Middle Eastern countries, operates religiously-based court systems for matters of personal status, and there is a separate, state-run court system that handles criminal and civil matters. For Samer, the Shari'a court was asked to declare him an apostate, in recognition that he had left Islam. The court duly obliged, annulled all his identity documents, and declared invalid every contract he had ever signed, effectively removing his 'legal personality'. *Identity Crisis* looks at this phenomenon in detail.[39]

Samer moved to a neighbouring country where he applied for refugee status with the UNHCR. This was successful. His links with Western Christians contributed to his being accepted for resettlement within the USA. However, his level of English was poor, meaning that, at least in the early months, he was extremely limited in what he could do and with whom he could communicate and interact. The person telling the story concluded that Samer had succumbed to the temptation of a supposedly better life elsewhere, thereby depriving the local Christian community of an effective member. He had been supported in leaving, not assisted in remaining.

In this version, Samer relocated ostensibly for religious reasons, but at a deeper level he relocated to seek a better life and exploited the phenomenon of persecution to achieve his goal. One tragedy is that this case established a precedent for the use of Shari'a courts against converts to Christianity in Jordan.

---

[39] Jonathan Andrews; *Identity Crisis* (2016, Gilead Books Publishing), pages 34-37

One couple who were victims of this precedent were Ramzi and Muna. In one week in March 2008 they went from living normally as a couple, raising their two children, to feeling and thinking that they were obliged to leave their country. Ramzi was physically assaulted by distant relatives, and his father applied to a Shari'a court to have Ramzi declared an apostate because of his conversion from Islam to Christianity. Custody of the two children would then be transferred to Ramzi's father.

Those who face religiously motivated persecution, or indeed any other form of injustice, are obliged to choose from one of three broad categories of response, which I categorise as 'accept,' 'resist' or 'flee'. The first action in supporting those who are facing injustice is to help them to clarify the facts of their situation, identifying and naming the source and form of the injustice and the motivation(s) of the perpetrator(s). This creates a clear statement of the situation, which facilitates an assessment of the options available – starting with a consideration of the likely consequences of quietly accepting the situation. Might it get worse, might the same be done to others or might the situation change for the better? This is the accept option. The alternative is to explore whether the injustice could be challenged – can the persecutor be presented with a statement of the effects of their actions, and be asked to correct the injustice? How might they react? This is the resist option, and an essential part of resisting injustice is being clear about why what is faced can be regarded as unjust; what laws, conventions or societal norms are being violated and why.

If neither the accept option nor the resist option are palatable, then the final option is to leave the situation. This is the flee option, and it usually has long-term consequences, and is frequently the hardest to implement. The flee option is often referred to as relocation in discussions of religious persecution, and as we shall see, relocation as a response to religious persecution should be regarded as the option of last resort – although there are situations in which it is the only viable option.

Ramzi and Muna were in such a situation, because the consequence of the Shari'a court declaring him an apostate would have been that Ramzi's custody of their children would have been removed. Ramzi and Muna were obliged to take the option of last resort.

They left Jordan, initially for Syria, before moving to a Western country with the assistance of a Christian organisation for whom Ramzi had done some translation work. The couple applied for asylum status and resettlement, but they grew frustrated at their situation, not least because their application appeared stuck in a never-ending paralysis of indecision. After several years, they made the decision to move to another country and restart the process in a different location. This move, their third, was somewhat risky; they moved to an Arab country, with the consequent risk of being forcibly returned to Jordan. There is also the risk that withdrawing from an asylum/refugee process in one country will automatically invalidate any subsequent applications made elsewhere; the expectation is that people apply in the first place of safety they reach, and that they remain there until their case is adjudicated. For Ramzi and Muna, their risk was rewarded. Their application to the UNHCR was accepted.

Their fourth move was to the USA, the country that granted them resettlement. They appear to be settling well, having secured employment and had their children complete their schooling. In their case the process was eventually successful, but it took five and a half years and a considerable amount of emotional, financial and other forms of support.

Alas, such timescales are not unusual for people who are obliged to leave their country due to religious persecution. They are an example of how people can end up replacing the certainty of turmoil with the turmoil of uncertainty. This is experience is all too common, and is why relocation is the option of last resort for those facing persecution; and why even within this option, the use of asylum and refugee systems is the option of last resort within the option of last resort.

We need to beware of a subliminal message embedded in these stories. Samer and Ramzi and Muna had links with Western Christians. This typically aids relocation to the West, but we must carefully note that it is not a sufficient condition for migration to happen quickly. There are all too many stories of false or unrealistic promises being made to people, creating expectations that are subsequently unfulfilled. Western Christian organisations have limited influence in the decisions made by resettlement programmes. They do not, as some are prone to think, have a stack of visas in their pockets.

A more pertinent message in Samer's story is the observation that this is the story of someone leaving who was an asset to the Christian communities in their country. Helping people to leave is not what indigenous Christian leaders want from Western (and other) Christians. Their consistent call is to enable people to stay. Ramzi and Muna are an example of the balancing tension that there are some for whom leaving is the only viable option.

So how do we assess who needs to relocate outside the region for true religious reasons? Firstly, we need to strongly discourage those who provoke a crisis as Samer did. Such people are less deserving of assistance. In Chapter 3 we noted the criteria of a threat of loss of life or liberty. To these criteria we need to add the threat of loss of custody of children, which was the reality confronting Ramzi and Muna.

Clearly there are pastoral factors in the cases of most people who believe that they need to relocate, and each situation must be handled with due sensitivity.

In July 2008 an organisation was contacted by a man who claimed that he needed to relocate because of his conversion from Islam to Christianity. The organisation contacted church leaders in his country to verify his claims. They were all dismissive, saying that if he did wish to migrate, then it was not for religious reasons. The organisation duly chose not to offer assistance, and heard a few weeks later that the man had quietly returned to his hometown. This illustrates the importance of involving local Christian leaders in such assessments.

Having looked at these case studies, let us describe how relocation works. We need to consider where people should move to, and the means of gaining initial entry and long-term residency. A further aspect is the question of how long people need to remain in a particular location. Most people who are forcibly displaced desire to return home as and when they can do so safely; those relocating to escape religious persecution are no different.

Ramzi and Muna's experience illustrates the use of interim destinations, by which I mean relocating somewhere as a temporary measure and as a stepping-stone to a third country. In this case they went through three countries – two Arab and one European – before reaching their final destination in the USA. Interim destinations have the benefit of allowing rapid relocation out of the victim's own country, thereby allowing people time to consider longer-term destinations and to plan and implement the process of getting there. The disadvantage is that it adds complications to the provision of support, and requires further relocations across national borders, each of which might prove stressful or problematic.

Those relocating need to gain initial entry to the country they travel to first. As with all migrants, the options for this are tourism, study or work, as we saw in Chapter 3. This affects the choice of location that those relocating can reach. (There is also the option of irregular methods of migration, although there are almost invariably serious consequences for this at some point; for the time being we will restrict our consideration to regular methods). Getting to a neighbouring country is straightforward for many people through reciprocal arrangements that grant entry on a short-stay, non-working tourist basis at the point of entry; travellers do not require a visa issued in advance. However, when travelling outside their region, many people must acquire a visa before travelling. This is especially the case for those from the Middle East. The evaluation of applications for such visas is becoming ever more rigorous. One reason is the political attention that is being given in many Western countries to reducing the number of people applying for asylum; not allowing people to visit makes it impossible for them to apply. Consequently, those I worked with on relocation methods sought to promote alternatives to migrating to the West. Sub-Saharan Africa, Asia and South America were all actively considered.

One option that is used on rare occasions is a humanitarian visa. This is a catch-all type of visa giving the authorities a means of action in exceptional circumstances. One case I know involved Tom (not his real name), an Iranian who had been resident in Cyprus for many years whilst an asylum application was considered. He became friends with an American migrant worker, who in turn knew people at his country's embassy. Over an extended period the embassy agreed that Tom should be granted a one-year residence permit in the USA on a humanitarian visa. An embassy official accompanied Tom to the airport and handed him an envelope saying "do not open it, do not lose it, simply hand it to the immigration officer when you arrive in the USA." As expected, he applied for asylum, which was granted. He settled well, assisted by his friend from Cyprus who by this time had relocated back to the USA. Such cases are very rare.

One story worth reflecting on is that of Maryam Rostampour and Marziyeh Amirizadeh, two Iranians. Their book, entitled *Captive in Iran*, explains why they chose to leave Iran following nine months of detention in Evin Prison in Tehran during 2009. They were formally acquitted following a court hearing in April 2010, but faced serious and credible threats by the authorities to their liberty and plausibly their lives. They moved to Turkey a few days later, an easy move to make since the two countries have visa-free travel for citizens of both countries. Their book gives a very brief summary of the eleven months they spent in Turkey applying for entry to the USA via the UNHCR system.[40]

Particularly instructive is their comment that their situation was very well documented online. One caveat we might add to this is that such material was overwhelmingly published on Christian news websites whose credibility may well be doubted by those evaluating their application. Several such websites operate to high journalistic standards, insisting on well-qualified staff, and at least two are led by people with experience in the BBC and other high-calibre media organisations; but such levels of professionalism are not always acknowledged as

[40] Rostampour & Amirizadeh; *Captive in Iran*, (2013, Tyndale) – pages 279-82 and 287-88 are relevant.

normal by those who are adjudicating applications to the UNHCR.

A second aspect to note is that Maryam and Marziyeh provided certificates of their baptisms as part of the evidence supporting their claims. Maryam's was issued by a church in Iran and appears to have been accepted without undue question. By contrast, Marziyeh's was issued by a Christian organisation, since she had been baptised during an earlier period in Turkey when she was studying Christian theology. This certificate was not readily accepted.

Another story illustrates the limitations of relying on baptismal certificates. A Catholic priest in the Middle East told me about a man who approached him asking to be baptised. The priest replied that he required him to attend a course of instruction in the Christian faith, to which the applicant agreed. The man faithfully attended, and part way through the course he brought a friend along with him who also wanted to be baptised. The priest was never sure whether they were genuinely converts, suspecting that they were endeavouring to acquire a baptismal certificate for other purposes, presumably to use in an application for refugee/asylum status on religious grounds. Nevertheless, he proceeded with the baptisms. The man who approached him first he never saw again. His friend, who only did part of the course, became faithful in worship and attended mass every week.

This story illustrates that the test of regular commitment to worship with other Christians in some form is one true mark of conversion. In Chapter 10 we will explore some of the different patterns of worship that have been observed amongst those who choose to become Christians. For those claiming the need to relocate because of religious persecution, my preferred method of checking who is genuine is to ask which church or Christian organisation they are in regular contact with, and then check with the leaders. The answer to this relies on an extensive network of personal contacts, and is hard to fake.

On one memorable occasion, twin brothers, Bill and Ben (not their real names), approached an organisation claiming that they needed to leave their country. They were duly asked to provide the name of a church or Christian leader to verify their claims. Their initial replies evaded this question, and they claimed that they needed assistance as a matter of urgency. When pressed they eventually provided a name, who, unsurprisingly, refused to support their claim. They had not chosen to become Christians. Help was declined. They approached other organisations, who contacted the first one for advice, and likewise declined. A few years later Bill and Ben made another approach, in which they acknowledged the lack of genuineness in their earlier appeal, claimed that they had now become Christians and gave the name of a church and its pastor that they were in regular contact with. This time, the verification process provided an affirmative response. Assistance was provided, although in this case they found a place of safety not far from their home.

This illustrates something that is true in many situations, namely that local solutions can be found. The principle is that people should flee the minimum distance to be safe. If the threat is from immediate family or local society, then there are often options other than leaving the country or the region. Such options are invariably simpler and quicker to implement than leaving the region.

In my experience, the approach of checking with local Christian leaders nearly always leads to a clear outcome of knowing whether someone is either not a true convert, a convert who needs to leave, or a convert who does not need to leave the area. Local leaders are usually open to finding local solutions to the problems faced by those who are under pressure because of their faith whenever possible. As we have noted before, there are a small number of cases where emigration is the only viable option.

One exception to this occurred in Egypt a few years ago. There was a spate of cases in which churches sent converts to Lebanon, asking Lebanese Christians to look after them. Such requests were often made at short notice, and it was pointed out to the Egyptians that there were limits to how many people could be supported. More constructively, they were asked what training or support they needed in order to be able to effectively support converts in Egypt, to enable them to stay rather than facilitate their leaving.

Why refugee/asylum systems are the option of last resort

Earlier in this chapter we noted three uses of refugee/asylum systems. Ramzi and Muna, and then Maryam and Marziyeh, had successful outcomes in migration eventually. Tom's situation was resolved by another approach. Why do I regard refugee and asylum systems as the option of last resort within the option of last resort? There are five reasons I want to discuss, as follows.

First, these procedures frequently take a long time. For Ramzi and Muna it took more than five years. The eleven months it took for Maryam and Marziyeh is much quicker than for most, although it probably did not feel quick to them as they went through the process. There can be a benefit in the delays, since applicants are granted leave to remain in the country of application pending a decision, and so their safety is reasonably well assured while applications are being considered. Lebanon is an exception to this. It is not a state party to the Refugee Convention and so legally the right to remain is not applicable, although many are allowed to do so in practice. There are, however, examples of people who have remained vulnerable, due to being pursued by family members, despite the fact that they are awaiting the outcome of an application to the UNHCR. All applicants to the UNHCR must remain in the receiving country, and in some cases movement within the country is restricted. An example of this occurred in May 2008, when an Iranian convert to Christianity named Mohsen relocated to Turkey with his family after he was arrested, beaten, released and then closely watched by the Iranian authorities. He applied to the UNHCR, and he and his family were restricted to remaining within one town whilst their application for refugee status was being considered, which is standard practice within Turkey and several other countries. It adds to the sense of vulnerability and can increase the risk of being exploited by armed groups or organised crime, including people traffickers and prostitution gangs. In his book *Asylum and Immigration*, Nick Spencer calls for their effective protection.[41]

Second, within the UNHCR system there is no guarantee as to where a successful applicant will be allowed to establish a new life. Applicants have at best a limited say in resettlement processes, which are themselves but one option for countries seeking to provide the "durable solution" that the Refugee Convention promises.

Third, while in the system, applicants are frequently not allowed to work, or are allowed to work only in certain industries, usually in jobs which are low paid and manual – the jobs that the nationals do not want. Those unable to work become dependent on state benefits or the generosity of donors. For many, the psychological implications of this are significant, and

[41] Nick Spencer, *Asylum and Immigration* (2004, Paternoster); see Chapter 7.

are an addition to the stresses they were experiencing before they relocated. Depression is a serious possibility. We noted in Chapter 2 the significant difference that is made when people are able to be part of the solution to their changed circumstances.

Fourth, there are low success rates, notwithstanding apparent rises in some European countries since 2014. The implication is that applicants are likely to be forced to return to their own country. Failed applicants, once they have returned to their own countries, frequently become marked people, and obtaining visas to other countries can become more difficult. This restriction can endure for many years.

In September 2006 I was told about an Iranian couple, both converts to Christianity, who had applied for asylum in Norway. The wife's application was accepted, but the husband's was rejected. He was deported, arrested on arrival in Iran and mistreated. He was eventually released, and immediately relocated to the Gulf. Of note here is the fact that one spouse being accepted did not guarantee the acceptance of the other, a somewhat unusual occurrence. The principle of family unity was violated. This principle is not guaranteed by the Refugee

Convention, notably if the principal applicant is not the head of the family.[42]

Fifth, specifically in religiously motivated cases, the officials handling applications, or the interpreters used during this process, may themselves be prejudiced against converts. There are examples of this causing unfair handling of applications from those who have left Islam. In Western countries there are examples of public servants who are themselves Muslim acting against such applicants, despite such behaviour being contrary to their conditions of employment. I was informed of one such incident in the UK in which a Home Office employee told someone that he should revert to Islam and go home. In cases like these, there is recourse to higher authority and in this case it was to put a request to the relevant Member of Parliament to support the referral. This often does resolve the injustice, although it adds to the stress on applicants. In Muslim-majority countries, many UNHCR staff and interpreters are Muslim, which has sometimes led to

---

[42] The "Principle of unity of the family" is recommendation B of the conference held from 2nd to 25th July 1951 at the UN in Geneva which drafted the Refugee Convention. Consequently it is a recommendation rather than an Article of the Convention.

similar problems; in 2005 an Iranian family's application to the UNHCR in Turkey was rejected when local officials failed to consider a court summons issued by an Iranian court that had formally charged one of the family with apostasy. Those supporting this family asked the UNHCR headquarters in Geneva to order the local office in Turkey to fully review the application. One unexpected consequence of this was that someone alerted a senior political figure in the USA, which led very rapidly to an offer to resettle the family. For the UNHCR, this made the decision to grant refugee status very easy, since the family would be resettled almost immediately, thereby ending the UNHCR's responsibilities to this family. Such stories show what can be done given the political will. We need to be aware though that stories like this are the exception to the normal pattern of delays and long timescales.

Asylum/refugee systems are the option of last resort, yet there are occasions when they are the only viable option, and forewarned should be forearmed. In 2016 I heard a presentation on how Christians in Turkey were assisting those who were obliged to use the UNHCR system there. A Jordanian attendee muttered several times, "that would not happen in my country." This reminds us that good theory is not always seen in practice. Relevant here is the fact that Turkey is a state party to the Refugee Convention, whereas Jordan is not. This alerts us to the need for in-depth training and awareness so that the relevant people are able to stand alongside those in refugee systems, and highlights the fact that the local knowledge element is crucial. In many places across the Middle East and beyond, such expertise is available.[43]

Samantha (not her real name) is an example of someone who was obliged to use a UNHCR application for refugee status and resettlement. She left her country by regular means because she feared her family's reaction to her conversion to Christianity. She then moved to Lebanon by irregular means, which was a necessity to avoid the possibility of her family knowing where she was. Her application to the UNHCR took more than five years, and included at least one rejection and appeal. Throughout the process she kept detailed records of all stages in the process, as well as all contact with local, government and UNHCR officials. These communications included threats to deport her, knowing that she would face the

---

[43] The presenter commended Patrick Sookhdeo (editor), *The Essential Guide for Helping Refugees* (2014, Isaac Publishing), subtitled *includes Status Determination, Training and Advocacy.*

wrath of her family who, if she returned, would be able to abuse and possibly murder her with impunity. She discreetly recorded one such threat on her phone, evidence that proved useful later in the process. This is a commendable practice.

Samantha was granted resettlement in a Western country. Within a month of arrival she was reported to be depressed, and this is not unusual following a prolonged period of living with intense uncertainty and the necessity of being discreet whilst working informally to support herself. She did adjust, and eventually became integrated to her adopted country.

Enabling people to stay – is extraction beneficial?

We noted in the Introduction the desire of most Christian leaders in the Middle East that Christians should be enabled to stay rather than being helped to leave. Appendix 1 gives a clear policy statement consistent with this request. It was written by the Religious Liberty Partnership (RLP), an organisation established to nurture collaboration amongst organisations that are addressing challenges to religious liberty. How do we enable people to stay?

One temptation is to break this into two categories, those who are recognised as Christians by their government and those who are not – in other terms, those whose religious registration is Christian and those who are converts to Christianity. One reason to do this is that the legal, social and family situations of the two categories are radically different. Yet the risk of doing so is that we are inherently reinforcing the segregation of society on religious lines, which is a root cause and clear expression of the pluralism deficit (see Glossary) that underlies so many of the challenges seen across the Middle East. Marginalisation, discrimination and harassment are all too common for many, although the intensity and form they take varies from place to place and over time.

For all Christians, legally recognised or otherwise, the desire of church leaders is that people stay, in order to be active participants in Christian communities. We should be aware that there are many more stories of perseverance than of flight and rescue.[44] Many do choose to persist in difficult situations, and as we have

---

[44] See, for example, Ron Boyd-MacMillan's book *Faith That Endures*, (2006, Sovereign World), pages 342-49.

noted before, there are stories of good news if one looks for them. The desire of Christian leaders in the region is to see more people become active participants in churches of all denominations. All Christians must constantly remember that Christianity originated in the Middle East; it was not imported from elsewhere.

I suggest that something that is crucial to enabling people to remain in the Middle East is for teaching about the faith to include the theme of being faithful followers of Jesus when faced with injustice. The central figure of our faith is Jesus Christ, the suffering saviour. This prompts some suggestions.

First, within the Middle East, many of the challenges for converts arise from the honour-shame dynamic in indigenous culture. Many of these problems pass if the initial phase is handled wisely. The mostly likely source of problems is the immediate family. Not overtly informing one's family of one's new faith often works well in avoiding this – instead allowing the difference that becoming a Christian makes to be seen in the person's life. I am aware of efforts by many who are working to dissipate anger and tensions between converts and their families, which requires continuing contact, something that is only possible for some people; Samantha's is one case where continuing contact was not possible. It is always a delight to attend graduation ceremonies at Christian theological colleges and see people graduating who are from Muslim backgrounds. For some, family members attend, often dressed in what appears to be a typically Muslim manner.

Second, should serious persecution occur, then there are three options: accepting, resisting, and relocating, as described earlier. In recent years, teaching and training on this has increasingly become part of programmes of instruction for new converts. Likewise, teaching on how to respond to injustice should be included in the teaching of all Christians in the Middle East from an early age. It is part of enabling people to be wise citizens who challenge injustice in all its forms for the benefit of society as a whole. It is about seeking truth and justice in a way that affirms and upholds the dignity and worth of all.

Third, relocating is rarely easy, frequently involves many months of uncertainty, and has long-term consequences. Relocating for a short period can have positive benefits, and there are several options for making use of the time away in honourable ways, notably through studying or vocational training.

Another option that works for some is to become a migrant worker.

Fourth, at this time in particular, Christians should keep in mind that many non-Christians are discreetly looking at alternative religious beliefs to those they have been taught by family and state. There are great numbers willing to ask Christians whom they trust about their beliefs. It is not helpful if the misconception that conversion inevitably splits families and leads to emigration is perpetuated unnecessarily.

A further story illustrating several of the long-term consequences of religiously motivated migration concerns an Iranian family. Timothy, Mary and their young son Joshua (not their real names) left Iran after Timothy was detained for approximately the fiftieth time and, more unusually, Mary and five-year-old Joshua were also detained briefly. Iranian Christian leaders urged them to leave. They relocated to Europe, where they enrolled as students, thereby securing student visas. One aspect of the discrimination that Timothy had suffered was that he had consistently been denied certificates for any study or training course that he had undertaken. He is by no means the only person to have faced this form of injustice. He, and those treated similarly, cannot prove their qualifications for any job. The study programme aimed to provide him with provable qualifications, and counselling support was provided as well. However, fully recovering from the many traumas he had faced took a considerable length of time. Mary made more progress with this, and with her studies, than did Timothy, who had been reluctant to leave Iran despite all that he had been through. What Timothy had done in Iran for many years was to act as pastor to numerous house fellowships. Iranian church leaders decided that the ideal plan for his family would be for Timothy to undertake formal theological study and then become the pastor of an Iranian fellowship somewhere. Appropriate theological study was not available in their initial location, which necessitated a second relocation, and the prolonged time needed for psychological recovery meant that those close to the family decided to delay such a move. Meanwhile, Joshua reached school age, and became a pupil at a local school. This required him learning his third language, following his native Farsi and some English. He rapidly became the most settled member of the family. This story illustrates some of the complexities of long-term support; notably the fact that pre-determining timescales is not always possible. The family continued to need financial support for a period of several years.

There are two further areas that we need to consider. First, we need to ask why is it that some Western Christians actively encourage Christians from the Middle East to migrate from their homelands to the West. Several possible answers come to mind; one is that many Western Christians struggle to see fellow Christians denied the ability to worship freely. The temptation to such a view needs to be tempered by the realisation that moving outside the region is fraught with difficulties; there are others with stories similar to Abdullah's.

A more positive rationale, which applies in some countries where are significant migrant groups who are Arab and Muslim, is that the authorities would like some Arab Christians to change the ethno-religious demographic balance. One can understand this. It needs to be noted, though, that Arabs of different nationalities are different in this. So, for example, France inviting Iraqi Arab Christians to join a community that comprises mostly Algerian Arab Muslims creates a challenging integration situation for everyone. The Arabic dialects are different, and the social customs vary by nationality.

This leads us to our second area, namely the need to be realistic about the aspirations of some Christians in the Middle East. We need to recognise that there are diaspora communities of Middle Eastern people in numerous countries outside of the region. These provide a *pull* factor which attracts others to come. I have met Arab church leaders working in several European countries, and many remark that they see it as God's provision that they have been sent ahead of those who feel obliged to leave in this period. They feel that God has prepared a place of worship for Christians leaving the region at this time.

Another reason for urging people – especially those who endure persecution – to remain is the risk that Christians stop practising their faith after they settle in the West. Descriptive studies suggest that many converts to Christianity who move to the West stop practising their Christian faith in their new locations. One study involved Muslims who became Christians in the Middle East and subsequently moved to Europe or North America. The evidence suggests that 85% to 95% of such people ceased practising their Christian faith. This study focussed on Arabs, and there are reasons why the situation might be different for Iranians. A similar study by Nik Ripken looked at those who moved to the USA having endured severe persecution somewhere, and in his analysis 90% were no longer practising their Christian faith ten years after they moved.[45] Helping Christians relocate to the West may well give them greater security, sense of safety and assurance of their rights and dignity. Whether it improves or harms their spirituality and religious practice is a very different question; for all too many it has a negative answer. There are always risks in migration. The question is, how well is this risk known?

This chapter has focussed on migration for religious reasons, and on situations that, in general, affect small groups of people. The number of converts to Christianity that actually need to move countries is a small proportion, even from Iran. For migration on a larger scale we need to focus our attention on Syria and Iraq. Here religion is one of many factors, and we can question whether violence, discrimination or a brain drain is having the greatest effect.

[45] See www.nikripken.com (accessed 20th March 2017) and his book *The Insanity of God* (2013, B&H)

Chapter 6
Syria and its Neighbours – are the displaced welcome?

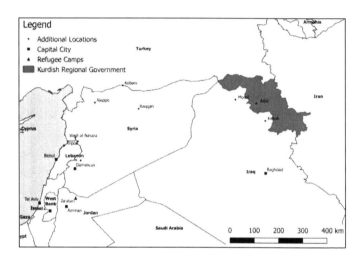

The conflict in Syria since 2011 has caused large-scale displacement directly affecting more than half the population; many are displaced within the country, while others have moved abroad. It has also attracted people to migrate to Syria, from within the region and from further afield.

This conflict has profoundly affected neighbouring countries. We will discuss the effects on them, taking them in the alphabetic order of Iraq, Israel, Jordan, Lebanon, and finally Turkey. The section on Lebanon will be brief because we examined this country in Chapter 1.

The conflict has shown what mankind is capable of. The following pages include powerful examples of what some people will do *for* and *to* others; sacrifice and service contrast with cruelty and oppression. Good news can be found amidst the bad if one seeks it.

Before we enter Syria, a historical note illustrates two recurring themes. In 1943, Elias Barzilai was the chief rabbi of Athens during the German occupation of Greece. Barzilai appears to have been aware that something had happened to the Jews of Thessaloniki, and it is clear that he was determined to do what he could to help them.[46] Amongst other actions, he asked the Greek Orthodox Archbishop Damaskinos Papandreou for help. Papandreou, afraid for the wellbeing of the people he was responsible for, replied that he was unable to prevent the Germans from doing what they wished, and nor could he allow church buildings to be used to provide refuge to large numbers of people. He did, though, offer to issue an

---

[46] Hitler's (so called) 'final solution' for the 50,000 Jews living in Thessaloniki is described in Victoria Hislop's *The Thread* (2011, Headline Review), pages 296-307.

order that clergy should do whatever they could to help individuals. Barzilai's own account states that he returned home and sent out an order to the Jewish community to flee to the hills.

On 25th September, members of the resistance took Barzilai to the hills of central Greece, where he spent the rest of the war, while thousands of other Jews fled. Barzilai was aware that there were people who would be unable to go into hiding because of age or infirmity. Alas, many of them were arrested and deported; presumably few, if any, survived the war.[47]

This illustrates the determination of religious leaders to support their community, and people of goodwill of different faiths working together as they are able, discreetly if not always publicly. It also shows that when forced mass displacement occurs, some people are invariably left behind because they are physically unable to relocate. They face severe consequences during a period of their lives when they are already vulnerable.

---

[47] Haaretz; *1943: Chief Rabbi of Athens flees the Nazis, saves the day*; 24th September 2016; www.haaretz.com/jewish/this-day-in-jewish-history/.premium-1.744047 (accessed 8th December 2016)

Syria – a most uncivil crisis

Our focus here is on migration. We will not attempt a comprehensive description of the causes and effects of the violence that has affected parts of Syria since 2011. Nor will we look at the historic context of the instability, except to note that stability – some might prefer the phrase 'relative stability' – was established by President Hafez Assad (father of Bashar) after he seized power in 1970. In this it is worth noting that several Syrian Christians have asked me not to describe the situation as a 'civil war'. They point out that there are all too many foreigners involved in the conflict, supporting the numerous participants. I have consistently followed this request as part of my commitment to respecting the local agenda; hence my use of the term 'crisis' to describe Syria's situation.

One point worth noting, since it is about migration, is that one of the contributory causes to the crisis was the response of various people to a drought that began in 2009. This profoundly affected rural agriculture and prompted many people to move to the cities in search of alternative work. Precise demographic data is not available, but some estimates state that as many as one million people were affected. It seems unlikely that this many people actually moved, but it is all too plausible that a large number of people did. This movement of people created an environment of disaffected, and mainly young, people desperate to find work. No doubt some sought to emigrate as migrant workers. We can presume that many accepted an approach by an armed group offering a job with a salary, whatever they thought about the aims and methods of their 'employer.'

One plea heard from those affected by the arrival of forcibly displaced persons is that those who have contributed to the crisis should also contribute to meeting the needs and aspirations of those affected by it. We can sense the element of natural justice in such calls. Christopher Phillips, in his book *The Battle for Syria: International Rivalry in the New Middle East*, notes that the crisis has returned Syria to the situation of the 1940s and 1950s, when various regional and global powers competed to bring Syria under their umbrella as a means of increasing their influence within the Middle East. The book shows how foreign powers have sought to shape the present crisis.[48]

[48] Christopher Phillips; *The Battle for Syria: International Rivalry in the New Middle East* (2016, Yale University Press); pages 5-6.

Many have migrated into Syria as combatants. The government is being supported by forces supplied by Hezbollah, Iran and Russia. Iran's contribution includes recruiting large numbers of mercenaries of other nationalities, including Pakistani and Afghan Shi'a Muslims who have fled into Iran to escape religious persecution in their own countries. Might we term them migrant workers, since they are being paid for their services?

The flow of fighters is by no means one-sided. Numerous armed groups opposed to the government have actively recruited people, and received volunteers as combatants and support staff from numerous countries. Their motives vary: some go seeking adventure, some are ideologically motivated, whilst others are migrant workers doing something for which they receive remuneration. Saudi Arabia is reported to have offered some men on death row a one-way ticket and travel permission to go to Syria and join an armed group.

Early in the crisis, a slogan was commonly daubed on walls that was translated, "The Christians to Beirut and the Alawites to the grave." From early in the crisis, an extremist religious agenda was displayed by some. What is significant here is that the Christians would be forced to leave, whilst another religious group were to be massacred. I have no wish to soft-pedal what has happened to some Christian communities in Syria and, as we shall see, in Iraq too. Yet it is a fact that other religious groups have been subjected to worse atrocities. This matches the violations of religious freedom seen across the Middle East; Christians are the most numerous group who have been affected, but others are more severely marginalised, exploited or abused. Worst affected are Baha'i – notably in Iran – and what are sometimes termed 'Muslims of the wrong type'. The latter refers to Muslims who are different from those of the rulers in a particular area. All too often this is Shi'a being oppressed by Sunnis; in Iran, it is reversed, and the Shi'a oppress the Sunni.

The slogan also introduces us to the fact that extremist groups are present amongst the participants in the crisis. The best known – or most notorious – call themselves Jabhat Fateh al-Sham, and Islamic State. These two organisations can be classified as violent extremist organisations (VEOs). Both have changed their names during the crisis. Jabhat Fateh al-Sham called itself Jabhat al-Nusra when it formed early in the crisis, and changed its name during 2016 to mark the severing of its links with the al-Qaeda network. Islamic State's original official title was The Islamic State of Iraq and ash-Sham. It was referred to as The Islamic State in Iraq and Syria (ISIS) and The Islamic State in Iraq and the Levant (ISIL) in some sources because the Arabic phrase Belad al-Sham can refer to Syria and also the entire Levant. The group re-titled itself The Islamic State in July 2014. It is frequently referred to as Daesh by many in the Middle East, a name which is derived from a transliteration of the group's initials in Arabic. This neatly avoids having to identify the group as having anything to do with Islam. Out of respect for the local context in the Middle East, I will use the term Daesh for this VEO.

One feature of the crisis has been the large number of participating militias and armed groups. There have been numerous mergers and splits, as well as groups renaming themselves, all contributing to make the crisis both confusing and hard-to-track. This has complicated the provision of military support, especially from those who are endeavouring to support those who are opposed to the government but do not subscribe to extremist ideologies or methods.

Another development was the establishment of de facto autonomy by the predominantly Kurdish areas of the north-east, to maintain coherent local administration. They established military forces to protect their communities. These forces at times expanded the territory they controlled, particularly in areas containing some Kurds that were being threatened or controlled by Daesh. Good local governance appears to have been established in these areas, including areas that are ethnically and religiously diverse.

One aspect of the crisis is that it has affected different parts of the country in profoundly different ways. Two stories illustrate the fact that, while parts of Syria have been devastated by the crisis, other areas have been spared violence.

During 2013, one Syrian told me that life was close to normal for him. He lived in Latakia on the coast where the restaurants and cafés served customers much as normal, and he and his friends could go walking on the promenade at midnight. The major changes since the crisis started were the doubling of the population of the city and a variety of economic effects such as price rises without wage rises. Life was very different for a relative who was living in a suburb of Damascus and had to observe a curfew each night. The contrast between these two Syrian experiences was very marked.

A Lebanese man explained that relatives of his wife continued to live in Syria. Their area was relatively safe; they lived in Wadi al-Nasara, often referred to in English as the Valley of the Christians. All the villages in the area had predominantly Christian residents. Like Latakia, they had seen an increase in the population as people relocated to the area from Aleppo and other areas affected by crisis.

I have no wish to downplay the level of violence in Syria, and the consequent human suffering and destruction of property. In August 2016 a photograph was widely circulated of Omran Daqneesh, aged five, sitting stunned and silent in an ambulance in Aleppo. He was covered in dust and bloodied. It put a name and face to the conflict that was engulfing parts of Aleppo at that time. Others have documented the effects of the crisis on the Syrian people in more structured ways. Katriona Hoover's book *Faces of Syria* uses the genre of printed photographs.[49] Kati Woronka's novel *Mourning Sham* explores some harsh

---

[49] Katriona Hoover; *Faces of Syria* (2015, TGS International)

realities of the effects of the crisis on the Syrian people. It includes the death, destruction and physical abuse of one human being by another, as well as the self-sacrificial acts performed by some in order to meet the humanitarian needs of the suffering, and to call for a resolution of the crisis. It highlights the struggles that are involved when seeking to bring hope and goodness into situations of pain, trauma and evil, using the novel to articulate insights derived from careful observation while living in Damascus.[50]

One evening during a visit to Lebanon in 2013, I was on the balcony of my room enjoying the air and distant views. The person in the neighbouring room was doing likewise. We got chatting about what we did and our reasons for being in Beirut. He explained that he was Syrian, and worked as a doctor. The next day he was sitting an examination at the German embassy as part of his application to work in Germany. The test was about language, not medicine. He did not spend long on the balcony, remarking, "I need to get back to revising." He was endeavouring to be part of the exodus, part of the brain drain that was

[50] Kati Woronka; *Mourning Sham* (2016, katiworonka.com)

steadily removing the people whom Syria could least afford to lose.

At the start of 2011 Syria was hosting two communities of displaced people; Iraqis and Palestinians. Numerous Iraqis had moved to Syria since 2003. Some remained in Damascus and other places, where they had established a new life for themselves. When the crisis began to affect the places where they were residing, many simply returned to Iraq. Others sought to move out of the region.

The Syrian government had been supportive of Palestinians for many years, providing accommodation, healthcare and other resources. They had not, however, granted them citizenship. The crisis interrupted the support that the government was able to provide. Some Palestinians attempted to leave Syria, but encountered significant difficulties. Neighbouring countries were willing to accept Syrians; but these people did not have Syrian papers, and a number of them were left stranded on the Syria-Jordan border. The ongoing failure to resolve the situation and status of Palestinians has continued to affect people, and we will return to this in Chapter 9.

Amidst the violence, Syria's Christian communities have been profoundly affected in several ways. First, Christians were forced to choose whether to support the government or those opposed to the government, or to attempt to remain neutral – with the risk of being unsupported if they were attacked. Other ethnic and religious groups faced the same dilemma, although it was particularly intense for Christians, who were frequently perceived as being in favour of the status quo under President Assad. In truth, the majority of Christians did continue genuinely to side with the Assad-led government, without condoning in any way the violence or other excesses perpetrated by some government personnel. Many Christians feared the imposition of the Islamist government which they believed could be installed were the Assad-led government to be removed. Christians acknowledge that President Assad has allowed the Church to operate within Christian communities, and that as an Alawite he is himself from a similarly sized religious community – at least according to the usually quoted demographic of 10-11%, although we noted in Chapter 5 that this figure was questionable for the Christian community.

Second, there were kidnapping attacks, many for ransom, some specifically targeting Christian leaders.

One high-profile case began on 22nd April 2013, when two bishops based in Aleppo, Yohanna Ibrahim of the Syriac Orthodox Church and Boulos Yaziji of the Greek Orthodox Church, were kidnapped when returning to Aleppo from a place close to the border with Turkey. At the time of writing, spring 2017, their situation remains unresolved.

Third, there were violent attacks on some Christian neighbourhoods or communities, and some church property. Consequently, Christians were forced to choose whether to remain where they were, relocate within the country, or attempt to emigrate. We should note that there was significant debate concerning the extent to which such attacks were religiously motivated or simply collateral damage.

During the autumn of 2013 most Christian leaders were highly concerned about the growing levels of sectarian violence. They considered that the Assad-led government would be justified in highlighting this and the increased vulnerability of Syria's Christians, although this did not mean that they necessarily endorsed any political agenda the government may have had in doing so. However, there were some Christians who were concerned that there may have been deliberate exacerbation of sectarian tensions, and that specific events may have been used by the government as propaganda tools. While they admitted that sectarian violence – especially that fomented by foreign militants – was a growing problem, they urged that such violence should not drown out the more moderate and conciliatory voices of many within Muslim communities. One Syrian Christian, who requested anonymity, noted that sectarianism was more intense in areas where foreign fighters have greater influence, "while even among Syrian Salafis[51] we are able to find some reasonable people who do not have any grudge against Christians," which is to say that in this case, those who migrated into Syria as combatants were causing the displacement of parts of the native population. As with so many cases in the Middle East, the Syrian crisis defies neat categories, and over-simplification and generalisations are frequently naïve.

Events in and around the town of Maaloula were illustrative of these complexities. The town's population included Christians and Muslims. Forces opposed to the government attacked the town and took control, and a number of Christians chose to

[51] Puritanical adherents of Islam, see Glossary

leave. The government conducted a counter-attack which allowed them to retake control of the town, but left opposing forces active in the surrounding hills. The government claimed to have acted in defence of the Christians, and some Christians retorted that civilians were killed by the less-than-discriminate use of military firepower and that the town remained subject to occasional mortar and sniper fire. The monastery overlooking the town was used as a sanctuary by some of those who were unable to leave due to infirmity. Some of the nuns present were kidnapped and subsequently released. The people that they had been caring for were left unsupported.

What effect has this had on the Christian presence in Syria? At several points I have heard church leaders lament that "all the Christians have left," while also remarking that, "my church is fuller than ever." The two phrases appear incompatible. What is going on? The first statement alerts us to the fact that many Christians have chosen to leave their homes. Some moved within Syria, to the Valley of the Christians and other areas perceived to be safe; others moved abroad. Another change was that Christians went to the church building nearest to their home even if it were of a different tradition or denomination from that of their usual place of worship. All were made welcome, with this change being embraced as a wise precaution when moving meant possible exposure to danger from unexploded ordnance, sporadic and random missile and mortar fire, or snipers. Another change was that amidst the violence, many were looking for sources of inner peace; indeed, people from other faiths started attending church services.

A number of churches have offered humanitarian assistance. Most are more than willing to assist anyone who approaches them. The idea of "meeting the need irrespective of the creed" is applied, as we saw in Lebanon in Chapter 1. The practice of supporting anyone in need is a powerful expression of Christ-like care for all peoples, and it is counter-cultural, since the prevailing culture is that one cares for one's own – members of the same family, clan or tribe. As with the Lebanese churches, provision of humanitarian assistance is not linked or connected to participation in worship; there is no inducement to non-Christians to convert.

Throughout the crisis, there have been regular calls by Syrian church leaders urging those outside the situation to focus their efforts on enabling people to stay. This should include working to resolve the crisis and avoiding making statements that, whilst well-meaning, serve to segregate society as a whole, including any that make religious affiliation a criterion in humanitarian support or migration systems. One clear example occurred in January 2017 when the Chaldean Bishop of Aleppo, Antoine Audo SJ, was asked for his reaction to (temporary) changes in the USA's immigration policy. He was quoted as saying:

> "We Christians of Syria and the Middle East do not like any speeches that make differences between us and Muslims when justice, peace and aid to those in need are at stake. Who makes these differences, feeds fanaticism and extremism... The measures and laws must be fair and must be applied equally to all, without discrimination. And as Christians, we ask to be helped not to emigrate, but to have peace in our countries, in order to continue our life and our witness in the land where we were born."[52]

[52] Fides News Agency; *Are US borders only open to Christians? "Who makes these differences feeds fanaticism" says Chaldean Bishop of Aleppo*; 31st January 2017; www.fides.org/en/news/61633-ASIA_SYRIA_Are_US_borders_open_only_to_Christians_Who_makes_these_differences_feeds_fanaticism_says_Chaldean_Bishop_of_Aleppo#.WJIn132O3IU (accessed 1st February 2017)

This is a reminder that the segregation of Middle Eastern societies on religious lines causes numerous problems, and that anything from outside the region reinforcing it is helping to maintain the dysfunctions that underpin many of the region's problems.

We will conclude our summary of Syria with a reminder of the brutality of the crisis. Amidst the violence, another form of forced migration was reported during 2016. This is the seriously unpleasant practice of kidnapping in order to harvest human organs which are sold on the international market. One report linked this to VEOs looking for new sources of income.[53] The Syrian crisis has displayed profound levels of brutality; it is anything but civil.

Let us pause for a lament. The following is from the prophet Habakkuk, and records the prophet speaking to God about the tumult that he saw unfolding before him:

> "Why do you make me look at injustice? Why do you tolerate wrongdoing? Destruction and

---

[53] Asia News; *Idlib, Children kidnapped for organ trafficking is the new Jihadi business*; 16th November 2016; www.asianews.it/news-en/Idlib,-children-kidnapped-for-organ-trafficking-is-the-new-jihadi-business-39152.html (accessed 16th November 2016)

violence are before me; there is strife, and conflict abounds. Therefore the law is paralysed, and justice never prevails. The wicked hem in the righteous, so that justice is perverted."[54]

God replied to Habakkuk; a response which we will reflect on in Chapter 10.

We will move on to a consideration of the countries neighbouring Syria. What is all too common is for these countries to carry a disproportionate burden in supporting the forcibly displaced. We shall see in Chapter 9 that this follows the typical global pattern, despite the formal aspiration for countries to share the burden.

One theme that emerges in this situation is the desire of many to return. This desire is by no means universal, and some have moved beyond the region. One anecdote describes four Syrians in Jamaica who had set up a stall selling Syrian food. They had a crowd of interested customers who were keen to sample the food and hear their stories. These four illustrate the desire of so many to be given a chance to

[54] Habakkuk 1:3-4

thrive somewhere. They are looking for opportunities, not aid; to contribute, not to be burdensome.

Iraq – being segregated?

The first stop on our alphabetic tour of Syria's neighbours takes us to Iraq. This is a country that has had its own patterns of displacement, seeing critical turning points in 1990 and 2003, as the invader of 1990 became the invaded in 2003.

In August 1990 Iraq invaded Kuwait. Numerous Kuwaitis fled the country, some driving across the desert to Saudi Arabia. The invasion was reversed by a USA-led coalition in the spring of 1991. Following this, some Iraqis rose in rebellion against the then-President Saddam Hussein. Violent internal conflict ensued in the south and north of the country, with many people fleeing cities and towns in search of safety in the marshes of the south, the mountains of the north, or across the border in Iran. The international community established no-fly zones in the south and north to stop the government using airstrikes as part of its campaign. A sense of calm settled on the country; we might call it 'peace' but that word is only applicable in the sense of the absence of violent conflict, not in the fuller sense of harmony. The no-fly zone in the north allowed the three northern provinces of Arbil, Dohuk and Sulaimaniyah to establish a de facto autonomous region, with its administrative centre in the city of Arbil.[55]

The international community imposed sanctions, the stated motivation of which was to prevent Iraq becoming a threat to its neighbours. These caused serious damage to the economy and public services, including the health system. One sign of this was a sharp rise in the child mortality rate.[56] Another was a serious brain drain, as some professional people chose to emigrate in search of a better life for themselves and their families. This contributed to the change in religious demographics that was noted in Chapter 5.

The removal of President Saddam Hussein in 2003 affected the whole of the country. Some parts of Iraq experienced an economic boom, seeing greater freedom and local decision-making, while other parts were affected by sectarian violence. One can debate

[55] Arbil is spelt Erbil, and occasionally Irbil, in some sources, with all three spellings being different transliterations of the name into Roman script. Arbil is the form used in official Iraqi sources. The Kurdish name is Hawlêr.
[56] See, for example, Madeleine Albright's book *The Mighty and the Almighty* (2006, MacMillan), Chapter 4.

whether it was the invasion itself or how the country was governed – or should we say misgoverned? – in the post-invasion period that led to the violence. One decision that has had long-term consequences was the removal from office of all senior administrators, and the disbanding of the army. This left numerous Iraqis, mostly Sunnis, with no means of supporting their families and few prospects.

The USA-led administration handed authority to new Iraqi rulers on 28th June 2004. One struggle in this was that many of those who were installed had returned to Iraq from exile abroad, and had little credibility or rapport with most of the populace. A new constitution was adopted in 2005, formalising the three northern Kurdish provinces as being an autonomous region administered by the Kurdish Regional Government (KRG) based in Arbil. The other major element of the new constitution was that it enshrined in law the rule that those who had held senior roles during the Saddam Hussein era could not hold public office again.

Sectarian violence erupted following the change in governance. Much of this violence pitted Sunni against Shi'a – one example amongst many being the forced expulsion of Sunnis from the Washash neighbourhood of Baghdad in 2004 by Shi'ite militias – although all religious communities were affected. The patterns of violence changed following a bomb attack in Samarra, a predominantly Sunni town north of Baghdad, on 22nd February 2006, which severely damaged the historic Shi'ite al-Askari mosque. This mosque is the burial site of the tenth and eleventh Imams, the leaders of the Muslim community in succession to the prophet Muhammad. Prior to this attack, most Shi'a heeded the call of Grand Ayatollah Ali al-Sistani to desist from retaliating against Sunni attacks. After the Samarra attack, calls for vengeance by Muqtada as-Sadr and others gained stronger support, and large-scale reprisals started to occur on a daily basis. Baghdad in particular became segregated, with each district comprising people from the same ethno-religious group.

We noted above that some Iraqis fled to Syria to escape sectarian violence in parts of Iraq. The scale was significant, as described by António Guterres, who was then head of the UNHCR, who reported in April 2007 that more than two million Iraqis were registered with the UNHCR in neighbouring countries, from an Iraqi population estimated at 25 million in 2003. This number, therefore, equates to approximately one in every 12 Iraqis having fled abroad, with the total rising at a rate of about 50,000 a month at that time. The two countries hosting the most were Syria with 1,200,000 and Jordan with 750,000, with smaller numbers in Egypt, Iran, Lebanon and Turkey.[57] At the time, I heard estimates from Jordanians that there were approximately one million Iraqis resident. The higher figure will include those who chose not to register for the reasons I described in Chapter 1.

Many ethnic and religious communities were affected by the rising conflict and the reduced rule of law, including parts of Iraq's Christian communities. One sign of the times was that the Chaldean Church closed its seminary in Baghdad in December 2006, reopening it in the Ankawa suburb of Arbil the following month. This church also relocated its administrative offices to Ankawa, which became known as 'the Christian suburb'.

The reduction in effective law and order, together with the general lack of security and high level of sectarian violence, led to a large rise in violent crime.

---

[57] New York Times; *The Flight from Iraq*; 13th May 2007; www.nytimes.com/2007/05/13/magazine/13refugees-t.html (accessed 31st January 2017)

Christians and other non-Muslim religious communities became the victims of targeted criminal activity, notably as part of a wave of kidnapping. Many who were kidnapped were well-educated professional people – Christians were perceived to have more money, or access to money from those in the diaspora, making them more lucrative targets. Furthermore, they were unlikely to respond violently, and had no large tribe to protect or avenge them. It was the widespread view during the 2000s that either a ransom would be paid (albeit not necessarily the amount first demanded) or the victim would be murdered. However, paying a ransom did not guarantee that the victim would be released. One example occurred in August 2010, when Luay Barham al-Malik, a Christian, was kidnapped in the Mosul area. His family negotiated with the kidnappers and paid a ransom. Alas, his body was found shortly afterwards.

Amidst the sectarian violence, religious extremists actively sought to impose their agendas in their areas of influence. One aspect of this was the desire to 'purify' areas by evicting those of different religious groups, in an overt exacerbation of the pluralism deficit. Christians became one group who were threatened or attacked by such extremists. There were several periods during the summer of 2006 when Christian residents of the Dora district of Baghdad were told to convert to Islam, leave, or be killed. In summer 2007, they were threatened with violence unless they removed the crosses from church buildings. Ostensibly this is overtly religiously motivated – however, it is possible that religious language was being used to cover other motivations, including inter-communal jealousy and the desire to seize property for the use of people who had been displaced from elsewhere, as in the segregation of Washash mentioned above. However, Christians in Iraq became increasingly convinced that religion was an essential part of the motivation behind the kidnapping of Christians.

During 2007 there was effective action to address the violence. An initiative known as the Sunni Awakening included proactive engagement of Sunni communities in addressing the violence within them. It created a sense of hope, to some, that they would be included in an Iraq that welcomed all its citizens. Alas, in subsequent years the government led by Prime Minister Nouri al-Malaki from 2006 to 2014 reverted to marginalising Sunni communities. The level of violence rose, and the political scene in Baghdad became increasingly polarised and paralysed. Several provinces sought, or simply acted as if they had, greater autonomy, and implemented development programmes for the benefit of residents.

This created the context for the arrival of Daesh in the summer of 2014. This group formed in Iraq, with its leadership drawn from senior army and administrative circles who had been summarily removed from their posts in 2003, and herein lies the source of this VEO's competence in military and governance matters. The group went underground during the Sunni Awakening, moved into Syria early in the crisis, and surged back into Iraq in the summer of 2014. They seized control of Mosul and surrounding areas, causing massive amounts of displacement, and proclaimed themselves 'The Islamic State.' Many of those who did relocate did so at very short notice. Most moved to the Kurdish Regional Government region, and many arrived with just the clothes they were wearing, with everything else, including wristwatches, confiscated at checkpoints operated by Daesh.

There was a strongly religious element to this wave of displacement. Christians and other non-Muslims were, typically, given the choice of leaving, converting to Islam or paying the jizya tax. In Islam, jizya is usually seen as an additional tax to be paid by non-

Muslims because they are being protected without contributing manpower to the military, and is sometimes denigrated as 'protection money'. As in many other situations, some of the elderly, infirm or young were not able to leave. Some were denied any choice in whether to leave or not, being enslaved and forced to serve the new masters. Some women were forcibly married, which we can justifiably describe as being made 'sex-slaves'. In parts of Mosul the homes of Christians were marked with a letter 'N', for 'Nazarene'. This mark meant that these properties could be expropriated, and any remaining occupants exploited. Alongside this, without downplaying what happened to Christian and Yezidi communities, we do need to acknowledge that the Shi'a communities suffered worse atrocities; they were murdered on the spot. In Syria we noted the extremist threat that Christians should be expelled and Shi'a killed; this threat was carried out in and around Mosul.

Of note is the fact that these events changed the nature of the Christian presence in the city of Mosul and the surrounding areas. It switched from being predominantly composed of legally recognised Christians meeting in officially recognised places of worship – church buildings – to being mostly composed of people from Muslim and other non-Christian backgrounds meeting in homes.

One effect of the rise of Daesh is the number of migrants living in the Kurdistan Regional Government's region. In 2003 the population of the KRG region was around five and a half million; in mid-2016 this had risen to more than seven million. Some of this increase is due to migrant workers who were willing and able to come and participate in the economic boom that occurred in parts of this area. Approximately 250,000 of these workers are Syrians, most of whom we could accurately describe as refugees, and who qualify for support from the UNHCR, and the majority of the new arrivals are Iraqis. Many of the Iraqis are forcibly displaced; but they are in their own country, and so are IDPs and do not qualify for support from the UNHCR, which simply refers them to the local and national authorities. International charities vary in their methods and procedures for responding to this; some only support refugees, while others are willing to include support for IDPs.[58] This is one area where the strict

[58] Hurriyet; *Iraqi Kurdish state dream crushed by low oil prices, political division*; July 2016; www.hurriyetdailynews.com/iraqi-

application of the definition of IDPs makes little practical sense.

In October 2016 the Iraqi government began a military operation to capture Mosul, forcing Daesh from the city. Those who were able to leave did so, overcoming considerable obstacles imposed by Daesh. Social workers reported that more than half the children they assessed were suffering from severe traumas; some had been forced to watch brutalities, including the public execution of relatives.[59] Also reported was the fact that, while many of those who fled Mosul had gone to Kurdish controlled areas of Iraq, some had chosen to go to Syria.

As towns were freed from the control of Daesh, returning residents found extensive damage to property due to a systematic scorched-earth policy which had seen most properties set on fire. This has implications for recovery: homes might be rebuilt, but

kurdish-state-dream-crushed-by-low-oil-prices-political-division.aspx? =101348 pageID=238&nid (accessed 6th January 2017)
[59] The Times; *My four-year-old son just wants to behead people*; 10th December 2016; pages 42-43.

lost family photographs and heirlooms will be irreplaceable. A new *normal* will need to be created.[60]

Every so often, the idea is discussed of creating an autonomous area for Christians within Iraq, with a location in the Nineveh Plain near Mosul usually being suggested. Appendix 3 considers such proposals, noting that what is required is good local, regional and national governance that works for all residents of an area and operates in a pluralistic manner.

Israel – abiding by the Hippocratic Oath?

Technically, Syria and Israel remain in a state of war, a situation that has persisted since 1973. It is illegal under Israeli law for Israeli citizens to visit Syria, and any Syrian attempting to visit Israel would receive a less than warm welcome at Tel Aviv airport, while there have been a few limited incidents of shells being fired across the Israel-Syria 'border'.

The term 'border' here means the line of control which is clear to everyone in the area. The

---

[60] For example, World Watch Monitor; *Devastation of liberated Iraqi Christian towns makes return seem further away than ever;* 15th December 2016; www.worldwatchmonitor.org/2016/12/devastation-of-liberated-iraqi-christian-towns-makes-return-home-seem-further-away-than-ever/ (accessed 1st May 2017)

internationally accepted border is that which was established in 1948 and adhered to until the Six Day War of 1967; there are elements of conquest and disputed historical claims in the derivation of many of Israel's boundaries.

The Israeli response to cross-border incidents is always militarily robust; if you fire at Israel then you can expect a response aimed at the point from which incoming projectiles were fired. This has proved a generally effective deterrent.

Israel has, on occasions, conducted airstrikes on Syrian territory. Israel's policy is not to comment on such actions. In most cases, the reports have presumed that the target was a consignment of weapons being supplied to Hezbollah in Lebanon via Syria. One notable exception occurred on 18th January 2015, when an Israeli airstrike in the Syrian Golan Heights killed an Iranian general, together with a senior military commander and five other members of Hezbollah. Reports at the time suggested that the most plausible explanation for the strike was Israel's desire to prevent the establishment of a missile base targeted at Israel as a deterrent against Israeli strikes on Syrian territory. On 28th January 2015, Hezbollah conducted an act of vengeance, killing two Israeli soldiers in a disputed area along the Israel-Lebanon border. Calm was established by a diplomatic exchange the following day.[61] Neither Israel nor Hezbollah want to repeat the war of 2006, which we discussed in Chapter 1.

On a more positive note, Israel does provide medical treatment to some people wounded in clashes that occur close to the Israeli border. More than two thousand wounded people have been transported into Israel and taken to hospital where they receive a very high standard of medical care. When they have recovered sufficiently – at least physically – they return to Syria.

In January 2017 the Israeli government announced that it was planning to admit one hundred Syrian children who had been orphaned during the crisis. They would enter with temporary residency status, and be accommodated in dormitories before being integrated into institutions run by the Education Ministry. After four years they would become eligible

---

[61] BBC; *Hezbollah sends 'anti-escalation message' to Israel*; 29th January 2016; www.bbc.co.uk/news/world-middle-east-31035647 (accessed 23rd February 2017)

for permanent residency status.[62] This is a small number, but those to be chosen are vulnerable people.

One evening in Jerusalem during 2014, a group of Israelis – both Jews and Arabs – described to me a visit they had made to Turkey, motivated by their desire to do something in support of those who had been directly affected by the Syrian crisis. Here is another example of well-meaning people seeking to make a positive difference. They had been to the Turkey-Syria border not far from Kobani, a town in Syria that was being fought over by Daesh and Syrian Kurdish forces (with the latter being supported by Western airstrikes). That battle ended with Daesh being forced to leave the town, and the town was left very severely damaged; almost all residents were forced to leave. The Israelis watched from a safe distance as they prayed. Elsewhere they had been involved in providing practical assistance to some displaced people.

[62] Jerusalem Post; *Israel okays historic plan to absorb child refugees from Syria war*; 26th January 2017; www.jpost.com/Israel-News/Report-Israel-okays-historic-plan-to-absorb-child-refugees-from-Syria-war-479650 (accessed 31st January 2017)

Jordan – how many migrants can it accommodate?

Jordan sits at a crossroads of migration. It welcomes migrant workers, some Jordanians work abroad, and the country has experienced the arrival of displaced persons at several points since independence in 1946. This section interweaves issues of migrant workers and the forcibly displaced, a reflection of the ways that regular and irregular migration can intertwine.

The formal title of the country is the Hashemite Kingdom of Jordan. The Hashemites are themselves migrants; they originated in what is now Saudi Arabia, being displaced when the al-Saud family succeeded in unifying the territory that is known as Saudi Arabia. The Jordanian Royal Family are from the Hashemite clan. So too was the monarchy that was established by British colonial authorities in Iraq; that one did not endure, being removed in a series of coups that led to the emergence of President Saddam Hussein.

Many Jordanian citizens are ethnically Palestinian. The other major ethnic group in Jordan has Bedouin origins, and refer to themselves as East Bankers, by contrast with the Palestinians, whose origins are to the west of the River Jordan. We noted in Chapter 2 that some Palestinians were forcibly displaced into

Jordan in the 1940s and in 1967, and that some were expelled in September 1970. Others have a longer-standing presence in Jordan.

The government treats its Palestinian residents in two distinct ways. Those who arrived before or during the 1940s have Jordanian citizenship. In contrast, those who arrived after the Six Day War of 1967 are classified as 'displaced persons', and do not have full citizenship. They are denied public sector employment, and in public universities, they are obliged to enrol as foreigners and pay their fees in US dollars, not the Jordanian dinar, a requirement that carries additional financial costs. They may, however, hold a temporary Jordanian passport, which must be renewed every two years.

The distinction reflects the decision made in 1988 by Jordan's late King Hussein that Jordan would disengage from the West Bank, allowing the Palestinians to work towards securing control of their own destiny. This decision was made at the request of senior Palestinian representatives. Effectively, Jordan surrendered sovereignty over the West Bank, a necessary step for the creation of a Palestinian state. Consequently, those originating from the West Bank have been displaced across a national border; they are not IDPs, and might be expected to return one day. Members of both categories are included in the UNHCR's count of refugees worldwide.

The next large-scale wave of displaced people to arrive in Jordan was composed of Iraqis, who arrived from 2003 onwards as discussed above, while more recently, Syrians started arriving in 2011. Some Syrians live in camps, of which Za'atari is the most widely known. It is situated in the north of Jordan, close to the Syrian border, and estimates of its population vary, with 90,000 being typical – making it the fourth largest town in the country.

Za'atari began as a few tents in 2011, but rapidly expanded. The facilities have been improved over time, including the provision of reliable electricity, and water being supplied to individual dwellings. An internal economy emerged, with one street of shops becoming known locally as the *Champs-Elysée*. A number of businesses operate in the camp, providing employment for some.

Za'atari operates on what is called 'closed camp' principles. All residents are registered with the UNHCR and are required to remain within the camp, only leaving when they have a permit do so.

Consequently, businesses within the camp can struggle to find business partners and customers outside the camp, and skilled tradespeople are restricted in offering their services. This restricts the fulfilment of residents' aspirations to become self-supporting, and keeps the camp dependent on aid.

The majority of displaced Syrians and Iraqis in Jordan, however, do not live in camps. Instead, they have found accommodation throughout the country.

There is significant debate about the effect of the 'visitors' on the economy. We considered similar complications in Lebanon in Chapter 1, and some are relevant to our discussion here as well. The official unemployment rate has reportedly risen from 13% in 2011 to 15% in mid-2016. The youth unemployment rate is much higher, possibly approaching 40%. The education system is producing more graduates each year than the economy can generate jobs for. This effectively forces some to seek work abroad. One estimate claims that as many as half of Jordan's qualified engineers work in the Gulf States.[63] The

[63] Of relevance to this section is an article published by the Washington Institute in December 2016;
www.washingtoninstitute.org/policy-analysis/view/jordans-

potential long-term effects of this brain drain are significant.

Not all foreigners resident in Jordan are forcibly displaced people. There are at least 600,000 migrant workers, many of whom are Egyptian, although some are from outside the Middle East. One feature of Jordanian society is that there are some jobs that Jordanians are reluctant to do, typically in construction, garment manufacturing, agriculture and domestic service. This is consistent with the patterns seen in Lebanon and the GCC countries, which we discussed in Chapters 1 and 4. Some Jordanians, mostly East Bankers, have a strong preference for public sector employment, even though many private sector jobs offer higher salaries. There is blatant discrimination in public sector employment: typically East Bankers get the jobs, while others do not. As in many countries, Jordan has sought to reduce the number of public sector jobs. This increases the competition for those positions that become available each year.

economy-was-always-shaky-the-refugee-crisis-has-only-made-things-wo (accessed 9th December 2016)

How did the government seek to accommodate the Syrians who arrived in towns and cities? One approach was to attempt to restrict the number of work permits that were available to Syrians. However, the government came under pressure from the EU to reverse this policy as part of attempts to limit the number of Syrians endeavouring to leave the region. It also proved problematic in practice. Skilled Syrian workers were willing to work for lower salaries than nationals, and many found work, raising an important question – at what point should we stop labelling them 'refugees' and apply the term 'migrant workers'?

The legal framework for migrant workers in Jordan compares favourably with those of other countries. One industry that has benefitted is garment manufacture, which employs 60,000 people, of whom 70% are migrant workers, fulfilling the requirement that every large firm's workforce includes at least 30% nationals. The theory behind this framework is good, but the same cannot always be said for the practice. It is reported[64] that some employers

[64] See, for example, Carnegie Institute; *Photo essay: migrant workers in Jordan's garment industry*; 5th January 2017; www.carnegieendowment.org/sada/?fa=66598 (accessed 11th January 2017)

routinely hold employees' passports, despite this being illegal, meaning some migrants suffer from unscrupulous practices such as unpaid overtime and verbal abuse in addition to the loss of their documentation.

We will record in passing that one factor that has allowed Jordan's garment industry to expand is that Jordanian garments have tariff-free access to the USA. We will return to the impact of beneficial trade agreements in Chapter 9.

One must wonder how the labour market will change, and what will be the consequences for Egyptians and other migrant workers in Jordan when it does. To Western observers, one of the root causes of the challenges around employment in Jordan is the expectations that are embedded in Jordanian society. Changing this will not be easy or quick. In Chapters 1 and 4 we noted similar issues affecting Lebanon, Oman and Saudi Arabia, and Jordan is not alone in needing to find authentic national solutions to the challenges it faces due to the rising aspirations of a growing population. The arrival of displaced people has exacerbated such challenges.

Returning to the topic of Syrians seeking safety, Jordan has exercised its sovereignty and enacted due control of the border crossings with Syria. One such crossing is at a place called Rukban, where a camp emerged on the Syrian side of the border accommodating 75,000 people, which the UNHCR refer to as Berm. Supplying aid to this camp has proved problematic, since Jordan regards the border area as a closed military zone, and restricts aid passing through. Tensions were heightened on 21st June 2016, when a suicide car bomb attack aimed at Jordanian border guards occurred in the area. The suspicion was that Daesh had infiltrated the camp from which the perpetrator had come. The UN and others have discussed the Berm camp with the Jordanian government, and negotiations are overshadowed by the realisation by all parties that Jordan has done far more for displaced Syrians than all countries outside of the immediate vicinity.[65]

In January 2016, one Jordanian reminded me that her country was hosting displaced people from 40

---

[65] Al-Monitor; *Difficult negotiations over future of 75,000 Syrians trapped in 'no-man's land'*; 17th August 2016; www.al-monitor.com /pulse/originals/2016/08/jordan-berm-syrian-refugees-trapped.html (accessed 19th August 2016)

nations. The figure of 40 surprised me; I was well aware of Iraqis, Syrians and Sudanese and could imagine that small numbers of Ethiopians, Eritreans, Somalis and Yemenis had found a way to get into Jordan, though I knew that Syrian displaced people were high-profile at the time, and that the support structures in Jordan appeared to be almost exclusively focussed on them. This emphasis was reflected in international media attention as well, and one issue that we will explore in Chapter 9 is that displaced people tend to be forgotten once media attention, and with it much donor funding, moves to the next crisis.

The UNHCR is one organisation that is supposed to be immune from such pressures, though theory and practice are not always the same, as we observed in the previous chapter. In December 2015, *al-Monitor* reported on claims of discrimination. The report illustrated several challenges that are faced when supporting displaced people, including the challenge of giving support with limited resources. Another such challenge is the legal framework within which support must be given – in this case, the Sudanese were not allowed to work and struggled to afford to pay for residency permits. Without these permits, they could not register their children in school. If UNHCR staff encouraged them to find work, the advice would be tantamount to telling them to work illegally, making them vulnerable to abusive treatment from unscrupulous employers, who would themselves be operating outside of the law.[66]

Lebanon – the most affected neighbour?

We looked at Lebanon in Chapter 1, where, amongst numerous other migration issues, we noted the presence of many Syrians. There are a few observations to add here.

On the measure of forcibly displaced people as a proportion of the population, Lebanon is the most affected country in the region, and probably the world. Its historical relationship with its neighbour Syria is one element of the dynamic surrounding the support that is given to Syrians within Lebanon. One positive comment on this is that it creates scope for forgiveness, healing and proactive engagement.

One aspect of displacement in Lebanon is the legal status of children born to displaced Syrians. Some are unable to register their children formally, resulting in

[66] Al-Monitor; *Is UNHCR in Jordan discriminating against Sudanese refugees?*; 2nd December 2015; www.al-monitor.com/pulse/originals/2015/12/sudan-refugees-jordan-unhcr-discrimination.html (accessed 16th November 2016)

children who have no official papers and are therefore stateless.

Prior to the crisis there was visa-free travel between the two countries. Attempts to restrict the arrival of further Syrian 'guests' – to use the Lebanese government's terminology – proved problematic. Official border posts can have additional checks added to their procedures, but the numerous tracks through the mountains are harder to control. The proximity of towns to the border is another complicating factor here.

One significant consequence of the crisis within Lebanon concerns Hezbollah. Since its founding in 1982, it has presented itself as Lebanese and focussed on defending the state of Lebanon and its people from whatever Israel might do. In 2006 it achieved widespread respect across the Arab world for its successes against the Israeli military during the summer conflict. In 2013 Hezbollah became an active participant in the Syrian crisis, in support of the Syrian government. It has sent military personnel, some of whom return as battle-hardened soldiers, while others returned as wounded veterans, and still others as corpses. The group's participation has transformed it into an organisation with regional force. From being perceived as a key player against the common enemy of Israel, it is now viewed in much of the region as a Shi'ite militia and, in parts of Syria, as an occupier. The long-term consequences of this remain to be seen.

Anecdotal evidence suggests that a particularly unsavoury form of migration occurs through Lebanon. It is reported that some Syrian Christian girls are kidnapped in Syria and trafficked to Saudi Arabia, where they are sold as wives to the wealthy. It seems likely that they become the second, third or fourth wife of those who are able to afford to maintain several. This practice is seen as forced conversion of Christian women to Islam, and it is able to operate due to the chaos of war, which allows the separation of families to occur without due record keeping or law enforcement. Similar stories are heard in Egypt and Jordan.

In the Middle East, claims of the kidnapping of Christian women, who are then forced to marry Muslims, are difficult to verify. Undoubtedly there have been situations in which a woman leaves her family without their approval to marry a Muslim in a genuinely loving and consensual arrangement, and the family then claims she was kidnapped to cover their sense of shame at her choice to leave her Christian family and community. Equally, there have been cases of women being tricked into compromising situations. The Syrian crisis creates a context of impunity from the law for assorted acts of violence and abuse, including kidnapping, human trafficking and forced marriage.

Turkey – economics and education

The topic of migration as it relates to Turkey would probably constitute a book in itself! In Chapter 2 we noted some of the forced displacements that brought Turkish and Caucasian people to this country, whose founding in 1923 included an exchange of populations with Greece. An ethnic group with a long-standing presence in the country is the Kurds, many of whom speak several dialects of Kurdish within their own communities.

In recent decades there has been much internal migration in Turkey. The general pattern of movement from rural to urban settings is one factor; Istanbul has become a mega-city, with significance on a global level. Part of this trend has been the migration of Kurds from the south-east to the major cities in western Turkey, which is typically motivated by people's desire for a better life for themselves and their children.

The Syrian crisis has had a profound effect on Turkey. It has had to re-evaluate its foreign policy principle of 'no problems with the neighbours' adopted during the 2000s when the Syrian crisis made it unworkable. Its policy towards Syria appears to have shifted during the crisis. In the early years, Turkey sought the removal of President Assad, and appeared to be supportive of various armed groups. This allowed its territory to be used as a conduit for fighters, support personnel, weapons and supplies. Exactly which groups it assisted, or allowed to be assisted, has changed over time.

One factor that is deeply significant to Turkey's government is the emergence of a de facto autonomous region within Syria governed by Syrian Kurds. The region has capable armed forces who are well able to defend their own communities (such as Kobani as mentioned earlier), and who are able to take the fight to Daesh. Turkey fears calls for greater autonomy for its own predominantly Kurdish area. Kurdish militancy within Turkey has a long history. A period of calm began in March 2013, and came to an all-too-violent end during the summer of 2015. The government restricted the reporting of this conflict, a practice that intensified following the attempted governmental coup on 15th July 2016. Parts of south-east Turkey have suffered extensive damage. One consequence is internal displacement within that part of the country, as well as movement westwards.

Turkey's response to the plight of Syrians has come to be a source of pride for many Turks. Access and border controls have varied during the crisis. Initially, Turkey thought that the numbers fleeing would be low, and that many could establish safe camps inside Syrian territory. As this was shown to be increasingly difficult, so more Syrians entered Turkey. The border is long and the terrain varies, and unofficial – or should we say illegal? – crossing points were established, although many were swiftly closed down.

In 2016, 2.75 million Syrians were registered with the UNHCR in Turkey. It can safely be assumed that there are others who have not registered. The vast majority of these are located in areas along the border, or in the major cities in the north-west such as Izmir, Istanbul, and the capital Ankara.

One curious fact is that there are now more people who speak Arabic as their mother tongue in Turkey than there are in several Arab world countries, including Bahrain, Kuwait and Qatar! If the Syrians integrate and settle permanently, then the ethnic and linguistic diversity of Turkey will have increased.

In January 2016, the Turkish government amended the law to allow Syrians to obtain work permits. This, along with other policy changes, implicitly recognises that Syrians are expected to remain present in significant numbers for the foreseeable future. Another motivation behind this change was to respond to pressure from civil society and business leaders. The latter pointed out that some companies were gaining an unfair competitive advantage by illegally employing Syrians on low salaries with no social security or health care benefits. The legal changes restricted all firms to having at most 10% of their staff as Syrians. The regulations require the employer to apply for a permit for each Syrian employed, and the employer must pay a fee for the permit and make monthly social security payments. In November 2016 it was reported that 10,000 Syrians had work permits and were working legally. In contrast, an estimated 600,000 to one million Syrians were working without permits. The employers of such people were liable for fines, although few local authorities were checking and enforcing the law. The general attitude of society was to applaud the employers for giving work to Syrians, and not to be concerned about the lack of due medical insurance and lower wages.[67]

There have been reports of some Syrians being exploited by unscrupulous employers. One such report, in December 2016, concerned agricultural work – an industry notorious for the use and abuse of migrant labour, and an area in which it is all too common that nationals do not want the jobs that employers have available. *IRIN News* gave an example of Syrians who had not been paid for four months.[68] Most Turks would be appalled at this. The issues of employment for the displaced are complex. We will return to this in Chapter 9.

In December 2016, Turkey reported that the state was providing education for 78,824 Syrian children in 2,000 temporary refugee centres. Many of the

---

[67] Al-Monitor; *Turkish companies flout law for cheap Syrian labour*; 30th November 2016; www.al-monitor.com/pulse/originals/2016/11/turkey-syria-legal-syrian-refugee-workers-cost-more.html (accessed 2nd December 2016)

[68] E.g. IRIN News; *The never ending harvest: Syrian refugees exploited on Turkish farms*; 15th December 2016; www.irinnews.org/photo-feature/2016/12/15/never-ending-harvest-syrian-refugees-exploited-turkish-farms (accessed 15th December 2015)

teachers were Arabic speakers, and the curriculum includes classes in the Arabic, English and Turkish languages. In addition, another 133,000 Syrian children are enrolled in state schools, where they are being educated in Turkish. Turkey is also providing some vocational training to Syrian adults.[69] Such initiatives are to be welcomed, although the provision falls well short of the total need.

Turkey is also host to significant numbers of Iraqis. Some live in camps in the south-east. They have been offered education for their children in state schools, although the parents typically decline. Attending school would mean learning Turkish, which would give some degree of integration to the children. It might also include compulsory religious education, contrary to the parents' wishes. Another factor is that the parents may simply be waiting to be resettled in Europe or beyond. Yet, rejecting the opportunity for education is likely to have negative consequences for their children's future.

[69] EMIS; *Turkey provides education to some 79,000 Syrian children*; 7th December 2016; www.emis.com/blog/turkey-provides-education-some-79000-syrian-children (accessed 9th December 2016)

Many within Turkey have applied to the UNHCR for refugee status. There are reports that some have been given dates for their initial interview in 2022 – six years after their application. This shows how the current crisis has overwhelmed the capacity of the UNHCR's offices in Turkey. Those within this system are likely to be there for a considerable period of time. They need to realise this (disappointing though it is), embrace their current situation, and accept the services, especially education, that are being offered to them.

Many NGOs, both national and international, operate in Turkey to support irregular migrants. Some also seek to provide humanitarian aid to those displaced within Syria. Such organisations operate under due licence agreements with the government. The registration systems have been subject to regular review and change, especially following the attempted coup of 15th July 2016, and NGOs are aware[70] that being seen as critical of the government or its policies will lead to their being closed down, and possibly lead

[70] For example, IRIN News; *Turkey steps up crackdown on humanitarian aid groups*; 27th April 2017; www.irinnews.org/news/ 2017/04/27/turkey-steps-crackdown-humanitarian-aid-groups (accessed 2nd May 2017)

to the arrest of staff members. People of goodwill are obliged to operate carefully here.

Turkey has seen major economic development since the turn of the millennium. It remains keen to attract both investment and people who can facilitate continued economic growth. To this end, in November 2016 the government announced that it was planning to introduce new regulations that would expedite citizenship for those investing in the country. To be eligible, people could purchase property of a certain value and retain possession for at least three years, or deposit funds in government bonds for at least five years, or invest in a business in such a way that it created jobs.[71] Turkey is more than willing to attract the migrants that it wants.

Having looked at reasons why some choose to migrate, we now move to look at two aspects of the journeys that those migrating typically take. People

[71] Hurriyet; *Turkey to grant expedited citizenship to investors*; 14th November 2016; www.hurriyetdailynews.com/turkey-to-grant-expedited-citizenship-to-investors.aspx?pageID=238&nid=106090 (accessed 15th November 2016)

who migrate for study or work use the global travel industry, mostly choosing to fly. Those being forcibly displaced rarely have access to such options, and typically travel by land or sea using informal means. They face the barriers that have confronted human beings since our earliest ancestors moved within and then out of Africa: namely mountains, seas and deserts. Our next two chapters look at the challenges that are faced, some well documented and others obscured by the very geographic features that are being traversed.

Chapter 7
The Mediterranean – playground or cemetery?

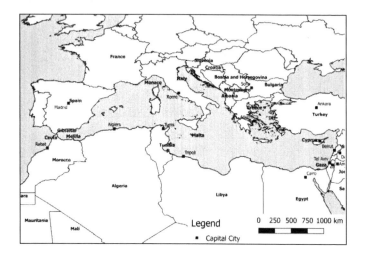

Some Syrians have made their way beyond the region. One route has been across the Mediterranean to Europe, mostly from Turkey to Greece. This route is commonly referred to as the eastern route, a term that also covers routes to Cyprus. There are others, of which the one from Libya to Italy is perhaps the best known. The term 'the central routes' covers this and other routes from Egypt, Tunisia and Algeria which aim for Italy. Then there are the western routes, typically from Morocco heading towards Spain.

We will look first at the eastern route, before considering the others and then reviewing what happens upon arrival in Europe. Having narrowed our focus in the previous chapter, we are now broadening our perspective – whilst the previous chapter focussed on Syrians, many of the people who are crossing the Mediterranean are of other nationalities. The motivations of those moving are also diverse: some are fleeing violent conflict, others political oppression and persecution, and still others the despair of very limited resources, opportunities and hope for the future. What is common amongst them is a strong motivation to face the risks of the journey and what follows.

In January 2017 the International Organisation for Migration (IOM) reported that 363,348 irregular migrants had crossed the Mediterranean and arrived in Europe during 2016. This was much reduced from the number for 2015. Hidden in the details was that arrivals in Greece were much lower – 173,561 in 2016, by contrast with 853,650 in 2015 – whilst those for Italy had risen from 153,842 in 2015 to 181,436 during 2016. A very small number of people landed in

Cyprus, just 189. Information for Spain was not available.[72]

Not everyone who sets off arrives in Europe. Some are intercepted or flounder close to their point of departure and are returned to shore. Presumably most await another opportunity to try again. Not everyone is so fortunate. IOM reported that 5,079 migrants were known to have died crossing the Mediterranean during 2016. These deaths were approximately two-thirds of the global total of reported deaths of irregular migrants. A further 1,144 died in North Africa, which we will cover in the following chapter – the Sahara is an unforgiving environment, and migration is a hazardous undertaking there.

The IOM noted that the casualty figures for 2016 were higher than in previous years. One factor is an improved methodology for collecting the data, although their informed opinion was that there had

---

[72] IOM; *Mediterranean migrant arrivals top 363,348 in 2016; deaths at sea: 5,079*; 6th January 2017; www.iom.int/news/mediterranean-migrant-arrivals-top-363348-2016-deaths-sea-5079 (accessed 10th January 2017)

been a genuine increase in the number of deaths.[73]
Elsewhere they acknowledged that data collection
was much weaker on the western Mediterranean
routes and a number of small craft may have
disappeared without trace; the deaths of all on board
would not have been included in the statistics.

A brief description of one aspect of maritime law will
assist our understanding. Maritime law states that
those seeking refugee status must cross borders
under their own control and direction. Anybody
assisting them in doing so can be charged with
people-smuggling. This is applicable to those piloting
boats or commanding a tugboat that is assisting
another vessel with migrants on board. This law is
one reason why smugglers typically put one of their
customers in charge of the boat, providing them with
minimal training – just one way in which smugglers
minimise the risks to themselves. This aspect of
maritime law also affects rescue workers. Typically,
they assess boats carrying irregular migrants from a
distance and wait for them to cross maritime borders

[73] IOM; *World fatalities of migrants, refugees approach 7,500 in 2016
as three-year total tops 18,501*; 6th January 2017; www.iom.int/
news/world-fatalities-migrants-refugees-approach-7500-2016-three-
year-total-tops-18501 (accessed 10th January 2016)

unaided. If they assess that the boat is in difficulties and there is a clear threat to people's lives, then rescuers can lawfully intervene immediately.

The eastern routes – to Greece and Bulgaria

In Chapter 1 we noted that most Syrians in Lebanon express the desire to go home, and are content to wait in Lebanon until they are able to do so. Some, though, choose to join the migration routes to Europe and elsewhere. One option is to travel through Syria to Turkey, a journey requiring two border crossings. An alternative is a boat to Cyprus, although the figures above show this to be rare.

One practice in Lebanon during 2015 was for Iraqis, and people of a few other nationalities, to acquire fake Syrian documents. The northern city of Tripoli was, anecdotally, a centre for such documents. The reason people do this is the perception that Syrians were being welcomed in Europe whereas other nationalities were not. Irregular migrants will, wherever possible and by fair means or foul, make their story fit the criteria for being accepted. Those making a living from irregular migrants will find ways to provide what is desired. The quality of the documents that these people received is open to question.

Similar practices emerged in Turkey, where they amounted just to one more fee that Afghans, Iranians and Pakistanis paid to smugglers.

The primary eastern route is from Turkey to the Greek islands. There are numerous possible starting points and destinations, and some of the routes are short; a few are swimmable given favourable conditions and good athleticism. Patrolling and preventing such migration is a complex undertaking.

In December 2015, Human Rights Watch (HRW) reported on violent means being used against boats of migrants endeavouring to travel from Turkey to Greece. In one reported incident a boat carrying migrants was disabled by deliberate damage to the motor, and the pilot was assaulted. That boat was fortunate – it was discovered three hours later by Turkish coastguards and all on board were rescued. HRW expected that violent assaults would stop following their first report on the subject, which was published in October 2015: they are a well-respected organisation whose reporting is based on high journalistic standards. One trusts that the second detailed report of December 2015 led whoever was organising and financing such practices to stop. HRW were careful not to make accusations. They did point out that a joint operation was in progress at the time involving Greek and Turkish coastguards as well as Frontex, the European Border and Coastguard Agency. In this context, 'border' means the EU's external borders.[74]

The statistics above showed a large drop in migrants arriving in Greece during 2016 compared to the previous year. There were a number of reasons for this. Improved prospects in Turkey, as described in the previous chapter, would be one. Reports of the difficulties facing those who had reached Greece would be another, and we will cover this later in this chapter. Another would be an agreement between Turkey and the EU, which was negotiated during 2015, with a joint plan of action beginning on 29th November of that year. On 18th March 2016 a second joint statement was issued, adding further elements to the programme.[75]

---

[74] Human Rights Watch; *Masked men continue to attack migrant boats on the Aegean*; 7th December 2015; www.hrw.org/news/2015/12/07/dispatches-masked-men-continue-attack-migrant-boats-aegean (accessed 22nd March 2017)

[75] EU; *EU-Turkey Statement, 18 March 2016*; 18th March 2016; www.consilium.europa.eu/en/press/press-releases/2016/03/18-eu-turkey-statement/ (accessed 21st January 2017)

The agreement has several major components. In summary, Turkey undertook to act to make departures more difficult, and to accept that those who arrived in Greece from Turkey from 20th March 2016 onwards would be returned to Turkey if their applications for asylum status were rejected. In return, the EU agreed to resettle somewhere in Europe one Syrian from a recognised camp in Turkey for each migrant returned; to provide three billion Euros of aid; to expedite negotiations on granting visa-free entry for Turkish citizens to all EU member countries; and to "accelerate" talks on Turkey's long-standing EU membership application. The EU's money was to be spent on helping refugees in Turkey become more self-sufficient, funding education initiatives for their children and supporting host communities. These are all laudable aims and principles.

The 2016 statistics would suggest that Turkey fulfilled its commitments to prevent or severely restrict departures. At the time of writing, the EU had not granted visa-free access and, whilst there was some progress on the membership application process in late 2015 and early 2016, the process came to a standstill following the attempted coup in Turkey on 15th July 2016.

The phraseology in the EU's statement referred to Syrians as being "under temporary protection" in Turkey. The continuing crisis in Syria suggests that they are unlikely to return home in the foreseeable future. Better phraseology for their situation would address integration. To that end, the agreement also included references to Turkey opening its employment market to Syrians – an undertaking that was fulfilled, as noted in the previous chapter.

In addition to its long, and often beautiful, coastline, Turkey has land borders with two European countries: Bulgaria and Greece. Both of these borders have been reinforced in recent years, though this does not prevent some irregular migrants endeavouring to cross them.

In August 2016 an unusual method of irregular entry into Bulgaria was reported. A group of mostly athletic young men climb or otherwise circumvent the fence along the Turkey-Bulgaria border, and when detected by border guards, one member admits to possession of a small quantity of illegal drugs. This person is arrested, and those with him remain in Bulgaria as witnesses to the crime. The criminal process takes a long time, allowing the migrants to seek ways of remaining in Bulgaria legally or making their way to other European countries. Without the drugs, the group would either be detained in a camp near the border or be returned to Turkey. Additionally, *The Times* reported that the Bulgarian Prime Minister had informed members of his Parliament that Bulgaria had returned 26,000 people to Turkey, all of whom had crossed the border illegally. Turkey accepted these people, despite there being no applicable EU readmission treaty in place covering Bulgaria.[76] Once more we see the lengths to which desperate people are willing to go to gain access to a place of opportunity.

In contrast, Bulgaria is welcoming some Syrians as migrant workers. They are given the appropriate visas in Damascus, enabling them to travel by regular means to Bulgaria, usually overland through Turkey. They fill vacancies created by the migration of Bulgarians within the EU.

Syrians, Iraqis, Afghans and Iranians are not the only people seeking to leave Turkey; some Turkish citizens are also actively looking for opportunities to move elsewhere. In August 2016 it was reported that

[76] The Times; *Migrants using drugs scam to enter EU, says Bulgarian PM*; 27th August 2016; page 37.

Canada, Spain, the UK and the USA were the most popular countries in which Turks were seeking to purchase property, and to which they were seeking to relocate. The EU countries of Greece, Ireland, Latvia, Malta and Portugal offer citizenship or residence permits to foreigners who purchase properties worth between €250,000 and €500,000 or buy bonds of at least €150,000 and keep them for five years.[77] Those with financial resources are given opportunities that are denied to those who do not have them. Some people are welcome, others are not.

The central routes – to Italy and Malta

The eastern routes are mostly quite short. In contrast, the central routes involve greater distances with increased chances of rough seas. The IOM report we referred to above noted that almost 4,600 of the 5,079 known deaths in the Mediterranean occurred on the central routes. Italy treats such incidents as murder, and carefully preserves all available evidence. This affords the deceased dignity in death where possible, although prosecutions appear unlikely.

[77] Al-Monitor; *How Turkey's coup turmoil has fuelled migration flurry*; 12th August 2016; www.al-monitor.com/pulse/originals/2016/08/turkey-coup-attempt-turmoil-fuels-migration.html (accessed 16th January 2017)

The figures for arrivals in Europe during 2015 and 2016 did not include Malta. One possible explanation for this is that Malta has a covert agreement with Italy that all intercepted boats will be taken there in return for granting Italy favourable exploration rights in its extensive exclusive economic zone (EEZ) of the Mediterranean. The Maltese government came under intense local pressure from its population during 2014, when the country had the highest per capita number of applicants for asylum status in Europe. Whilst there were no arrivals by sea, a number, mostly Libyans, continue to arrive by air. The issue of burden sharing within Europe will be addressed later in this chapter.

One change that occurred on the central routes during 2015 was in the type of boats typically being used. For those departing from Libya, few were wooden, as had been the case previously. Instead, wooden boats had been replaced by inflatable rubber dinghy-style boats. The change reflected a deliberate action in Libya to destroy wooden boats. Such actions were presumably funded by European countries. The death rate probably rose, although precise statistical evidence is not available.

The largest national group on the central route during 2015 was Eritreans. They had migrated through Sudan, and then either Egypt or Libya, to reach the coast. They were fleeing from political and ethnic harassment and persecution, with some also facing religious persecution.[78] This illustrates the fact that much of the irregular migration on this route is from Africa; those from the Middle East typically use the eastern routes.

The western routes – to Spain

During the 2000s, Morocco effectively closed the routes through its territory. One consequence of this was that migrants switched to travelling to Mauritania, hoping to board a boat aiming for the Azores. This is a seriously dangerous crossing. Little has been reported about it in recent years, and one suspects that the Mauritanian government took action to stop its territory being used for such purposes, and probably received covert assistance from Western governments to do so. This would have been handled within a general framework of countering extremism

[78] IRIN News; *For Eritreans, Egypt is the new route to Europe*; 6th June 2016; www.irinnews.org/feature/2016/06/06/eritreans-egypt-new-route-europe (accessed 16th January 2017)

and violence. We will look a little further at Mauritania in the following chapter.

The rise in irregular migration since 2011, together with the increasing dangers of moving through Libya (which we will explore in the next chapter), have brought the Morocco route back into focus. There are two ways in to Europe when taking this route: by boat across the Strait of Gibraltar, or by forcing one's way into Ceuta or Melilla, two Spanish enclaves on Africa's northern coast. For the latter, border fences were heavily reinforced in the 2000s.

Reaching Europe – a place of welcome?

Those who successfully cross the Mediterranean arrive in Europe, landing in one of several countries all of which are members of the EU. The EU's Dublin Principle requires applicants for asylum to apply in the first country that they enter. This is consistent with the international norm that those fleeing should apply for refugee status in the first safe country they reach and that those whose case is accepted will be resettled somewhere. We will return to this in Chapter 9.

Systems were established in these countries to register arrivals, including the use of biometrics such as fingerprints. Some migrants endeavoured to avoid being registered at the point of entry, preferring to make their way to other countries within Europe, and apply for asylum where they wished to settle. One story illustrates the fact that exploitation occurred. Agents in some Balkan countries informed irregular migrants that "When you reach Germany you will be given a house, a car and a job," and then asked "Would you like to buy a train ticket to get there?" The promise was not true.

Prior to 2015, movement within much of Europe was straightforward. The Schengen Area removed all checks on national borders within the zone, thereby facilitating the free movement of people and goods amongst participating states. One reaction to the wave of migrants entering during 2015 was the reintroduction of checks and the erection of fences on some national borders. This led to the emergence of camps for migrants near to border crossings.

In August 2016 *The Times* described how some people were retracing routes and resurrecting methods for crossing the Italy-France border which were used by resistance fighters during the Second World War. The occupants of a camp near the border regularly try to cross the border; some paying local guides to show them routes. This creates a further opportunity for some people to enter the people-smuggling 'business' and make money from irregular migrants.[79]

One camp near a border was located on the edge of Calais, France, and was known as The Jungle. The Jungle was being treated by the authorities as a closed camp. Residents found outside the camp had their shoes confiscated and were returned to the camp. Within the camp itself, leaders emerged for each ethnic and national group present, and acted as liaison points for those seeking to be of assistance. As for the risks of another sea crossing, either by stowing away on a boat across the English Channel or on a train through the Channel Tunnel, the most common remark was, "We will either die slowly here or quickly on the journey." When asked why they were reluctant to formally apply for asylum in France, most remarked that they were being treated worse than dogs; consequently none would choose to remain in France. One effect of this attitude which was seen during 2016 was that an estimated 80% of the support to residents was being provided by British

[79] The Times; *Migrants retrace French resistance routes to reach UK*; 13th August 2016; page 38

people. The attitude of most French people they had encountered was of wanting them to go home – or at least, anywhere other than here. Welcoming migrants, some of whom had been forcibly displaced, appeared to be the option of last resort.

In October 2016, the residents of the camp were dispersed throughout France, and the camp was demolished. In November 2016, the French government increased the support it was giving for migrants to make a voluntary return to their own country. The figure offered was raised to €2,500, with the offer valid until the end of 2016. A government official was quoted as saying that the offer appealed to Afghans.[80]

Turkey is not the only country with whom the European Union has an agreement that focuses on irregular migration. On 5th October 2016, the EU announced that it had signed one with Afghanistan which included the repatriation of Afghans whose claims to stay in Europe had been rejected. The announcement was made at an international

---

[80] RT; *'Best Offer': France to give €2,500 to migrants who return home voluntarily*; 24th November 2016; www.rt.com/news/368086-france-migrants-home-voluntarily/ (accessed 28th November 2016)

conference at which various governments worldwide pledged a total of US$3.75 billion in aid to Afghanistan over a four-year period. The EU's pledge was €1.3 billion, worth US$1.46 billion at that time. As always with pledges at such conferences, promises and actual payments are not always the same. Many of the national delegates praised positive developments in Afghanistan. Few made any reference to the presence or scale of the conflict that was affecting parts of the country; at the time, government forces were struggling to ensure security in Kunduz, a state capital. One article on the conference was entitled *Europe Makes Deal to Send Afghans Home, Where War Awaits Them*. The title is all too poignantly true; European governments, including the government of the UK, are too willing to send people to places where they are likely to have few good options.[81]

The EU denied that its aid contribution was linked to the repatriation deal. Sceptics will not be convinced by such claims. The EU's own data stated that 213,000 Afghans entered the EU during 2015, of whom

[81] New York Times; *Europe makes deal to send Afghans home, where war awaits them*; 5th October 2016; www.nytimes.com/2016/10/06/world/asia/afghanistan-eu-refugees-migrants.html (accessed 17th October 2016)

176,900 applied for asylum status. Of these, at least half had been rejected, although appeal processes might not have been exhausted. Consequently, thousands of Afghans face being forcibly returned under the terms of the agreement at some point. We can note in passing that this reflects the low acceptance rates generally seen in such processes.

Appendix 4 looks at deportation. One key point is that re-entry to the country of origin is rejected in some cases, and an effect of an agreement such as this is that the recipient country has undertaken to admit those returned to it, accepting the assurance that only those who are genuinely its citizens will be returned. There is usually an undertaking by the recipient government to refrain from acting harshly against those being returned. What difference such assurances make in practice is open to question.

France was not the only country from which Afghans chose to return home; 3,200 voluntarily left Germany from January to November 2016, while in the same period, 5,000 Iraqis chose to make voluntary returns from Germany. We noted in Chapter 5 that not everyone who arrives in Western countries settles well. For some the transition proves too difficult. The cultural differences are large, and language can be an issue for many. Some prefer the instability of home to the uncertainties of abroad, especially in places where establishing a new 'normal' life proves problematic. The statistics from Germany record that more people returned voluntarily than were deported, and the numbers for both types of return were higher in 2016 than during 2015.[82]

The UK's approach to the arrival of irregular migrants into Europe has been interesting. There were several elements to its approach. One was to be generous with aid funding, deliberately allocating this to the countries neighbouring Syria, and focussing on education. The UK made a commitment to accepting 20,000 Syrians over a five-year period, selected from official camps in the neighbouring countries, consciously choosing those with the greatest needs. The Prime Minister who announced this, David Cameron, argued that this was to act as a disincentive to irregular migration. The response of the UK's people has, arguably, been more generous than that of their government. Numerous people and organisations have become involved in local

[82] BBC; *Germany Migrants: record number opt to leave – most to Balkans*; 28th December 2016; www.bbc.co.uk/news/world-europe-38449841 (accessed 20th January 2017)

initiatives to provide a welcome to those who arrive, and aid to those elsewhere. One example is the support for residents of The Jungle. Meanwhile, very few have argued against the government's position.

We noted in Chapter 2 that one factor which helps people to settle in new locations is the ability to worship according to their beliefs. In some of the camps within Europe this has been possible, with The Jungle being one. However, it has been problematic in others. There are people endeavouring to conduct a comprehensive survey with a view to asking the EU and member states to act decisively to resolve problems. Anecdotally, most issues arise when residents of a camp act in a similar manner to how they would in their own country, with those who regard themselves as a majority suppressing the rights of others. Allowing such practices to occur within Europe is not helpful for the integration of people into European society.

Religious freedom in Europe is much appreciated by many who are able to enter, settle and integrate. In August 2016, *The Economist* quoted Mohamed Taher Sabri, imam of a large mosque in one of Berlin's poorer districts, stating that "Germany's constitution is a 'God-given' document which enables all kinds of religion to flourish and offer moral guidance." *The Economist* noted that, "not many Muslim countries tolerate such diversity." The dilemma that emerges is how to know which strands to encourage and which to be wary of. The article noted that political comment about global events can complicate international relations, citing as an example a sermon preached in some mosques in Germany which referred to the attempted coup in Turkey during July 2016.[83]

We need to remind ourselves that many non-European migrants are welcome in Europe. Foreign students are one category, and those who are coming to work in the healthcare sector are another.

In 2014 the Maltese government introduced The Individual Investor Programme to attract financial investments from wealthy individuals by offering them Maltese passports – effectively citizenship – in return for donations to a development fund, and acquiring property in the country. The programme requires applicants to give a €650,000 contribution to a national development fund and provide a €150,000

---

[83] The Economist; *Through the politics of Islam, Germans and Turks are deeply intertwined*; 19th August 2016; www.economist.com/blogs/erasmus/2016/08/germany-turkey-and-islam (accessed 22nd August 2016)

investment in government stocks or bonds. Applicants must also own property worth at least €350,000 in Malta for at least a year to establish a 'residency link' to the country. There is apparently no requirement to actually live in the property, or anywhere else in Malta. Fulfilling these criteria entitles the individual to apply for a Maltese passport. Maltese passport holders enjoy visa-free travel to at least 166 countries. A spouse or a child costs an additional €25,000, or €50,000 if the dependent has reached the age of 18. The Maltese government claims that it rigorously scrutinises applicants to ensure that only those it deems suitable are actually granted a passport. Government figures indicate that many families are using the scheme: 202 applicants secured citizenship for 503 spouses or children in the first two years.

This programme is controversial within the EU, as are those of several other EU members. [84] Critics argue that these programmes amount to selling access, and violate the principle that citizenship in a country other than that of one's birth needs to be earned.

[84] Politico; *Malta slammed for cash-for-passports program*; 17th August 2016, updated 23rd August 2016; www.politico.eu/article/malta-cash-for-passports-program-individual-investor-programme/ (accessed 31st January 2017)

Finally, we must note that such practices are not restricted to Europe. In Chapter 6 we noted Turkey's plan to grant citizenship to those investing in the country.

The Mediterranean Sea is hazardous to some, as well as being a popular tourist destination for many Europeans. Next we look at a vast ocean of solid but shifting sand. The desert of the Sahara also proves to be harsh and unforgiving to those who flounder while attempting to cross it. In this case there are people of ill will seeking to use abhorrent methods to exploit the vulnerable, and there are far fewer well-resourced people of goodwill endeavouring to rescue those in distress. In many places the systems for maintaining law and order are flawed, weak or non-existent, creating a context for unscrupulous people to exploit the vulnerable.

Chapter 8
The Sahara – place of retreat or flight?

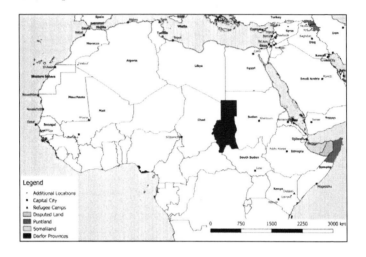

The desert has played a significant part in the history of Christianity. Numerous monasteries are located in deserts, and arguably, these have played a significant part in maintaining the Christian presence in parts of the Middle East. A long-term pattern seen in Egypt has been that Christians were actively engaged in society whenever possible, and retreated to desert monasteries during periods of severe oppression. In the desert, the faith was maintained, and the faithful were prepared to emerge strengthened when conditions allowed.

Today, many people attempt to cross the Sahara heading for the North African coast, and a boat to Europe. At the start of Chapter 7 we noted that 1,144 people were known to have died whilst moving in Africa during 2016. Having crossed the desert, they then face the sea. We will see examples of people who become settled – in some sense – en route through Africa, and others who realise the dangers and difficulties, abort their planned migration to Europe, and return home. In some places, the transit routes across the Sahara have become two-way.

One evening, sitting in a comfortable hotel in southern Europe, Sam (not his real name) described his journey to Europe. In outline, he was driven in a pick-up truck across the Sahara. The truck was crammed beyond capacity, with everyone instructed to hang on tight; anyone who fell off would be left where they landed. Each 'passenger' was given a small bottle of water. The journey took several days, with the only stops being to transfer fuel from containers to the vehicle's tank. At one point they passed another truck that had broken down. They sped past without stopping; Sam presumed that all involved had perished. Sam was well aware that he and those who travelled with him had been lucky. Not only had the truck been reliable, but they had had no problems with any formal border checks, and nor had they encountered any unofficial checkpoints operated by armed groups.

Sam went on to describe the struggle to find a boat, and the traumas of the sea crossing. On arrival in Malta he was taken to a detention centre. He was released after a few months and began establishing a life on the island.

People-smuggling is a very lucrative business. A comprehensive description was provided by Peter Tinti and Tuesday Reitano in their book *Migrant, Refugee, Smuggler, Saviour,*[85] as we noted at the end of Chapter 3. They note that people-smuggling is a dynamic industry that adapts rapidly to changing circumstances. The three common motivations for irregular migration all apply in parts of Africa. First, violent conflict affects some parts, rooted in the actions of governments or armed groups. Second, poor and oppressive governance affects some people, notably in Eritrea, which is sometimes described as "the North Korea of Africa". Third, inadequate economic development, with limited jobs and opportunities, affects many. Changing patterns of

[85] Peter Tinti and Tuesday Reitano; *Migrant, Refugee, Smuggler, Saviour* (2016, Hurst Publishers)

agriculture due to changing technology and climate change prompt some to move to urban areas in search of gainful employment. In many situations these motivations intersect. For example, the tourist trade in the Sahara desert was decimated by the emergence of Al-Qaeda in the Islamic Maghreb (AQIM for short), an armed group linked to the al-Qaeda franchise. During the 2000s they were involved in the high-profile kidnapping of a few Westerners. The security situation has been improved but, at the time of writing, tourism had not recovered.

Economics is the underlying issue here, in terms of the inadequate supply of jobs and opportunities. Widespread corruption, including police seeking bribes, and a lack of transparency, are also pertinent factors. Such considerations constitute a significant *push* factor, and many urban and rural youth actively consider applying for a visa to France, the UK, Canada or elsewhere in search of a better job and living conditions. The urge to leave their country is so strong that some are ready to risk dying at sea or in the desert. The phenomenon is known to some as the *haraga* (literally: 'the ones who burn the frontiers').

This chapter now takes a geographical survey around the north of the Sahara, from the Atlantic to the Indian

Ocean. It focuses on those countries that are members of the Arab League, a supra-national body (see Glossary), though most of these countries have citizens who are not ethnically Arabs. In places this causes tensions, a sure sign of a pluralism deficit affecting the harmony of all.

Mauritania – can the displaced return?

Mauritania is a microcosm of migration issues, being profoundly affected by urbanisation, and as both a host country for the displaced and a source country for some who have fled to neighbouring states.

The urbanisation trend is increasingly pronounced. Typically, men leave their villages to look for work in regional towns or the port cities of Nouadhibou and Nouakchott, the capital. This has created a situation where some villages now have no working-age men, causing numerous social problems. It is presumed that there is a significant gender imbalance in urban areas. Amongst the social issues are abandoned wives and families, and high divorce rates. This trend is exacerbated by the fragility of many rural agricultural communities, as in recent years drought and floods have affected parts of the country.

During 2012, a large number of people fled into Mauritania from Mali, establishing camps near the border. In July 2012, the UN reported that the M'bera camp housed 80,000 people, which made it the fourth largest conurbation in the country. (This is similar to Za'atari in Jordan, as we observed in Chapter 6.) In April 2013, Doctors Without Borders (also known as Médecins Sans Frontières) described conditions in the camp as appalling. The UNHCR challenged some of the factual accuracy of this description, claiming to have addressed the shortage of toilets so that there was one per 30 residents, not one for every 3,000 as claimed. This is an example of reporting by a widely respected NGO leading to remedial action. In 2016 the UNHCR released a map of the camp, illustrating that it continues to be home to numerous Malians.[86]

Internal conflict from 1989 to 1991 resulted in 75,000 Mauritanians fleeing to Senegal, while a smaller number of Senegalese people fled into Mauritania. These people were treated as 'refugees' on both sides of the border. Mauritanian law does not allow the granting of refugee status, so those who had been

---

[86] Relief Web; 21st April 2016; http://reliefweb.int/map/mauritania/mauritanie-camp-de-refugi-s-de-mbera-au-24-mars-2016 (accessed 31st May 2017)

forcibly displaced into Mauritania might be an 'applicant for refugee status' but nobody can be described as a refugee in Mauritania in the legal sense of the term.

In 2013, 30,000 Mauritanians remained resident in Senegal, an example of how long some people are displaced for. A return programme for Mauritanians operated from 2007 to 2012, organised by the UNHCR. Some of those who made use of this service encountered two significant challenges upon arrival in their own country. One was that educational facilities were limited, prompting some families to return to Senegal, where they had appreciated the schooling provided for their children. The second concerned the issuing of Mauritanian identity documents. We noted in Chapter 6 that some Syrians in Lebanon were unable to register the birth of children. Establishing legitimate legal identity should not be difficult, but frequently is. Enabling the displaced to return is often complex, and ensuring the right conditions are available as people arrive requires detailed planning and careful execution. In Mauritania, some returning citizens were unable to support their land ownership claims because of their lack of official identity documents.

Displacement from rural agricultural contexts is especially problematic for families. Children learn the necessary skills for this work by watching and working with parents and others. In situations of displacement, this cannot happen. In some camps better education may be provided than would have been available in the rural context, and in such cases, the children not only lack the skills to return to rural settings, but have acquired knowledge and aspirations that make them unwilling to learn the skills of their parents and others in their community. Such factors become more significant the longer people are displaced.

In the previous chapter we briefly mentioned Morocco as the western route across the Mediterranean. We noted that it had changed its border controls to prevent those who are migrating from entering Morocco. One result of this was to push that transit route further south, with people heading to Mauritania and then for a boat journey aiming for the Azores – a very small target in the expanse of the Atlantic Ocean.

One trick of the trade on this route was for migrants to deliberately throw their passports overboard when boats were intercepted. Their intention was to make it very difficult for anybody to repatriate them because there was no documentary proof of their nationality.

Morocco and Western – or is it Moroccan? – Sahara

Moving north from Mauritania, we come to what is known internationally as Western Sahara, an area whose status the UN regards as disputed. Historically, Spain withdrew as the colonial power in 1975, at which point both Mauritania and Morocco, the two neighbouring countries, claimed sovereignty of the area. An independence movement, known as the Polisario, had initiated an armed conflict in 1973, which endured until a UN-administered ceasefire was established in September 1991. During this period of conflict, Mauritania renounced its claim to sovereignty, whereas Morocco asserted its claim in 1979 by declaring that it had annexed the area, making it a province of Morocco known as Moroccan Sahara. The annexation is not recognised internationally. In 1984 the African Union (AU) officially recognised Western Sahara as an independent country; consequently Morocco withdrew from membership, making it the only country on the continent that was not a member. In January 2017 Morocco re-joined the AU, despite the continuing disagreement over the area's status.

Since 1991, Morocco has controlled approximately 80% of the territory in Western Sahara, with the Polisario controlling the remainder. The latter refers to itself as the "Sahrawi Arab Democratic Republic". The Sahrawi are the pre-eminent indigenous tribe.

The conflict caused some displacement; an estimated 90,000 Sahrawians are still living in five camps near Tindouf in south-west Algeria. These people are able to return to their homeland, but only if they recognise Morocco's control of the area, and this is a price that many are unwilling to pay. Consequently, they continue to live in the camps despite being well aware that they could have a higher standard of living back 'home'. They make this sacrifice to maintain their sense of identity, and to express their long-term desire for the independence of their homeland.

This is an example of a long-running situation with little prospect of resolution. Morocco continues to actively develop the area, and encourages its citizens to migrate there. It actively encourages exploitation of the mineral resources and fishing along the coast. After oil was discovered off the coast of Mauritania in 2001, the Moroccan government encouraged prospecting for oil off the coast of its province of Moroccan Sahara.

In the previous chapter, we noted that Morocco has sought to prevent irregular migration to Europe from its northern coast. In 2013 it revised its policy towards irregular migrants within its territory, replacing the previous practice of deporting people with an offer of registration and the right to work, albeit under a status which means that no social security benefits would be provided. Those who are moving through, or attempting to do so, are almost exclusively from sub-Saharan Africa, and a significant proportion of them are women. This is different from the general trend of single men migrating. Single women typically travel in groups in an attempt to provide some degree of protection, yet they remain very vulnerable; those seeking to assist them report abuse, including rape.[87]

Algeria – recovering from internal displacement

We leave the Atlantic Ocean and move eastwards along the southern shores of the Mediterranean, first to Algeria and then to Tunisia. Both continue to have

[87] News Deeply; *The dark reality for women migrants in Morocco*; 17th February 2017; www.newsdeeply.com/refugees/articles/ 2017/02/17/the-dark-reality-for-women-migrants-in-morocco (accessed 2nd May 2017)

their economic struggles, including insufficient suitable jobs for graduates. Both have been used as starting points for journeys across the Mediterranean in the past, and in recent years both appear to have taken effective action to stop such journeys.

Algeria clearly illustrates the prevalence of urbanisation. At independence in 1962 it was estimated that 69% of the population lived in rural settings. In 2016 70% lived in urban settings; the percentage in rural settings has more than halved in fifty years.

Algeria has recent experience of internal conflict and displacement. Conflict during the 1990s resulted in at least half a million, and possibly as many as one and a half million, people being internally displaced in 1992 – the peak year in terms of displacement. The higher figure represents 4% to 5% of the population. Many people relocated to the outskirts of cities, creating slum areas with high unemployment, poverty and some malnutrition. This was unplanned and largely unmanaged urbanisation. The government has striven to respond adequately throughout this century, and it is understood that many have been able to return home, although no survey has been undertaken in recent years to confirm this.

Algeria is notable in that fewer of its citizens have migrated to Syria to join Daesh and other armed groups. Many commentators regard this as a legacy of Algeria's internal conflict during the 1990s, and another possible explanation would be that any extremists who wish to fight take the shorter journey to join AQIM, which is generally understood to operate in Algeria as well as Mauritania, Mali and Niger.

Tunisia – receiving returning jihadists?

Tunisia is where the Arab Spring first erupted in late 2010 and early 2011. Its long-standing President Zine el-Abidine Ben Ali stepped down and promptly left the country, migrating to exile in Saudi Arabia, where he lived in comfort, though he was confined to a plush and expansive villa. The country moved from being effectively a one-party state to a multiparty democracy. The government changed several times in the following years, always with a peaceful transition of power, albeit with various levels of political brinkmanship. The 2015 Nobel Peace Prize was awarded to the National Dialogue Quartet of civil society organisations in Tunisia, in recognition of the constructive role taken by civil society in supporting Tunisia's political transitions.

Prior to 2011, expatriates living in Tunisia described it as a friendly and open place to live and work, a country that had made commendable progress in many areas including education and women's employment. The only area of life with serious restrictions was the political sphere, where criticism of the president or government was strictly taboo. The Arab Spring ended this restriction for Tunisians.

The Arab Spring affected other countries in profoundly different ways. Conflict in neighbouring Libya prompted a significant number of Libyans to seek sanctuary in Tunisia, and some remain living in camps near the Libyan border. Those with the means to do so have moved elsewhere in Tunisia or have transited through the country as they left North Africa to establish a new life elsewhere.

Tunisia has experienced several violent incidents. During 2013 there were two political assassinations, and in 2015 there were two violent attacks affecting tourists. On 18th March, three gunmen attacked the Bardo National Museum in Tunis, killing 21 foreigners and a local police officer. On 26th June, a lone gunman attacked tourists on a beach near Sousse, killing 38 people. The two attacks badly affected the country's tourism industry, which was struggling to recover from a large downturn in response to the widespread protests and disturbances at the start of the Arab Spring in 2011.

As 2017 began, Tunisia was facing a new political challenge. An estimated five thousand Tunisians have joined armed groups abroad, including Daesh in Iraq and Syria, as well as groups operating in Libya. These Tunisians have migrated, presumably with a variety of motivations, including some who have moved for ideological reasons, and others who have moved for adventure or simply employment. Some were starting to return, prompting a public debate on how they should be treated, including calls from some for their citizenship to be revoked, thereby denying them access to the country.

Underlying this was concern that some returnees might perpetrate violent attacks in Tunisia. Comments posted on-line by people presenting themselves as Tunisians threatened such criminality. The government was keen to fulfil its legitimate duty to protect citizens and affirm that it had heard the public's calls for action, pointing out that another option was imprisonment in Tunisia for crimes committed abroad. [88] It was also clear about its international commitments and its strong desire to maintain good relations with a broad spectrum of other governments. Such links were essential to economic wellbeing.

This illustrates the dilemmas faced by numerous governments in how to handle migrants returning when they have been participants in violent conflict and their loyalties are open to question. Identifying them is likely to be problematic without a trusting relationship with their friends and associates at home, and it is worth noting that some who join Daesh become totally disillusioned with its ideology and methods, and that such people may present no threat on their return. Also relevant in this context is the development of de-radicalisation programmes in a number of countries.

Libya – smugglers becoming traffickers

Moving eastwards we reach Libya, a country much changed since 2011. Colonel Muammar Qaddafi, who

---

[88] Al-Monitor; *How will Tunisia deal with thousands of returning Jihadists?*; 17th January 2017; www.al-monitor.com/pulse/originals/2017/01/tunisia-return-islamic-state-fighters-syria-controversy.html (accessed 19th January 2017)

ruled from 1969 to 2011, brought stability, but allowed no serious dissent to his continuing rule. During his period of rule there were a large number of migrant workers in Libya. One policy of his later years was to enable more nationals to be effective in the workplace. He facilitated and paid for higher education abroad, notably for Libyans studying for MBAs. Following Qaddafi's removal in October 2011, many migrant workers left the country. Large numbers of migrant workers leaving over a short period had a significant detrimental effect on the country, and the communities that they left. This caused serious problems in several areas, notably the health service (because many of the nursing staff were from Asia) and with bread supplies (since most of the bakers were Egyptians).

People-smuggling is a profitable trade in Libya. Under Colonel Qaddafi, it was effectively a state-sanctioned and state-controlled industry. A few well-connected operators controlled most of the migrant transit from sub-Saharan Africa towards Europe. Qaddafi used his control of this trade in his dealings with Europe, using the threat of allowing mass migration from Libyan shores as part of his negotiating strategy. It is widely rumoured that he requested security equipment to monitor Libya's very extensive desert borders, thereby pushing control of irregular migration to the desert. After the removal of Colonel Qaddafi in 2011, smuggling became a more chaotic business: anyone with a few strategic connections could take part in this multi-million dollar industry.

The dark side of this business comes when migrants can no longer pay for transit. Often in such cases migrants are held in illicit detention centres, tortured, sold into labour camps, sold as sex slaves, or killed. The operators exploit the vulnerable, switching from the consensual arrangements of smuggling to the worst of brutal practices as traffickers. One witness of sex trafficking in Libya reported that unscrupulous agents "would simply take the girl they wanted. They had no conscience, no morals, not an iota of mercy even though she was a mere child." Another reported that, "One just disappeared and they never found her again, despite her father and brothers searching for her. Another was found three months later, cut, raped and lying in the middle of a park. She had been left for dead."

The exploitation of irregular migrants is rampant. In October 2016 the *International Business Times* reported that more than 70% of people who migrate through Africa are exploited, based on a survey of those who made it to Europe.[89] The desert contains dangers from the evil actions of some humans, as well as the dangers that arise from the natural world.

Egypt – systemic discrimination or violent attack, which does more harm?

Moving eastwards, we come to Egypt, which has coastlines on the Mediterranean and the Red Sea. We have noted that several thousand Egyptians were migrant workers in Libya, and in Chapter 6 we noted that many others work in Jordan. There are also large numbers in Saudi Arabia and the small Gulf States. The disruption in Egypt which forced long-standing President Mubarak from office on 25th January 2011 prompted many Egyptians to consider becoming migrant workers. One estimate stated that 100,000 secured work somewhere and migrated, of which 60,000 were Muslims and 40,000 Christians, suggesting that the brain drain effect is disproportionately higher for Christian communities, since the 40% figure given for Christians here is

---

[89] International Business Times; *Anti-Slavery Day: Why migrants crossing the Mediterranean are victims of slavery and trafficking*; 18th October 2016; www.ibtimes.co.uk/anti-slavery-day-migrants-crossing-mediterranean-among-most-vulnerable-trafficking-1586816 (accessed 20th October 2016)

higher than all of the range of demographic figures (6-20%) given in Chapter 5.

For irregular migrants, Egypt is both a host and a transit country. In November 2016 I asked an Egyptian church leader how many Sudanese and other migrants were resident in his country. "The estimate is four million," he said, an amazing figure. The word 'estimate' is significant here, as many outside observers regard this figure as exaggerated. The UNHCR operates in Egypt, and has a formal programme for Syrians, all of whose applications for refugee status are accepted. Some Sudanese register, but many do not, and their applications for refugee status are far from automatic. Some are genuinely in need of protection, but others are probably economic migrants in search of work.

For many years, some Sudanese have endeavoured to travel through Egypt to Israel. Typically, they crossed the Sinai Peninsula and then the border into Israel. Once in Israel they were treated reasonably well, and a viable community emerged in the Tel Aviv area. The numbers of Sudanese reaching Israel have reduced dramatically since 2014, however; one factor was that Israel started constructing a fence along the border. The migrant issue appears to have been the primary motivation for this, although a second motive was a desire to make cross-border attacks by armed groups more difficult.

A second deterrent has been the deterioration of law and order in some parts of the Sinai Peninsula; armed groups have emerged whose activities include kidnapping irregular migrants and extorting money from their families. Like the Sahara, this area of mostly desert can be a dangerous place. Egypt has taken extensive action to protect the Red Sea coastal areas, including resorts such as Sharm el-Sheikh, from the effects of lawlessness in other parts of the peninsula; tourism – which is to say, short-term regular migration – is strongly desired.

Violent attacks in and around the city of el-Arish, on the northern coast of the Sinai Peninsula, have prompted some residents to flee the area. There was a spate of incidents in 2012, and another series in February and March 2017. One observation made in 2017 was that if extremists wish to fight the government then they attack police and security service personnel; whereas if their aim is to embarrass the government then they murder some Christians. The bomb attacks on two churches on 9th April 2017 fit this pattern. An Egyptian bishop speaking in Washington DC in May 2017 remarked that, whilst violent attacks on Christians garner much publicity, it is the systemic, daily discrimination in education, public sector employment, provision of public services, building permissions and other legal processes that has the greater effect on Christian communities.

Another migration route that has opened in recent years is boat travel to Europe. This emerged in response to abusive practices suffered by migrants when transiting Libya. Starting from Egypt substitutes the dangers of a longer sea crossing for the risk of meeting armed groups when transiting Libya's desert areas.

Sudan – transition, transfer and transit

Moving southwards from Egypt, we come to Sudan. This country has seen much internal conflict with consequent forced displacement since gaining independence in 1956. Many people have relocated to study or to work, either internally or abroad, whilst others became irregular migrants in neighbouring countries and beyond. The borders, and arguably the nature, of the state, changed in July 2011 when South Sudan seceded to become an independent country.

Our focus here is on migration, within, from and through Sudan, though we will include brief details of the background that are pertinent. Two individual stories introduce the dynamics of Sudanese migration.

Mary (not her real name) was born in what is now South Sudan. Her parents moved the family to Khartoum because they thought the education for their children would be better there. I have no doubt that this proved to be true. Mary moved again when she chose to go to university in Egypt. In due course her qualifications enabled her to secure a job, and subsequently residency, in a European country. In one sense, she is part of the brain drain from Sudan. She is also the product of her parents' desire to provide quality education to her and her siblings, and her family is an example of urbanisation in the sense that they migrated to a city in the expectation of better opportunities.

Alan (not his real name) also has an instructive family history. Both his grandfathers were Cypriots who moved to Sudan as young businessmen. They met and married Sudanese women, settled permanently in Sudan, and raised their families. Alan's parents met and married. When conflict and limited opportunities prompted Alan to seek a better life elsewhere, he used his ancestry to secure residency, a job and citizenship in Cyprus. His Sudanese wife was able to join him. There is a two-way aspect of this story – migration to and from the region – when it is viewed over three generations.

One area of continuing conflict encompasses the three provinces on the western side of Sudan which are collectively referred to as Darfur. In June 2016 it was reported that there were more than 300,000 Sudanese living as forcibly displaced people in neighbouring Chad. Most had been there for more than a decade, and the camps had become towns, albeit ones with limited infrastructure. We might note in passing that Chad was also hosting more than 70,000 people who had been displaced from the Central African Republic. One way of identifying the camps (or towns) of Sudanese was billboards advertising the services of several humanitarian aid organisations. Yet by 2016, many of these organisations had curtailed or even closed their operations, primarily due to a lack of funding. Other situations using the term 'refugees' were attracting more media attention, and more resources, forcing the residents to adapt and become self-sufficient. It is also a prompt to us that support polices need refining;

long-term sustainability needs to be established which does not rely on excessive outside support.[90]

Several factors converged in Darfur to create lethal levels of violence. At its peak, the casualty rate for conflict in this part of Sudan was estimated to be 10,000 deaths per month, some from direct military action and some due to the shortage of food and medical care. In contrast, 3,709 civilians were reported killed in sectarian violence during October 2006 across the whole of Iraq, during a period of intense sectarian conflict.[91]

On 17th December 2006, a statement by Madeleine Albright, Joschka Fischer and 13 other former Foreign Ministers published in *The Financial Times* provided a succinct commentary on Darfur which is all too applicable to other parts of Sudan. Their statement included:

[90] IRIN News; *Sudanese refugees in Chad must adapt or starve*; 9th June 2016; www.irinnews.org/feature/2016/06/09/sudanese-refugees-chad-must-adapt-or-starve (accessed 19th January 2017)

[91] IRIN News; *More than 3,700 civilians killed in October, UN reports*; 22nd November 2006; www.irinnews.org/report/61960/iraq-more-3700-civilians-killed-october-un-reports (accessed 28th February 2017)

"The Darfur conflict is more complex than often characterized. It does not simply reflect, but rather cuts across tribal, Arab versus African ethnic, and farmer versus herder stereotypes. It is coloured by local grievances and aggravated by greed, which takes the form of banditry and competition for scarce resources...The primary cause of the ongoing crisis, however, remains the callousness of the governing elite, intent on preserving its own privileges and indifferent to its population."[92]

The reference to "African versus Arab" reflects the fact that migration has taken place over centuries. There are linguistic and cultural differences amongst the numerous tribal groups throughout Sudan, including those within the Darfur region. It is cultural background and cultural influence during the last four centuries that has resulted in some groups being *Arab oriented* and others *African*, including the Fur tribe from which the name Darfur is derived. Most tribes originate in Africa, with the exception of the Beni

---

[92] Financial Times; *Sanctions would force a change of policy in Sudan*; 17th December 2006; www.ft.com/content/328e41fc-8e13-11db-ae0e-0000779e2340 (accessed 28th February 2017)

Halba, and some Razeigat, who originate in Arabia and who are the product of migration.

Many people in Darfur resented the central government in Khartoum not providing the region with a fair share of national resources; a complaint echoed by those in other parts of Sudan. In Darfur, some tribes resorted to violence against the government. The government responded by arming militias from other tribes and granting them impunity within Darfur. It chose not to deploy the army, primarily because it could not rely on the loyalty of junior soldiers, many of whom were likely to be sympathetic to the tribes involved. A secondary reason for this was that the army was needed to tackle conflicts with similar roots in other parts of the country.

Sudan is a transit country for irregular migration. This flow of people includes Somalis, some of whose stories we will cover in Chapter 10. The most common nationality of those passing through is Eritrean. They face the challenges of the long journey, vulnerability to kidnappers, and the arbitrariness of officials. There are stories of people getting through the country only by bribing police. Others have been kidnapped and held to ransom, with the perpetrators evading prosecution by bribing the police.

The EU has concluded an agreement with Sudan which includes limiting the movement of people through Sudan towards the Mediterranean and thence to Europe. The agreement includes an arrangement with Eritrea under which Sudan can return Eritreans found in transit. In Chapter 7 we mentioned similar agreements with Turkey and Afghanistan. In some respects this agreement is more problematic; Sudan is not noted for gentle, respectful treatment of those to whom the government takes exception; Darfur is not the only example of serious abuses of power, which are all too well known amongst organisations focussed on various aspects of human rights. In 2016 it was reported that 900 people had been detained in a single day and returned to Eritrea. One individual noted that he had passed through by bribing the police but that this practice had not worked for a relative: the authorities, it seemed, had received a better offer.[93] In the following chapter we will note

---

[93] IRIN News; *Sudan and Eritrea crackdown on migrants amid reports of EU incentives*; 25th May 2016; www.irinnews.org/news/2016/05/25/sudan-and-eritrea-crackdown-migrants-amid-reports-eu-incentives (accessed 17th January 2017)

some positive aspects of the EU's endeavours to address migration towards Europe.

It is worth reflecting on the changing nature of the Christian communities in Sudan. Prior to 2011, the majority of Sudanese Christians originated in what became South Sudan. They, or in many cases their parents or grandparents, had migrated to Khartoum to escape conflict or for better educational or work opportunities, as did Mary and her family at the start of this section. The government forced those of southern origin – predominantly Christians or animists – to be citizens of either Sudan or South Sudan and, if the latter, to leave and reapply for their jobs as foreign migrant workers. Many felt obliged to leave Sudan, despite having never lived in South Sudan; in no true sense was it 'home' to them.

Somalia – instability and inward investment

I am including Somalia here because it is a member of the Arab League, although Arabic is not the national language, and because it illustrates several factors pertinent to the issue of migration by regular and irregular means.

Somalia has been without an effective national government since January 1991. There have been a number of attempts at international intervention and mediation since then, but instability and inter-tribal violence are prevalent in some parts. The country has 18 provinces, some of which have committed themselves to active participation in larger administrative structures. Two of these are Somaliland in the north-west and Puntland in the north-east, though there are several others, and the arrangements change over time. The motivation for this is invariably to create a functional tier of governance, in an attempt to make up for the deficiencies created by the dysfunction of the 'national' government in Mogadishu.

Somaliland has a different history from the rest of Somalia. It was formerly a British colony or protectorate, whereas the rest of Somalia was an Italian colony prior to independence in 1960, and it declared its own independence from Somalia in 1991, though this is not recognised internationally. The territory has a constitution, a functional government and an established legal and policy framework. In July 2010 there was a peaceful transfer of power from one president to another following an election.

For Somalia as a whole, the population of nine to ten million is remarkably homogenous, being approximately 85% ethnically Somali, linguistically Somali-speaking and religiously Sunni Muslim. The divisions are clan, sub-clan and extended family-based, with an ever-changing mix of loyalties, alliances and enmities. The instability has the potential to cross the nation-state borders into neighbouring Djibouti, Ethiopia and Kenya, all of which have areas in which ethnically Somali people constitute the majority of the population.

Violence and instability, together with floods and droughts, in parts of Somalia have left many people displaced, either within the country, in neighbouring countries, or beyond. Internationally, people have moved across the land borders to either Kenya or Ethiopia, or have travelled by boat to Yemen. This route has been used by Sudanese, Eritreans and Ethiopians as well as Somalians, and is a dangerous crossing, with many people drowning in the attempt. On this sea crossing some smugglers pilot the boats themselves, pushing their customers into the sea close to the Yemeni coastline. Most migrants make their way to shore safely, although reportedly on occasions some have drowned because they were dropped in deep water and were unable to swim. This practice is different to that seen in the Mediterranean in the previous chapter.

Yemen, or rather parts thereof, descended into violent conflict in 2015. This profoundly affected patterns of irregular migration. The movement of migrants on the transit route across the Gulf of Aden switched to being from, rather than to, Yemen. Yemenis seeking to leave their country were joined by irregular migrants who were resident in Yemen and wished to return to Africa. At the time of writing, most Yemenis who had made this difficult journey had settled in Ethiopia.

Some displaced Somalis have migrated to Somaliland. In international terms they are IDPs, since they are within the international boundaries of their own country, although the authorities in Somaliland regard them as applicants for refugee status.

Somaliland faces the dilemma that it needs greater economic development, and better international trade links, but faces significant restrictions due to its disputed political status. It has a growing number of educated young adults seeking employment. Either they will find jobs locally or they are likely to join the trails of economic migrants seeking work elsewhere.

One development opportunity would be to expand the facilities of the Port of Berbera and improve transport links with Ethiopia, notably with a new railway line.

This would benefit Ethiopia as well, since it would create more export routes; but the pertinent question is whether such investment can happen without Somaliland being recognised as independent. The arguments that militate against independence include the border with Puntland being disputed and, on occasions, fought over. The African Union is understood to be opposed to independence, presumably because they wish to avoid setting a precedent that would allow small areas to think that they can solve their problems by independence. Within Africa, the experience of South Sudan following independence from Sudan in July 2011 is not encouraging. An independent Somaliland would risk a flare-up of internal tribal tensions following the removal of the need to maintain a united front against the Somali federal government. The alternative is to find routes for inward investment to those parts of a country that are stable despite the instability of other areas. This challenge is likely to recur in Syria and elsewhere, and hopefully the example of the KRG area of Iraq is a positive example of what can be done when there is political will to support inward investment.

The theme of the importance of good governance to address the *push* factors in migration occurs again in the Somali example.

Dadaab, Kenya – the world's largest camp

Dadaab, in north-eastern Kenya, is commonly cited as the world's largest refugee camp. At one point it had 450,000 residents, mostly but not exclusively Somalis. It is a closed camp, like Za'atari in Jordan in Chapter 6. The authority responsible, in this case the Department of Refugee Affairs (DRA), issues special movement passes to permit residents to travel outside the camp. Without that document, they must remain within the confines of the camp.

The Kenyan government has long sought to close the camp. This objective attracted greater attention in 2015 when, on 2nd April, five gunmen killed two security guards and 147 students in an attack on a campus in Garissa. Kenya was stunned by the atrocity, which was blamed on the Somali armed group ash-Shabaab.[94] The residents of Dadaab, two hours by road from Garissa, were left in no doubt of the coming

---

[94] This armed group is named 'al-Shabaab' in many sources. Under the rules of Arabic grammar, the correct name would be ash-Shabaab. I use this term in deference to my Arabic-speaking friends.

clampdown when Deputy President William Ruto warned that "the way America changed after 9/11 is the way Kenya will change after Garissa."[95]

The immediate consequence of this was that the DRA stopped issuing travel permits, and one result was that some residents of Dadaab who were students at universities in Garissa, Nairobi and elsewhere were unable to sit their examinations, while others who had been offered places at university were unable to start their courses. Some appealed to the UNHCR, asking them to intervene on their behalf. The Kenyan authorities refused.

The Garissa massacre exacerbated long-standing concerns about instability within Dadaab. Parts of the camp had become no-go areas for the authorities after humanitarian staff were kidnapped, and these areas appointed local administrators who acted on behalf of their neighbourhoods. Some of these people paid a high price for their service to others: they were targeted by ash-Shabaab or other extremists, and a

[95] IRIN News; *Dadaab refugees caught in the middle*; 18th February 2016; www.irinnews.org/analysis/2016/02/19/dadaab-refugees-caught-middle (accessed 17th January 2017)

number of them were killed. The situation led to calls within Kenya for the camp to be closed.

Several proposed timetables for closure have been announced. To date, all deadlines have slipped. In November 2016 the Kenyan government announced that the camp was scheduled to be closed by May 2017. To achieve this, the government planned to move non-Somali residents to other camps, whilst all Somalis in the camp would be obliged to leave Kenya. The UN was offering cash payments to anyone willing to return voluntarily. The mood in the camp was that one should take the offer rather than risk being expelled with nothing. There are serious questions here about the assessment of the conditions in Somalia, which should have evaluated the general socio-economic-political conditions as well as the local situation. Assessing the conditions like this in southern Somalia might be straightforward for Mogadishu, where international engagement has seen improved governance and a reduction – but not an eradication – of violence. However, similar evaluations in rural contexts are much more difficult to complete, and would need to include agricultural conditions as well as security and public services such as schooling.[96]

This timetable could not be realised. At the time of writing, the Kenyan government strongly desired to close the camp, but had not yet been able to do so. The practical issues needing to be addressed made this a complex undertaking. Drought in parts of Somalia, part of a wide scale drought in many east African countries, was a further complication.

This is an appropriate place to conclude our tour around the Sahara desert. The question of who can return safely arose at the start, in the example of Mauritania, as well as in the example of Somalia and Somaliland. At roughly the mid-point we remarked on whether those who remained in Tunisia were willing to welcome certain returning migrants.

---

[96] IRIN News; *Reprieve but no solution for Kenya's Dadaab refugees*; 16th November 2016; www.irinnews.org/analysis/2016/11/16/ reprieve-no-solution-kenya%E2%80%99s-dadaab-refugees (accessed 17th January 2017)

Together with the previous chapter, this leads us to look at the international system for handling the forcibly displaced. How did this system arise? What was it designed to do? Which aspects are working well, and what shortcomings have emerged? There is much being done or thought about to manage regular and irregular migration, but what else needs to be considered? Who is involved practically, and who is involved at policy levels? One significant challenge is to create a system that effectively supports those who do need to move, whilst clearly and quickly rejecting those who seek to make use of such systems for inappropriate reasons. This is unlikely to be a straightforward challenge. It is, though, one of the most vital and pressing challenges of our time.

Chapter 9
Fit for Purpose? – past, present and future

In September 2016 the UN held a summit on migration. The closing communiqué was entitled The New York Declaration for Refugees and Migrants, and described the commitments made collectively by all member states. The press release highlighted three undertakings. First, to start negotiations aimed at agreeing a Global Compact on Safe, Orderly and Regular Migration, to be adopted by the UN in September 2018. Second, to develop guidelines on the treatment of migrants in vulnerable situations. Third, to achieve a more equitable sharing of the responsibility for, and burden of, hosting and supporting the world's refugees, by adopting a global compact on refugees in 2018.[97]

The third commitment is an acknowledgement that the current system for handling forcibly displaced people does not share the burden equitably; it has always been the case that neighbouring countries

[97] Available on a UN website: https://refugeesmigrants.un.org/sites/
default/files/un_press_release_-_new_york_declaration_-
_19_september_2016.pdf (accessed 25th January 2017)

carry a disproportionate share of the consequences of migration from any particular country. In Chapter 7 we noted that the EU has struggled to achieve burden sharing amongst its members, at least in terms of where people are accommodated while their claim for asylum status is evaluated.

In Chapter 4 we noted the story of Stephen, who became an illegal migrant who worked to support himself. He entered legally, became illegal, and left through a legal channel, and is an example of the ways in which regular and irregular migration intertwine. He illustrates why a holistic approach, linking regular and irregular migration, will be beneficial.

Further commitments were included in the UN's press release, albeit that they were not highlighted on the first page. Two of these were commitments to prevent and respond to gender-based violence, and to "ensure that all refugee and migrant children are receiving education within a few months of arrival."

One wonders how successful the proposed negotiations will be. Stating ambitious goals during a conference is relatively straightforward; agreeing programmes to implement ambitious solutions will be difficult. In the area of burden sharing, the longstanding practices of many are contrary to the stated objective of greater equity. I found the comment in the opening paragraphs of the press release saying, "when we have ended conflict," to be idealistic. The UN has been seeking to achieve this since its founding in October 1945; the Syrian crisis is the latest demonstration of its limitations in resolving conflict.

One organisation that responded to the UN's initiative was Amnesty International who released a report on 4th October 2016 entitled *Tackling the global refugee crisis: From shirking to sharing responsibility.*[98] The report's introduction includes:

> "This report documents the precarious situation faced by many of the world's 21 million refugees, the vast majority of which are hosted in low and middle-income countries, while many of the world's wealthiest nations host the fewest and do the least. If all – or most – countries were to take a fair share of responsibility for hosting refugees then no one country would be overwhelmed and the lives of

[98] See www.amnesty.org/en/documents/pol40/4905/2016/en (accessed 5th October 2016)

refugees would be significantly improved. Amnesty International is calling for all countries to put in place refugee resettlement programmes and to increase safe and legal routes for refugees to enter the country. The organisation is also proposing that countries agree a specific system for responsibility sharing, based on the use of reasonable criteria such as national wealth, population size and unemployment rate."

This report gives a figure for the number of refugees worldwide. In addition to these 21 million people, another 44 million people are displaced within their own countries. The total number of forcibly displaced people was 65 million. These figures are the UN's assessment of the global situation at the start of 2016.[99] Of note here is that the IDP figure is slightly more than double that of the number of refugees.

Amnesty's call is for more effective resettlement programmes and burden sharing. It outlines a set of criteria to determine what a fair share might look like

---

[99] UNHCR; www.unhcr.org/uk/figures-at-a-glance.html (accessed 21st February 2017)

for all countries, albeit that unemployment statistics are far from reliable in some countries.

On 9th March 2017 Louise Arbour was appointed to the post of UN Special Representative of the Secretary-General for International Migration. Ms Arbour's career includes being CEO of the International Crisis Group (2009-14), UN High Commissioner for Human Rights (2004-08) and Chief Prosecutor of the International Criminal Tribunals for the Former Yugoslavia and Rwanda (1996-99). She brings an impressive depth of expertise with human rights in complex situations to the role.

Having summarised the present, we will review the history of the international system for addressing the needs of the displaced, noting that it has been adapted over time.

UN agencies – UNHCR, UNRWA, IOM and World Refugee Year

The system for managing irregular migration was established by the UN following the Second World War. In 1949 the UN established the United Nations Relief and Works Agency for Palestine Refugees in the Near East (UNRWA) to oversee provision of support for displaced Palestinians. The original mandate was to provide jobs on public works projects and direct relief for 652,000 Palestinians who had been displaced by the events surrounding the creation of the state of Israel in 1948. The mandate is renewed every three years by the UN General Assembly and revised when necessary. At the start of 2017, the UNRWA was providing education, health care and social services to an estimated five million people, the survivors and descendants of those displaced in the 1940s. It operates in Jordan, Lebanon and Syria as well as the Gaza Strip, West Bank and East Jerusalem.

At its inception, the UNRWA provided assistance to Jewish and Arab/Palestinian people who were displaced within the state of Israel by events prior to and during the establishment of Israel in 1948. The Israeli government assumed full responsibility for these people in 1952; the UNRWA's mandate has been restricted to Palestinians ever since.

In 1950 the UN established a second agency for refugees. The United Nations High Commission for Refugees (UNHCR) is responsible for aiding other refugees around the world. Its mandate is to help them to lose their refugee status whenever possible, by integration into their current country, resettlement in a third country, or repatriation.

There is a marked contrast here: the UNRWA's mandate is to support people where they are without seeking an alternative status for them, whereas the UNHCR's mandate is to assist people in resolving their situation and status so that they no longer need support.

A second distinction concerns the children of those who are granted refugee status. In the case of the UNRWA the status passes automatically to offspring, whereas under the UNHCR it does not. For Palestinians, this ensures some level of provision to allow them to acquire legal papers for their descendants. In contrast, we noted in Chapter 6 that some Syrians in Lebanon are struggling to register the births of children, making them stateless.

One subtle point to note is that the UNHCR's figures for forcibly displaced people, referred to above, differentiate between Palestinians and all others.

The Syrian crisis illustrates the challenges involved in registering displaced people. Many Syrians who flee choose not to officially register for refugee status. Some have sufficient financial resources and the contacts necessary to be self-supporting. Some fear reprisals against them or their families if it becomes known to the authorities in Syria that they have left the country. Others fear that being registered makes them vulnerable to being forcibly returned. Keeping records current also has its challenges. Those who do register sometimes cease to be in contact with UNHCR staff. Some find that they are able to return to Syria, if not necessarily to their home, and neglect to inform the UNHCR of this. This is understandable if an opportunity to return occurs at short notice.

A third UN institution is the International Organisation for Migration (IOM), whose reports we referred to in Chapter 7. This organisation has had several names since its founding on 5th December 1951. The original title was the Provisional Intergovernmental Committee for the Movement of Migrants from Europe, which describes its founding purpose of assisting with the resettlement of people who had been uprooted by the Second World War. The name has changed several times since then, before settling on IOM in 1989. Its mandate has broadened to be worldwide.

Its head office is in Geneva, close to the UN offices, which also include the UNHCR's headquarters. It has had 'permanent observer' status at the UN since shortly after it was founded, and in August 2016 the

UN General Assembly voted to formally recognise the IOM as a 'UN Partner Organisation'. The IOM duly assumed this status on 19th September 2016 during the UN summit on migration that produced the New York Declaration. One consequence of this vote is that it formalised IOM's role as a humanitarian assistance agency.[100]

On 28th July 1951 the UN General Assembly formally adopted the Refugee Convention. In Chapter 3 we noticed that this restricted the term 'refugee' to those fleeing their country prior to 1st January 1951. The intention was to address the then-current situation. Inherent at that time was a presumption that the establishment of the UN reflected a global consensus to end violent conflict amongst nations, and that consequently there would be no further sources of violently displaced persons. This utopian ideal remains unfulfilled. The 1967 Protocol removed the restriction.

The Convention remains a very useful document, which one trusts will be the starting point of the

---

[100] IRIN News; *How will joining the UN change IOM?*; 12th August 2016; www.irinnews.org/analysis/2016/08/12/how-will-joining-un-change-iom (accessed 27th January 2017)

negotiations initiated by the New York Declaration. In particular, the question of the legal definition of a refugee remains pertinent.

Four Articles of the Convention in particular are relevant for what follows in this chapter. Article 22 addresses education. It states that access to primary education should be the same for refugees as for nationals, and that access to secondary education should be the same as for expatriates with work-related residency. This requires host nations to open their education systems to newly arrived forcibly displaced people. There is clearly a capacity issue in doing so, which it seems reasonable to request international assistance in meeting. One significant factor in this is language. If the host language is the same as the displaced then integration is likely to be much quicker. In the Middle East many Syrians, for example, share a language with Iraqis, Jordanians and Lebanese, while the situation in Turkey is very different, since to attend local schools, displaced Syrian children need to learn Turkish. In Chapter 6 we noted that some Iraqi families decline the offer of education in Turkish for their children.

One option for finding additional staffing is to look for qualified teachers amongst the displaced, a practice that we saw in some 'tented communities' in Lebanon in Chapter 1. The New York Declaration's objective of ensuring access to education within a few months is commendable, and one trusts that the resource implications are met. One route to achieving this would be greater use of NGOs, and notable in much relief and disaster response work is the high proportion that is undertaken by FBOs. This needs to be encouraged and facilitated, whilst ensuring that appropriate standards are maintained in terms of curriculum and child protection.

This commitment should be broadened in three ways. First, to include higher education. In the previous chapter we saw that Somalis in Kenya were denied opportunities to participate in university education. Second, to include vocational training in electrics, plumbing, nursing, sewing, etc. Third, to be broader in its scope than simply enabling academic study, for example by recognising the benefits of sports activities for teaching teamwork, improving physical health and introducing the role of mentoring. Another example would be the value of creative arts, which can make a positive contribution to post-trauma processes.

Education gives children a future, but possibly not a future in the place from which their parents were displaced. It also leads to the need for more jobs for those leaving education. Vocational training often needs to be complemented by micro-enterprise; that is, the granting of small scale loans that enable people to become self-employed. This is particularly significant in contexts where women are obliged to become head of their household. Typical in post-conflict situations is that the number of 'female-headed households' rises, due to men having moved away from their family as combatants, with the inevitability that some become casualties and never return.

This leads into the issue of employment. Article 17 of the Refugee Convention addresses the employment of refugees. It states that national labour market considerations should be taken into account, and that refugees should be allowed to seek work after three years' residence.

Article 18 addresses self-employment. It stipulates that refugees should be permitted to exercise their trade in the same manner as other resident expatriates, and the same applies to the establishment of companies. Article 19 makes similar provisions in respect of due recognition of professional qualifications.

The significance of enabling people to work should be recognised. It is part of enabling people to be part of their own support and actively involved in creating a new *normal* for themselves, their families, and their communities. It is essential for reducing dependency on humanitarian aid, a form of support that is likely to end at some point, as we saw for some Sudanese people living in Chad in Chapter 8.

In Chapter 6 we noted that Jordan's garment industry benefitted from having tariff-free access to the USA. Consequently, it provided jobs for 600,000 people, many of them migrants. The relevance here is that one way of creating jobs in countries hosting displaced persons is to grant them free trade agreements for appropriate industries. The weakness of the Jordan example is that many of the employees were migrant workers from Asia rather than displaced Iraqis, Syrians, or others. Perhaps Jordan should consider adjusting how expatriate workers are recruited by its garment industry.

One strength of the New York Declaration is that it encompasses both regular and irregular migration.

This is to be welcomed, not least because neat categorisation breaks down at various points, one of which being the fact that people migrate using irregular means because they have no good employment opportunities, meaning that improving employment opportunities becomes a means of reducing the *push* factors that cause irregular migration in the first place.

In Chapter 8 we described how Somaliland's endeavours to boost its economy with inward investment, and hence provide more jobs for its people, were hampered by its legal status. Similar considerations apply in other places where there are contested claims of sovereignty. For Somaliland, it is a declaration of independence that has not been recognised. For other locations, the terms *disputed* and *occupied* have legal significance: for occupied territories it is illegal under international law for the controlling state to move its citizens into the area or develop the area for its own benefit, while in a disputed territory there are no restrictions on the actions of the controlling state. So, for example, Morocco's development of Western Sahara is legal under international law because the area's status is labelled *disputed* by the UN. One complexity of the situation of the West Bank and the Gaza Strip is that their status at the UN is *occupied* whereas the Israeli government asserts, argues and acts as if their status is *disputed*.

We have noted economic considerations at several points, including in Chapters 1, 4 and 6. The issues here are complex. One aspect is the observation that pluralistic approaches enrich the community. Marwan Muasher's book *The Second Arab Awakening and The Battle for Pluralism* examines the effects on the Middle East of a deficiency of pluralism. Muasher is a former Foreign Minister and Deputy Prime Minister of Jordan. He sees this as the crucial challenge emerging from what was first termed the Arab Spring and which he refers to as the Arab Awakening.[101]

Many of those migrating from Africa are moving due to changed agricultural patterns. It seems likely that such changes will affect more people as the effects of climate change become more apparent in more places. The implications of this for migration are profound. This needs to be seen in a wider context of changing patterns of employment. Agriculture is one industry where greater mechanisation, and increases in the

[101] Marwan Muasher; *The Second Arab Awakening and the Battle for Pluralism* (2014, Yale University Press)

size and scale of farms, mean that fewer workers are needed even if crop yields rise. The pattern we have seen is typically that men migrate from rural to urban contexts within their own country – Mauritania being one clear example. If they cannot find work in one urban context then they might try another, larger, town or city. Should they exhaust options in their own country then they seek to emigrate. Wherever possible, they do so using legal means, turning to irregular methods as the option of last resort.

Mitigating such trends requires greater effort to be put into sustainable development in the places which people feel obliged to leave. Urbanisation and a modern version of an industrial revolution are occurring in many countries. This revolution needs to be successful, because the alternative is ever more people endeavouring to migrate. [102] It is worthy of support, and one trusts that such considerations form part of the negotiations to fulfil one of the New York Declaration's commitments.

---

[102] See, for example, Inter Press Service; *War on climate terror (II): fleeing disasters, escaping drought, migrating*; 11th August 2016; www.ipsnews.net/2016/08/war-on-climate-terror-ii-fleeing-disasters-escaping-drought-migrating/ (accessed 27th January 2017)

There is additional synergy here with another UN initiative, namely the Sustainable Development Goals which were adopted by the UN General Assembly on 25th September 2015.[103]

Returning to the history of the international systems, the UN General Assembly designated the period June 1959 to June 1960 as World Refugee Year. This was an attempt to raise greater awareness of the plight of the estimated two and half million recognised refugees at that time, and saw calls for greater efforts at solutions, including improving local integration and improving resettlement internationally. At the time, many people in Europe who had been displaced during the Second World War remained in makeshift accommodation. It is instructive that in the late 1950s, resettlement was regarded as having taken too long, which shows that burden sharing was proving problematic. Within Europe, the World Refugee Year proved successful. Almost all the camps were closed, with former residents either resettled or moved to more modern accommodation. Political will was

[103] UN; https://sustainabledevelopment.un.org/sdgs (accessed 3rd March 2017)

exerted to effectively address the needs of Europe's displaced.

The programme of World Refugee Year also addressed displaced people in the Middle East – Palestinians – as well as in Hong Kong and China, and included encouraging more countries to formally sign the 1951 Convention. One publicity mechanism was the issuing of special postage stamps by several countries. The stamps, together with the publicity about them, used visual images to show the journey from darkness, poverty and despair to a new life with bright hopes for the future. Today, many migrants are attempting to make the same journey.

Within the Middle East, programmes were less successful. The Palestinians did receive some relief packages and funding for development projects. But there was no political will to actually resolve their situation, and we will return to this later in the chapter.

It is time to focus on some positive developments which attempt to improve the capacity of systems for resettlement.

Sponsorship Schemes – Canada, UK and beyond; integration or inclusion?

In 1979, Canada established a Private Sponsorship Scheme to facilitate resettlement of those with official refugee status. It has endured because it has proven popular and successful. In July 2016, the UK announced the introduction of a similar scheme, to be known as Community Sponsorship. The first two families to be resettled using this process arrived during 2016. Australia, Brazil and Germany have schemes along similar lines, and the UNHCR, in partnership with the Global Refugee Sponsorship Initiative (GRSI), is encouraging other countries to introduce similar programmes.[104]

These schemes involve both the government and civic groups. Groups apply to the authorities to be accepted as a sponsoring body. They need to demonstrate that they have the resources, expertise and commitment necessary. The government then selects the refugees

[104] For details of Canada's scheme see; www.cic.gc.ca/english/ resources/publications/ref-sponsor/ and for the UK's scheme see www.gov.uk/government/publications/apply-for-full-community-sponsorship (both accessed 22nd February 2017); for details of GRSI see UNHCR; 16th December 2016; www.unhcr.org/uk/news/press/ 2016/12/58539e524/global-refugee-sponsorship-initiative-promotes-canadas-private-refugee.html (accessed 4th May 2017)

to be resettled, and allocates each individual or family to a group that acts as their sponsor.

These schemes increase the capacity of resettlement systems by enabling more citizens and groups to become involved. One reason they are credited with being effective is that they break down barriers – those resettling in a new country are obliged to meet, interact with and relate to a group of nationals. In turn, the sponsors are obliged to learn about the new arrivals' journey and origin.

For the UK's Community Sponsorship programme, the sponsor is responsible for the individual or family for one year, and responsible for their housing costs for two years. The sponsors undertake to meet the refugees on arrival in the country, provide a culturally sensitive orientation, find suitable accommodation, assist them with English language learning, facilitate access to medical and social services, and support them towards employment and self-sufficiency.

One often hears about helping forcibly displaced people to 'integrate' into their new setting. In many uses, the word 'integration' is used to imply that the displaced must adapt to their host community; that they make all the adjustments. This puts the onus on those that have left traumatic situations to do all of what's necessary for them to thrive. An alternative term for what needs to happen would be 'inclusion', which carries the implication that the host community should make some adaptations to be truly welcoming of the displaced. The displaced still do most of the adapting – learning new languages, legal frameworks and social norms is vital, and it is essential that they learn the language and the legal framework under which they have come to live. However, the idea of inclusion keeps the hosts aware that they, too, might adapt.

In Canada and the UK, engagement in inclusion began mainly with churches and other Christian groups offering to be sponsors of displaced persons. Subsequently, synagogues, mosques and other religious groups became engaged, in a clear example of the positive contribution being made by FBOs. As we remarked in Chapter 2, such groups play a prominent role in assisting the forcibly displaced.

We have also noted the significance of enabling the displaced to be able to worship as they wish. In many cases, this will be more complex than it appears for irregular migrants reaching the West; churches and mosques vary widely, and finding a good fit might prove problematic. This is an area where the idea of inclusion, rather than the idea of integration, can assist; the religious community that the displaced seek to join can be encouraged to make some adjustments in order to better meet the needs and aspirations of the new arrivals.

Buried within the array of systems which migrants must learn and move through is the complex question of how governments decide whose claims for refugee/asylum status are valid and to whom they should offer resettlement. Assessing those who have arrived can also be problematic, and this is one reason that Europe is working intensively to reduce irregular migration.

Europe – the good, the ugly and problematic asylum systems

Since 2014 the EU has increasingly sought the cooperation of African and Middle Eastern states to reduce irregular migration towards Europe. What is known as the Khartoum Process was launched in November 2014 to provide "A platform for political cooperation amongst the countries along the migration route between the Horn of Africa and

Europe."[105] Following this, a broader initiative was launched on 29th June 2016, when the EU's Council of Ministers adopted the Partnership Framework with Third Countries under which 16 countries of origin and transit for migrants were to be invited to cooperate with the EU's goals on curbing irregular migration. The EU was offering development aid, trade agreements, investment deals, improved visa application systems and other benefits to governments who were willing to negotiate and implement a results-orientated agreement. Unstated in the deal was the converse: namely that non-engagement or non-cooperation from any country would be reflected in the EU's policies and procedures towards that country. The budget for the programme was reported to be eight billion Euros over four years.[106] Some of this appears to be money already allocated to humanitarian and development aid, as those items have been brought under this umbrella to a certain extent.

[105] See http://www.khartoumprocess.net/ (accessed 31st May 2017)
[106] For comparison, the EU's budget for 2016 was €155 billion; assuming that €8 billion over four years is evenly spread, then this amounts to 1.3% of the EU's annual budget.

The EU presented its first two reports on the programme on 18th October 2016 and 14th December 2016. Both gave clear evidence of the scale and intensity of the diplomatic efforts being made by EU institutions and some member states to secure agreements and oversee effective action. One initiative has been to reduce smuggling from Niger, addressing some of the issues we summarised at the start of Chapter 8. Claims were made that the agreements had already reduced migration through the Sahara, which would in due course reduce the number of journeys across the Mediterranean.[107]

One regrettable feature of this approach is that it treats migrants as bargaining chips; people have become an object in a barter exchange, with disastrous results for their dignity, safety and human rights. The desire of African governments to gain maximum benefit from the situation in political, financial and a range of other areas is understandable; arguably it is in their national interest. Several were presenting their (for want of a better term) 'shopping

[107] See http://europa.eu/rapid/press-release_IP-16-3473_en.htm for the first report and https://eeas.europa.eu/sites/eeas/files/second-progress-report-1_en_act_part1_v11.pdf for the second (both accessed 24th January 2017)

lists', many of which included vehicles and other equipment to improve border patrols. One suspects that a lot of these resources would be utilised in a brutal manner. This concern could be addressed by providing an effective monitoring system for how equipment funded by the EU was used.

On the other hand, one positive consequence of the process is that it has given the EU a route for dialogue and engagement with the governments of Sudan and Eritrea in particular, which are fairly isolated in many international circles. In inter-governmental affairs, everyone is obliged to engage with the leaders of other states whatever they think of their character, ideology and policies. Some of these policies and practices are the root cause of many people seeking to migrate by irregular means, and create a large *push* factor for some of their citizens. In Chapter 8 we noted the arbitrariness of the Sudanese government's treatment of those who seek to transit through Sudan. Eritrea was observed to have improved its border controls and patrols, with the dual motivation of celebrating the 25th anniversary of its independence and being seen to be acting as a good partner of the EU.[108]

This is a concerted effort to address some of the *push* factors, notably by trade and investment programmes. It also seeks to increase the *pull* factors of destinations other than Europe. In addition, the inclusion of visa application systems for the nationals of participating countries is commendable, and should include student visas and other means of supporting the education of their citizens.

The Partnership Framework includes several Middle Eastern countries, and in the case of Jordan and Lebanon, the EU's existing engagement is being brought within this broader framework.

In the case of Iran, there is linkage to the EU's developing trading relationship with Iran as part of the Joint Comprehensive Plan of Action (JCPOA), which was negotiated in 2015 and signed in January 2016 and concerned Iran's nuclear programme. In Chapter 2 we noted that at the turn of the century, Iran was probably hosting more displaced people

---

[108] IRIN News; *Europe tries to buy its way out of the migration crisis*; 30th June 2016; www.irinnews.org/analysis/2016/06/30/europe-tries-buy-its-way-out-migration-crisis (accessed 24th January 2017)

than anywhere else in the world, with approximately half a million Iraqis mostly living in western Iran and three and a half million Afghans, many of whom were living in the east of the country. The Iraqis were Shi'a displaced from southern Iraq by Saddam Hussein's government, and most returned home following his removal in 2003. Of the Afghans, one and a half million were migrant workers in regular employment, one million were officially registered as refugees, and the remaining million had no legal status in Iran.

In November 2016 it was reported that more than one million Afghans had returned to Afghanistan. In Chapter 7 we noted that France's programme for assisting voluntary returns appealed to Afghans, and that the EU had an agreement allowing Afghans to be repatriated. In the overall picture, this made only a small contribution, since the bulk of those returning had been living in Iran or Pakistan. People were leaving Iran because the government had stepped up its efforts at removing those in its country who did not have legal status, and were leaving Pakistan because the government and the UNHCR had been offering inducements to those who might have been willing to return. The package for those leaving from Pakistan included a grant of land as a means of becoming self-sufficient, and one trusts that training was provided to ensure that people had the knowledge and skills to farm effectively. Endeavouring to provide for those returning is commendable; we saw a counter-example in Chapter 8, where Mauritanians were returning home but subsequently deciding to return to camps in a neighbouring country.[109]

One aspect of handling those that do reach Europe is the complexity of assessing asylum applications. Even for Syrians, we need to ask why can some move within their country and live safely, while others are obliged to emigrate. The answer depends upon numerous factors related to family, extended family, perceived or actual links to political parties, militias, or armed groups, as well as each person's socio-economic background. Western systems are evidence-and-rules based, yet in many situations being able to produce evidence is problematic for applicants. Western officials need to have detailed knowledge of the situation in each country from which applicants are arriving, and maintaining the information that

[109] Voice of America; *Over 1 million Afghan refugees return home*; 16th November 2016; www.voanews.com/a/over-one-million-afghan-refugees-return-home/3598412.html (accessed 27th January 2017)

underpins the evaluation of asylum applications is a complex and time-consuming activity.[110]

We must accept that some irregular migrants make their stories fit with what they think will get them accepted. For example, when it was thought that unaccompanied children would be given priority, then some families sent a child who had been briefed to claim that they were an orphan. If and when the child was accepted, then at some point an application would be made for the parents to enter under family reunification principles. Such a subterfuge needs to be explained as something that arises from the chaos and fear of a crisis situation. Another potential risk in this area is seen amongst migrants who claim to be converts to Christianity purely to support an asylum claim. We noted in Chapter 5 that regular participation in worship is the key criterion for this, and it is often the case that adherents of Christianity of the same nationality are best placed to identify who are genuine converts and who are not. The methods used for this confirmation are rooted in trusting relationships; it is not clear how applicable they are to

[110] See, for example, Dave Smith's *Refugee Stories – seven personal stories behind the headlines* (2016, Instant Apostle), e.g. the chapter Maron's Story.

the need to deal with larger numbers of people, or to address political or ethnically-rooted reasons for migrating.

In April 2017, Pope Francis drew attention to the conditions in many of the holding centres in various parts of Europe housing irregular migrants. In off-the-cuff remarks he used the term "concentration camp" for a facility in Lesbos, Greece, and we need to ask how much of an overstatement this is. Clearly, Europe's camps are not about seeking high death rates from malnutrition, slave labour, brutal mistreatment and mass murder. Yet, equally, they are not intended to be attractive, or places of hope. They show that processing asylum claims is problematic.[111]

One problem seen in some facilities is that freedom of worship is denied to some residents. A typical pattern is that communities of a particular nationality mimic the conditions of their home country, so that

[111] Zenit; *Pope's homily at mass for memory of "new martyrs" or 20th & 21st centuries*; 24th April 2017; https://zenit.org/articles/popes-homily-at-mass-for-memory-of-new-martyrs-of-20th-21st-centuries/ (accessed 3rd May 2017). See also New York Times; *Was the Pope Wrong to Compare Refugee Centres to Concentration Camps?*; 25th April 2017; www.nytimes.com/2017/04/25/opinion/pope-francis-compares-refugee-centers-to-concentration-camps.html (accessed 2nd May 2017)

restrictions that exist on freedom of religion or belief (FoRB, see Glossary) in the home country are replicated in camps. Allowing this militates against the subsequent integration of migrants into European societies. Officials of all facilities need to ensure that European norms are respected, while irregular migrants need to be made aware that failure to abide by the law – including those laws underpinning the principle of pluralism – makes them liable to being returned to their country of origin.

The challenge of supporting, welcoming and integrating irregular migrants can serve as a disincentive to irregular migration. The UK's policy and practice for Syrians, of selecting the most vulnerable people to be resettled from near to their original source, addresses these challenges. It does, however, rely on working closely with the authorities and international agencies which are providing support structures. One aspect of this is the importance of trusting their evaluation of who is most vulnerable, and most likely to benefit from resettlement.

Europe's collective response to irregular migration since 2014 illustrates all too well that attempts at equitable burden sharing are problematic.

Burden sharing – always problematic?

A further anecdote from the 1930s and 1940s illustrates why equitable burden sharing is significant by its absence today.

One individual who sought to move himself and his family away from danger was Otto Frank, father of Anne Frank, the author of *The Diary of a Young Girl*. Otto applied for a visa for himself and his family to move to the USA. Despite previous residence in the USA, his application was refused, along with many others. Having exhausted all options, he took his family into hiding, which though it is not cross-border migration, is a form of relocation. The family lived in hiding for two years before being discovered and detained. Otto was the only family member to survive. His daughter's diary has become a literary classic. It came out of trauma and tragedy, one aspect of which was the denial of Otto's request to migrate to escape a danger that he foresaw.

The arguments for rejecting European Jews in the 1930s and 1940s included fears about their taking jobs from nationals, fear of infiltration by people planning to commit serious crime, as well as concerns about the financial costs. Alas, such arguments are all too similar to those heard in much of Europe and the

USA since 2011. This was articulately pointed out in August 2016 by Nicolas Kristof, a *New York Times* columnist, whose parents arrived in the USA as refugees. He wrote:

> "The reasons for the opposition then were the same as they are for rejecting Syrians or Hondurans today: We can't afford it, we should look after Americans first, we can't accept everybody, they'll take American jobs, they're dangerous and different. In the 1930s and '40s, though, a world war was underway and Jews were widely seen as potential Communists or even Nazis. There were widespread fears that Germany would infiltrate the U.S. with spies and saboteurs under the cover that they were Jewish refugees."[112]

His point is that the arguments which were advanced about infiltration, both then and in our own times, are exploiting fears about the possible abuse (by a tiny few) of welcome and inclusion to crush the legitimate pleas of many. The observations which were made

---

[112] New York Times; *Anne Frank today is a Syrian girl*; 25th August 2016; www.nytimes.com/2016/08/25/opinion/anne-frank-today-is-a-syrian-girl.html (accessed 26th August 2016)

earlier suggest that these fears are inappropriate in our time. The threat that was seen in Tunisia in Chapter 8 was from nationals returning home, not from Libyans and others entering. The spread of extremist ideology is no longer limited by geography; it is spread online, and addressing this is probably a book in itself! Suffice it to say that tackling Islamic extremist ideology requires the active participation and leadership of relevant Muslim religious scholars and leaders at community, national and international levels.

The apparently self-evident point – that no country can admit everyone – must be addressed, though accepting that argument does not mean that we must deny entry to all. And we must also ask what is required to support those who remain close to the source of conflict.

Burden sharing amongst the international community has never worked; the load invariably falls disproportionately on countries which border conflict zones. It is no accident that many large camps are close to national borders. We have seen that this is the case for Za'atari in Jordan, Dadaab in Kenya, the camps hosting Libyans in Tunisia and those near Tindouf in Algeria.

My observation is that forced migration receives some attention at the time the crisis first gains public attention, but tends to rapidly fade out of view. For example, how many people are aware of the 90,000 people living in camps near Tindouf who we encountered in Chapter 8? Or Malian residents of M'bera camp in Mauritania? We also noted that camps of Sudanese people living in Chad were being forced to become self-sufficient as external support was reduced by the financial considerations and limitations of those who had been supporting the camps. In the midst of this, a consistent theme is that the displaced long for an opportunity to thrive. Camps that endure for several years need to become functional communities, operating like towns with the infrastructure to become established and then the ability to trade legally, buy supplies, and sell what they produce. Residents need to be able to commute to work in nearby locations. Internet access is also essential for communication and the facilitation of online, knowledge-based business, and all of this needs to become the normal practice soon after a camp emerges; waiting to be compelled by the inevitable decline of donor funding is less than helpful.

We have observed several programmes that seek to support host countries and enable transit countries to adapt so that some migrants can choose to remain and contribute. Migrants, particularly irregular migrants, are looking for opportunities; so anything that boosts job creation and fair trade is a positive development. Most initiatives for this benefit host communities directly, as well as helping migrants.

In August 2016 it was reported that 27,800 people had been arrested for illegal entry to the UK between January 2013 and April 2016.[113] This count excluded people who had been detained at the official entry points (since such people are handled by members of the UK's Border Force), and those who overstay their visas. These 27,800 people were presumed to have entered by stowing away in lorries. In global terms, this number is tiny for a forty-month period.

One could argue for improved border controls, which in this case would be greater checking of vehicles at the UK's ports. The principles of diminishing return on investment, and cost-benefit analysis, are

---

[113] BBC; *Illegal UK entries surpass 27,000 in three years*; 30th August 2016; www.bbc.co.uk/news/uk-37215764 (accessed 25th January 2017)

important to apply here. Improving security along national borders and coastlines is always possible, but the number of people who will be detected at the point of entry will diminish quickly once all the simple-to-implement steps have been taken. Further, it is important to realise that the 'smuggling industry' will rapidly adapt to any changes.

During 2016, attention was drawn to the number of migrants present in the USA with no legal status, with the number of 11 million being claimed. Such numbers are always an estimate based on extrapolation from what can be counted; almost by definition, nobody has a complete record of people residing illegally in a country. The figure of 11 million is approximately 3% of the USA's population. The equivalent estimate for Europe is approximately 1%.

One people for whom burden sharing has never worked – and arguably has not been intended to work – is the Palestinians.

Israelis and Palestinians – responding to injustices

In our historical survey in Chapter 2 we discussed the dispersal of the Palestinians within the Middle East and the migration of Jewish people to and within the region, and these people reside at the centre of the Middle Eastern context. Let us summarise what we have seen, and then look ahead. There are stories with lessons for us all, especially about how to handle injustice in migration that has occurred in the distant past but is still within living memory.

We will look at the continuing situations of some of the Jews who moved to Israel in the 1940s and 1950s, before turning our attention to the Palestinians.

Israeli Jews who originated in Arab countries are known in Israel as Mizrahim. In the decade after 1948, they endured much discrimination. One of the more extreme forms of discrimination was the deceitful removal of babies, who were given to Jewish parents of European origin. One example of this is the story of Gil Grunbaum. He was adopted at birth, with his biological parents being informed that their child had died. His biological parents were never shown their child's body or grave, or given a death certificate, and the adoption paperwork had some irregularities, notably the absence of the biological parent's consent. Mr Grunbaum discovered the truth about this late in life. His is one of numerous such stories, with estimates for the number of such cases running to 5,000.[114]

Collectively the situation is referred to as 'the Yemeni babies', although the affected parents were from several predominantly Arab countries, including Iraq and Tunisia. One story of someone who was born in Yemen is that of Yona Yosef, who took her then four-year-old half-sister for a routine medical check-up, and never saw her again. The clinic told Yona to go home, and said that her sister Saadia would be returned shortly. As a recently-arrived immigrant, Yona was unaware of what due process and protocol should have been, and assumed that the clinic's staff would be trustworthy.[115]

The point we need to make here is that the Mizrahim had been forcibly displaced, and Israel, their new home, was supposedly a place of safety. The reality

[114] Jonathan Cook, an Israeli journalist based in Nazareth, Israel; *The shocking truth of Israel's disappeared babies*; 5th August 2016; www.jonathan-cook.net/2016-08-05/the-shocking-story-of-israels-disappeared-babies/ (accessed 8th August 2016)

[115] Washington Post; *A 70-year old mystery: Yemeni Jews say young relatives were stolen in Israel*; 8th August 2016; www.washingtonpost.com/world/middle_east/a-70-year-old-mystery-yemeni-jews-say-young-relatives-were-stolen-in-israel/2016/08/05/385c8d4f-0831-48a9-aaba-a3c9ff3c275c_story.html?utm_term=.1aa568802ec7 (accessed 25th February 2017)

was that they encountered suspicion, discrimination and exploitation. Was one motivation for this behaviour that the best interests of the babies and young children would genuinely be served if they were living with better off families rather than those who arrived penniless and with several children? At least one Israeli NGO works to assist individuals and families to discover the truth about themselves and their relatives. In June 2016 Israeli Prime Minister Benjamin Netanyahu instructed one of his ministers to open all relevant files and "discover the truth," noting that, "The issue of the Yemenite children is an open wound that continues to bleed in many families who do not know what happened to the babies that disappeared". One commends this search for truth.

The issue here is the terms on which migrants are made welcome. In this case, they were welcomed into the country, but this brutal form of social engineering was applied to the next generation. The question that arises from this is whether this is an example of an attempt to integrate people which leads to abusive methods. An approach rooted in inclusion is more likely to recognise and reject abusive methods such as these. The enriched whole needs to be more than the sum of its components; pluralism, when it is enhanced, works for the benefit of all.

What is also of note here is that nowhere in the reporting about these events is there any reference to people asking for compensation. The process of investigation is about discovering truth – coming to terms with what has happened, and facilitating individuals, communities and society as a whole to move forward in a healthy way.

Switching our focus from Jews to Palestinians, we have to conclude that if the international refugee system was established to support Palestinians, then it has clearly failed to resolve their situation, or rather, the situation for some of them. The UNRWA continues to be required; a fact demonstrated by the renewal of its mandate every three years.

One aspect of the situation in which Palestinians find themselves is the question of the right of return. The international norm is that the displaced should be able to return to where they were prior to being displaced, but in this situation, this principle is highly problematic. The debate here centres on when in history one takes as the baseline for who should be where. The Palestinian claims are rooted in the events of the 1940s, while the Jewish claims are based on having been displaced in the more distant past. Why use the Second World War as the defining point? One factor in the complexity of this on-going situation is that the international norms were established following this conflict and cannot be applied retroactively, as we noted in Chapter 2 concerning the Armenian Genocide. The implication is that the Jewish claims cannot be recognized within international norms despite the wide acceptance of their historic foundation. Reconciling the competing claims continues to be problematic to all parties.

Most pragmatic assessments accept that those who were displaced from what is now the internationally recognised state of Israel will not be able to return, and nor will their descendants. Yet formalising their resettlement and status in other countries is not without its problems – and, further, some Palestinians desire, if not a return, then due compensation.

This situation is one where correcting past injustices and compensating for forced displacement of a previous generation is, in practice, very difficult. Amidst the complexities of the Israel-Palestine question, this is only one factor.

An alternative approach, it seems, would be to find healthy ways to move on. This is easily said by an outsider, but not easily done by those involved.

Elsewhere, correcting past injustices is also a major challenge. We have touched on such issues in Cyprus, Western Sahara, Sudan and Somaliland. The Armenians appear generally resettled in numerous locations, and we noted in Chapter 2 that Turkey and Armenia have discussed normalising relations. Turkey has acknowledged that violence occurred, and is asking all parties to accept the past and move forward in a healthy manner; but healing historic wounds affecting whole societies is a major undertaking. It is an area where Christianity and Christian communities have a contribution to make, and Russ Parker's book *Healing Wounded History* offers some insights.[116] The key criterion is whether those involved are willing to participate in processes of reconciliation and healing.

This moves us to our final chapter, which provides a personal view of how God is at work in the Middle East. One area is the role of Christians – alongside other people of goodwill – who are seeking to bring

[116] Russ Parker; *Healing Wounded History* (republished 2012, SPCK Publishing)

healing, forgiveness and reconciliation, and to be builders of peace and community. To participate in this way, they need to remain in the region.

Chapter 10
How is God at Work in the Middle East?

This chapter is written from a Christian perspective. Religious terminology is defined for the benefit of readers who are adherents of other faiths or none, and then it consciously looks for good amidst displacement. Good news is to be celebrated and enjoyed, but not to the exclusion of acknowledging where pain, loss and trauma are part of the story. True recovery may well be aided by dwelling on something good, or finding a benefit somewhere. Yet true recovery usually also involves much time, emotional energy and wise support from those who are able to listen with empathy. This may not ever be an easy or cost-free process.

This chapter begins with a brief overview of the Old Testament, framing the story there as one that is about migration. There then follows a discussion of the conundrum of how a loving God can allow pain and suffering to exist in his creation. These considerations lead into a survey of what God is doing in the Middle East in this period of history, the superficial view of which might be that his Church is hard pressed, and his people are being forced out. Beneath the surface of popular news, however, a different picture emerges, one of a Church which is being transformed by its participation in supporting the forcibly displaced and its welcome of those who convert to Christianity. The chapter concludes with a brief reflection on the words 'ambassador' and 'home'.

The Biblical text

Taking a big-picture view of the Old Testament, its narrative is framed by two occasions of mass migration by God's chosen people, the Israelites. The first is the exodus from Egypt and subsequent arrival in the land that was promised to their patriarchs, Abraham, Isaac and Jacob. The second is the exile to Babylon. Much of the historical narrative of the Old Testament is driven by the question of why God would allow his people to be displaced.

Abraham, a significant figure in Judaism, Christianity and Islam, was born in Ur of the Chaldeans, near Basra in modern day Iraq. He was a wandering migrant, who moved first to Haran, located in modern-day Syria, and subsequently moved again to what was then called Canaan, which is modern-day Israel and the West Bank. Abraham also spent time in Egypt, where his descendants went during a famine. They settled there and became established. This created the context for the exodus under the leadership of Moses.

In Chapter 5 we noted that some adherents of Judaism seek to worship at the tomb of Joseph. Joseph's life is summarised in Genesis chapters 37 to 50, and his story includes several elements which are relevant to migration. He was people-trafficked into Egypt as a slave, probably while in his teens. He excelled in his work, becoming a trusted employee – a migrant worker – before becoming the victim of a false accusation and being thrown into prison. Whatever 'rights' he had were ignored, but he excelled again, becoming responsible for a section of the prison. In due course, he came to the attention of the ruler, Pharaoh, and was appointed to a senior national leadership role. At this point, he is regarded as a highly valued migrant worker, providing a service that no national can perform. Some years later he meets his brothers, who had initiated this sequence of events by selling him to traffickers. Joseph presents this twenty-plus-year sequence as God's doing not theirs (e.g. Genesis 50:20); what was intended for harm has become a means of providing for the family during a severe famine. Joseph acts as a saviour; he does not take revenge. It is no surprise that some adherents of Judaism treat Joseph's tomb as a place of pilgrimage, and want to worship there.

The exile to Babylon is described in the historical and prophetic books of the Old Testament. The book of the prophet Jeremiah is one such book. The general theme that emerges is that the Israelites lost sight of the purpose of being God's people while living in their own land, and needed to rediscover it while in exile. An entry on the Institute of Middle East Studies (IMES) blog in June 2016 picks up on the themes of the book of Jeremiah:

> "In times of war, destruction, expulsion, defeat, and captivity due to the Babylonian invasion, the biblical story informs us that the prophet Jeremiah was instructed to execute two commands. Firstly, God had asked him to invite the Israelites not to fight back, lest they fail and die, but to seek the peace of the city to which they had been carried (Jeremiah 29:1-7). In other words, they are to settle down in Babylon, the land of the enemy, to build houses and to prosper; they are explicitly requested to restructure their religious and social life due to the pressing change they had faced. Secondly, God asked the prophet to undertake an

escrow[117] to buy a piece of land in the war zone of enemy territory while he was imprisoned (Jeremiah 32:1-25). At one point, the Israelites had thought that Jerusalem was the invincible city, especially since the temple implied the presence of God, the mighty warrior, who would act on behalf of His people. But, "as the wind scatters the cherry blossoms," their convictions were scattered with the third wave of Babylonian deportation. This is when the temple and their homes were flattened to the ground and they were driven out of the land. Regardless of the reasons behind their captivity, they were asked both to prosper and to hold on to the promise of restoration."[118]

Moving to the New Testament, known to Muslims as the Injil, it becomes clear that Christians have been part of the general pattern of migration since the earliest days of the founding of the religion. The New Testament records the murder of Stephen (Acts 7:54-

[117] An escrow is a transaction between two parties with the finance provided by a third party.
[118] Walid Zailaa on IMES blog; *Hope: an ecclesiological identity or a prophetic act?*; 30th June 2016; https://imeslebanon.wordpress.com/2016/06/30/hope-an-ecclesiological-identity-or-a-prophetic-act/#more-3983 (accessed 16th November 2016)

60) and the oppression of the church in Jerusalem that followed (Acts 8:1-3). Many responded by leaving the city, and the text records that they spoke of their beliefs about Jesus wherever they went. There are numerous other examples in sacred texts and history books of Christians choosing to migrate to escape actual or threatened persecution. The Huguenots left France in the seventeenth century. The Pilgrim Fathers who went from the UK and the Netherlands to what became the USA were motivated by their desire to find freedom of religion. Some English Catholics established the state of Maryland to provide an escape from persecution at the hands of Protestants. Likewise, Anabaptists left parts of Europe and were instrumental in establishing Pennsylvania. Arguably, the long-standing interest of the USA in issues of religious freedom originates from this aspect of the country's creation.

Kenotic Creation – the challenge of suffering

One challenge to Christians, and indeed adherents of all faiths, is posed by the overt suffering seen throughout the world, including both natural disasters as well as the evil perpetrated by some humans on others. As we have seen, both phenomena prompt migration. From 2003 to 2015 I worked in the field of religious freedom, addressing religiously motivated persecution. In the numerous cases of people across the Middle East who choose to become Christians, this form of injustice is a common experience. In religious terms, they respond to God and then suffer injustice as a direct consequence. How can a God who is described as loving and sovereign allow this? This is covered by a branch of theology and philosophy called 'theodicy'. One approach is to say that it is a consequence of the freewill that God granted to human beings, but how can one balance the two: the sovereignty of the creator and the genuine freewill of humanity?

Before answering that, we need to affirm that freewill is desirable; that it is a good gift. Free will is essential for love, which is a free gift, offered by the lover to the loved. For humans to be able to love God in a meaningful way, they must have freewill. One can also argue that freewill is essential for art and science. It enables human beings to act outside of deterministic constraints to create new and beautiful things; and to observe and measure phenomena, and form and test hypotheses; art and science respectively.

Returning to the issue of God's sovereignty, the solution that appeals to me is 'kenotic creation'.[119] Kenotic is a Greek word, meaning 'emptying'. One occurrence in the New Testament is Philippians 2:7, where the term is used to describe how Jesus voluntarily gave up some attributes of divinity during his lifetime on earth. This voluntary surrender of some aspects of divinity was for a defined period of time and a specific purpose.

Kenotic creation expresses the view that God acted in a similar manner when he created the universe, the earth and humanity. He gave up some aspects of sovereignty in order that human beings would have genuine freewill. God's purpose is that he wants people to be able to respond to his love and choose a loving relationship with him. True freewill means that such a response cannot be forced, controlled or assumed. Some will choose to reject love. Consequently, there is scope for humanity to use their innate freedom to act in ways that are evil.

How does freewill operate in the physical sphere? If mind activity requires brain activity, then how do our

---

[119] See, for example, Clark Pinnock's *Most Moved Mover* (2001, Paternoster) for a fuller treatment of this theology.

brains, part of the natural world, function in a way that allows us to be creative and unpredictable? We need a brief digression here into some aspects of physics. In scientific terms, God created a universe where quantum mechanics and chaos theory both apply. Quantum mechanics operates at very micro levels. In normal living, nature is essentially predictable, operating according to physical laws and principles which are established in creation and discovered by humanity. It is this predictability that allows life to function as we know it. Does this mean that creation is predictable, at least for all practical purposes? This is where chaos theory helps us, since it states that a miniscule change in one location, time or event can lead to a big change somewhere else. One practical illustration of this is the fact that weather forecasting is a complex discipline because small changes in the situation in one location and time can lead to large differences in later events.

The physical universe created by God operates in a non-deterministic manner, and herein lies the root of natural disasters, which we could term 'natural evil'. A further level of enquiry is useful here. The earth's surface is not static; the process of creation is constantly continuing. The movement of tectonic plates explains earthquakes; it also explains the formation of mountains. Volcanoes contribute to some mountain formation and also to the spreading of rich nutrients over large areas. Storms, rivers, ice, wind and other weather events shape the natural environment, and without them, the earth may well be just a large swamp. Creating the earth we inhabit involved large-scale, complex interactions of dynamic forces. We lament the effects, and support the victims, of natural disasters; we also praise the creator for the beauty of the earth. Freewill requires an element of non-determinism, and so too does the beauty of the earth.

In theological language, this leads us into the issue of God's providence: how often does God intervene in his creation? Here we need to avoid the extremes of total determinism – which is incompatible with the created order – or deism, whereby God is completely passive and just watches what he initiated. God will respect the integrity of the structures he built into the universe, yet will intervene when and where he chooses. He appears to me to intervene in small ways, minor miracles some would say, many of them unobservable as he protects some from danger. Major interventions are rarer.

Let us conclude our brief synopsis of the biblical text and short description issues around theodicy and providence with a look at one Bible passage that helps us transition to a search for what God is doing amidst current events. One of my favourite Bible stories is in Daniel chapter 3, which describes Shadrach, Meshach and Abednego, three Jewish men displaced to Babylon, being thrown into a furnace. They were loyal to the ruler politically, but had refused to worship his image because doing so would violate a key tenet of their religious beliefs. I find their words to king Nebuchadnezzar instructive:

> "King Nebuchadnezzar, we do not need to defend ourselves before you in this matter. If we are thrown into the blazing furnace, the God we serve is able to deliver us from it, and he will deliver us from Your Majesty's hand. But even if he does not, we want you to know, Your Majesty, that we will not serve your gods or worship the image of gold you have set up."[120]

This combines an explicit acknowledgement that God is able to protect them with the realisation that he might choose not to do so. God is the almighty;

[120] Daniel 3:16b-18

whether or not he chooses to intervene in any particular situation is not our decision. The three men in this story illustrate an expectation that God's people are to remain faithful to him whatever their circumstances. We must be content with the answer that God gave to Job, as described in the Old Testament book of the same name: God has a big universe to run (Job chapters 38 to 41). Therefore, we must humbly bow to God's wisdom, as his providence has concerns way beyond the human.

So what is God doing in the Middle East today? He seems to be watching attentively as some of his people are moved from one location to another. He seems to be changing the structure of his Church. He is undoubtedly at work in numerous small, largely unperceived, ways to protect some from harm and enable others to be in the right place at the right time.

One Syrian who was speaking at a small gathering in 2012 wondered whether the removal of Christians from the region was justified because they had lost their effect on society as a whole. This is not a common thought amongst Christians from the Middle East, and even less so amongst those in the region – the speaker had emigrated some years previously.

For some Christian communities who have been displaced en masse, the life and witness of the Church has been re-established in a new location. In Chapter 6 we noted that the Chaldean Church in Iraq moved its seminary from Baghdad to Arbil, where the Ankawa suburb came to be known locally as 'the Christian suburb'. In August 2016 there was a service of celebration when three young men from Qaraqosh, near Mosul, were ordained to the priesthood in a camp near Arbil.[121]

During 2016, Sarah (not her real name), an Iraqi Christian who grew up in Mosul, explained how she fled to the Kurdish region in response to Daesh's conquest of Mosul and the surrounding area in 2014. She remarked that, apart from any physical damage, the community harmony in her area of Mosul had been destroyed; different ethnic and religious communities would no longer trust one another. Sarah continued:

> "But as a Christian, I am aware that Jesus spoke about forgiveness and reconciliation. This is just

[121] Asia News; *Erbil celebrates three new priests, witnesses of Christ amongst refugees*; 12th August 2016; www.asianews.it/news-en/Erbil-celebrates-three-new-priests,-witnesses-of-Christ-among-refugees-38293.html (accessed 31st January 2017)

what my community in Mosul needs. Where will the community find such attributes? Surely, it can only come from the Church and Christian people. So, as a human being I struggle with the thought of returning but as a Christian I know that I should. So, when it is safe for me to return I will do so in order to speak about, and demonstrate in how I live, forgiveness and reconciliation."

Sarah is seeking to be a trendsetter in responding to the situation. In Chapter 1 we noted that some Lebanese church leaders were calling for Christians to be trendsetters in responding to displaced Syrians in Lebanon.

These stories relate to those who are recognised by their state as Christians. Another effect of current events is that people are choosing to become followers of Jesus; that is, to become Christians. In Chapter 5 we noted the rise of small house-based fellowships or churches in parts of Iran.

Converts whilst journeying

Some years ago an Iranian couple wished to visit a family member who was living and working in the UK. I will call the couple Timothy and Mary. They applied for a visa to the UK. The application took some time to process, though the reasons for this were not clear to them. Timothy became frustrated and decided to take matters into his own hands. He acquired false passports for a European country and bought flight tickets for his wife and himself to Cyprus, which at the time was on the verge of becoming a member of the EU. They duly arrived in Cyprus, but the documents were not good forgeries and the subterfuge was identified by immigration officials.

Timothy and Mary were detained at the airport. They were convicted and sentenced to time in prison. Christians in Cyprus working to support prisoners became aware of them and provided some support. Mary received a short sentence, on the grounds that she had not been proactive in acquiring the documents. When she was released she began meeting regularly with Christians. She decided to become a Christian, adopting the religion of her friends for herself. Several months later, Timothy was released. He and Mary were allowed to stay in Cyprus for a short period. Effectively, the authorities decided against deporting them, almost certainly because of the significant costs involved, since there were no direct flights from Cyprus to Iran. (Appendix 4 examines deportation.)

Mary introduced Timothy to her new friends, explaining how they had cared for her during his time in prison. Timothy was impressed, and began exploring the Christian faith for himself. He made the same decision as his wife. They were baptised together in a discreet service in a church in Cyprus, with another Iranian acting as translator for Timothy, who had limited English, and the priest, who spoke no Farsi.

A few days later they returned to Iran of their own accord. Their attempts to short-circuit the visa application to the UK had led to several months in prison, to meeting people who became friends, and to their choosing to become adherents of a different religion.

What happened next? Their Christian friends were obliged to self-censor their communication for the sake of Timothy and Mary. Why? Because contact with Westerners, and with Iranians in the West with whom they had no natural family or business connection, would attract suspicion and attention from the Iranian authorities.

Another story of someone who became a Christian while migrating is Muhamed. He left Somalia for the usual reason of limited opportunities. He made his way by land to Sudan, and then to Libya. The journey took some considerable time. The first life-changing event Muhamed experienced was that he met and married a Somali woman. She became pregnant as they moved into and through Libya. They were amongst the unlucky ones who were detained by an armed group and later by officials. During this time, Muhamed's wife experienced difficulties with her pregnancy, and Muhamed pleaded with one of the guards for medical care for his wife. One guard replied, "The prophet was not black." The couple lost the child. The overt racism in the guard's reply appalled the couple and, in my understanding of Islam, will appal many Muslims.

The couple were released some time later, and joined the crowds seeking to earn enough money to pay for the boat trip to Europe. Muhamed's wife became pregnant again, and the pregnancy was advanced when they were able to acquire a place on a boat. The boat got into difficulties but was fortunate to be spotted in time by a Maltese naval vessel. The couple, and those with whom they were travelling, were rescued. The Maltese authorities took Muhamed to a detention centre, following normal practice. His wife was taken to a hospital, where she was well cared for and gave birth to a healthy child.

At that time, Malta had an arrangement with the USA to resettle Somalis. The process required three interviews and two medicals; the thoroughness of this due diligence invariably took at least a year. This couple became two of the beneficiaries of that programme. Their journey from Somalia to the USA took several years, and included much uncertainty and a number of traumatic incidents.

The guard's comment to them in Libya increased the couple's growing sense of disillusionment with Islam. They continued to believe in and pray to God as they started exploring alternative religious beliefs. In Libya they had met some expatriate Christians who they asked to explain Christianity to them. In Malta they sought and found Christians who encouraged them in their journey from Islam to Christianity.

The displaced exploring Christianity

In Chapter 6 we looked at the displacement caused by the Syrian crisis. Amidst the violence, trauma, destruction and displacement, many Syrian churches have been involved in meeting the needs of the desperate. One example was reported in August 2016 during an intense period of violence in parts of Aleppo. An article published by Lapido Media described the violence and use of siege tactics, amidst which churches of all denominations were meeting the needs of some of those displaced from other districts of Aleppo. One church was providing cooked meals to several thousand people. The churches were receiving financial support from abroad to support their activities.[122]

Since 2011, many displaced people have started exploring the Christian faith. One pattern is that small discussion groups form, where the Bible is read, discussed and evaluated. More than half of such discussion groups stop meeting; others, though, continue. Those who choose to adopt Christianity are then faced with decisions about the social effects of their religious conversion. Typical responses fall into three broad categories.

Some choose to integrate as fully as they can into Christian communities. They attend recognised churches, seek formal membership in the church, and

[122] Lapido Media; *Aleppo Horror: be careful whose side you are on*; 24th August 2016; www.lapidomedia.com/western-media-aleppo-horror (accessed 2nd February 2017); section entitled *Hope*

become as actively involved as their other commitments allow. They adopt Christian social norms and dress codes, although this is a slow process for many. This approach is not available to everyone. One obvious requirement for this is that there is a local Christian community whose leaders are willing to accept the presence and participation of those who have converted to Christianity.

Other converts to Christianity endeavour to find a balance between Muslim and Christian societies. They will not integrate into Christian communities, but remain in the Muslim communities that they were raised in whilst distancing themselves from overt Islamic religious practices, such as attending a mosque, reading the Qur'an, and participating in Muslim prayers. The dynamics of having been forcibly displaced assists with this, since some of the social norms of 'home' have been discarded or modified in the changed circumstances.

The final group are harder to define and, within some Christian circles outside the Middle East, are the most controversial. They remain overtly within Muslim communities, rejecting outward signs of Christian communities including the use of the term *Christian*. They will use the name Isa rather than Jesus for the founder of Christianity. Their dress code does not change. They meet for worship in homes or social centres, but avoid any appearance of creating what would be recognised by others as a church building. Their motivation is to demonstrate to their neighbours what following Isa (to use their terminology) looks like.

Such works of God are often complex and surprising. Simplistic descriptions and neat categorisations are rarely applicable. In his book *More Drops – Mystery, Mercy, Messiology*, George Verwer appeals to his fellow Christians – especially those who are active in non-Christian communities – to be more accepting of how God appears to be at work.[123]

At the end of the Syria section of Chapter 6, we quoted the prophet Habakkuk berating God about the tumult that he saw unfolding before him. God replied:

> "Look at the nations and watch – and be utterly amazed. For I am going to do something in your

---

[123] George Verwer; *More Drops – Mystery, Mercy, Messiology* (2015, CWR)

days that you would not believe, even if you were told."[124]

The changing nature of the Church in parts of the Middle East amazes many of those who are closely involved.

Final words – ambassadors, home; discomfort, anger, tears and foolishness

This chapter ends as it began, with a discussion of two further aspects of Christian thought.

The New Testament describes Christians as 'ambassadors' for Christ.[125] I fear that the word ambassador is misunderstood by many Western Christians. We are used to ambassadors of countries being welcomed, and treated with honour and dignity. They are migrants doing a job, and enjoy some significant privileges in return for fulfilling their duties. This was not the case in the Roman Empire of the first century. An ambassador for a community was sent to the emperor with a message. He (and they were all male then) would need to wait, possibly for months or even years, in Rome for an appointment. If

[124] Habakkuk 1:5
[125] Ephesians 6:20 and 2 Corinthians 5:20

his message caused any offence then the messenger could be executed on the spot. Being an ambassador was costly and risky. This is the practice of the times which underlies the biblical imagery. For some Christians in the Middle East today, being a true ambassador of Christ is costly and risky.

We also need to ask: what is our understanding of 'home'? The New Testament speaks of this world as not being our true home; saying that rather, our true home is with Jesus in the age to come. We are passing through, on a journey, often thought of as a pilgrimage. We balance our citizenship in this world with our citizenship in heaven.[126] It is the latter that is secure for eternity; the former is transient.

Both of these New Testament concepts affect our understanding of the importance of enabling people to stay without being displaced.

Some respond to the risks by choosing to stay, while others seek to relocate. As an outsider, one respects the decisions made by individuals and families, but one also senses the effects of individual decisions on the sense of community amongst Christians, and

[126] Philippians 3:20

indeed other communities. Removing people from such risk is not necessarily appropriate. The Church throughout the Middle East is not strengthened by the extraction of Christians; it is built up by enabling people to stay. Where relocating is the only viable option for individuals or families, then the request of church leaders in the Middle East is that people should stay within the region. Enabling people to become strong disciples is a long-term endeavour. For most of us, this requires persisting in our religious practices when life is not easy, and it is no different for migrants.

We noted in Chapter 5 the real and present dangers to the spiritual health and religious practice of converts to Christianity if they leave the lands of their birth. For such people, balancing the risks to their physical, mental, emotional and spiritual health is rarely easy, especially if they face serious injustice because of their conversion.

We will end our journey through migration from, to and within the Middle East with a prayer, after which we will summarise our observations and the recurring themes in the stories of the people we have met during our journey.

This set prayer is from the Franciscan order founded by St Francis of Assisi. It appears in several different forms on a number of websites.[127] It is intended for use as a closing blessing or benediction at the end of a service, the point of transition from worship to living out the ethical implications of one's faith in daily life in a world which combines beauty and mess, joy and pain, and justice and injustice.

> "May God bless us with *discomfort* at easy answers, half-truths and superficial relationships, so that we may live deep within our hearts.

> "May God bless us with *anger* at injustice, oppression and exploitation of people so that we may work for justice, freedom and peace.

> "May God bless us with *tears* to shed for those who suffer from pain, rejection, hunger and war, so that we may reach out our hands to comfort them and turn their pain into joy.

[127] The version used here is from A Heart For Justice; 7th October 2010; http://aheartforjustice.com/2010/10/07/a-franciscan-blessing-may-god-bless-you-with-discomfort-anger-tears-and-foolishness/ (accessed 30th May 2017), second edition on the webpage.

"And may God bless us with enough **_foolishness_** to believe that we can make a difference in this world, so that we can do what others claim cannot be done to bring justice and kindness to all our children and the poor."

Amen.

Conclusion

Mankind has always been on the move, although the means and mechanisms have changed over time. The barriers of deserts, oceans and mountains continue to be significant. Modern airliners and cruise ships may whisk some of us across them in serene comfort; others are obliged to undertake hazardous journeys by foot, truck and flimsy boats. People move for adventure, for leisure, for study, for trade, in search of work, or for a job that has been arranged in advance. Others are obliged to relocate to escape persecution for religious, ethnic, tribal, political or other reasons. Some move in response to natural disasters or changing agricultural patterns, whilst others are forcibly displaced by man-made conflict.

The Middle East has been a crossroads for trade and migration for millennia. It remains so, with many residents on the move as part of the general trend of urbanisation alongside those who are seeking better education or employment opportunities. Much of this movement is within a country and some of the remainder is within the region, notably to the Gulf States. Many migrate to the Middle East, with significant numbers working in almost all the countries of the Middle East. Saudi Arabia and other GCC countries are assessing the effects of the presence of many migrant workers, with a view to meeting the changing aspirations and needs of their indigenous populations.

In addition, the region is a source and host for many forcibly displaced people. The most high-profile examples concern Syrians (since 2011) and Iraqis (from 1990 onwards, with significant developments in 2003, 2006 and 2014). In both countries, some parts are more affected than others, causing many to become forcibly displaced persons and others to become migrant workers. Many long to be able to return safely to rebuild and resume their lives; anything they do where they are is seen as a temporary stopgap. Others have moved further afield in an attempt to establish a new *normal* life. This is a long journey – in all senses of the phrase – and many have succeeded only in reaching interim points along the way. It is also the case that some of those displaced from elsewhere are moving into and through the Middle East and North Africa. Egypt, for example, hosts numerous Sudanese, as well as people of other African nationalities who are moving through, or attempting to do so.

Forcible displacement is not a new phenomenon in the Middle East. The Armenians are, mostly, well settled and well established in numerous locations across and near to the Middle East, as well as further afield. The Jews who were displaced from many Arab countries had access to Israel, whose government assumed full responsibility for their welfare. The Palestinians are, collectively, more varied in their status – some have integrated and inter-married in several countries, whereas others remain living in settings officially called camps – albeit ones typically made of concrete – decades after they were displaced. Others have migrated outside the region.

Migration always carries a degree of risk: it works out very well for some, while others struggle for years. Knowing who to trust, who is reliable, and who is seeking the mutual benefit of hosts and migrants is difficult; there are all too many unscrupulous people who are only too willing to exploit the vulnerable for their own short-term, selfish benefit and profit. We have observed historical examples of people engaging in social engineering, forcing their views on newly arrived migrants who are ignorant of their rights in the society they are entering. For some, places that were supposed to provide safety, sanctuary and a new life proved to be less than was claimed.

Many people who are forcibly displaced replace the certainty of trauma with a turmoil of uncertainty. Creating a settled, secure, new *normal* life typically takes years, even decades. Many people are offered some support, which, while required in the initial phase, is not necessarily what they most want. Instead they want opportunities to care and provide for themselves, their families and communities. Perhaps the most underused resource available to the forcibly displaced is they themselves. They may well arrive with little more than the clothes they are wearing, but they bring with them their skills, competences and experience of life. They have much to offer and contribute; the majority crave the opportunity to do so.

One factor that helps many to come to terms with what has happened, and the new situation that they find themselves in, is the opportunity and space for worship. All too often this proves problematic. An experience which is far too common is for the social dynamics within a camp to deny some people the right to worship, and the authorities in some host countries are not always alert to this. Wider recognition of the need would be a positive development.

There is always opportunity in disruption. The people-smuggling industry understands this, and adapts rapidly to changed circumstances. Some Christians, together with other people of goodwill, also respond quickly, bringing humanitarian aid, disaster relief and listening ears to those who need help and long to tell their story.

The international systems for handling forcibly displaced people date from the late 1940s and early 1950s. Some aspects of the systems have worked well, but it is notable that the expectation of burden sharing has never been effectively implemented to the satisfaction of those countries hosting large numbers. This issue is becoming increasingly widely recognised, and there have been some fine words spoken about addressing it. The spread of Personal Sponsorship Schemes has the potential to increase the capacity of resettlement programmes globally, yet the scale of forced displacement means that all too many remain displaced for years, running into decades, before they are able to establish a new *normal* life somewhere.

The establishment of the international mechanisms overtly put Jewish and Palestinian displacement in the Middle East as a separate category from all other ethnic groups. Further, the mechanisms for these groups were there to support them in their displacement, not to enable them to achieve a new status. The state of Israel took on responsibility for Jewish people, and it has given them a new citizenship and a place to belong. The Palestinians, collectively, have no such well-resourced champion, although many Middle Eastern countries have contributed to enabling some Palestinians to achieve a sense of normality.

What is much clearer is the desire to reduce the numbers of people who are looking to migrate by irregular means. Some measures are geared towards making the journey harder, in an attempt to reduce the numbers of those willing to try. Some of these measures are brutal, almost violent. One consequence of these measures is to increase the dangers faced in irregular migration, and we must assume that these measures have led to increased death rates. They are also unlikely to have had much effect in the long-term: the desperate, aided by ever more resourceful people smugglers, will always find other routes. Some migrants, regular as well as irregular, whose situations are or become intolerable, will resort to desperate measures.

Much more constructive are efforts that are made to support source, host and transit countries. The approach undertaken by the EU, for example endeavours to combine trade and investment deals with the promise of better visa systems for regular migration.

The framework of *push* and *pull* factors is a long-standing method of describing migration. One hopes that Western countries never lose the characteristics which make them attractive destinations; they have innate *pull* factors which are objectively desirable, including the clear and stable rule of law and societies which value pluralism, embracing and thriving upon the contributions made by a vibrant diversity of peoples. Around the globe, the informed, able and well-resourced know where dependable legal frameworks and cultural norms lie. It also remains the case that within post-colonial dynamics there is frequently a strong attraction to go to the former colonial power; it is an attractive patron and the land of opportunity to many. For some there is a justice element: you came to us when it suited you, so we should be allowed to come to you when we wish.

What is to be welcomed are efforts to address the *push* factors in the places which people are seeking to leave. Give people a sense of hope, with realistic opportunities where they are, and they will gladly stay part of that community. Better education and greater job opportunities are crucial, as is the spread of clear, consistent governance. Providing these as urbanisation and changing patterns of agriculture affect more people in more locations will be an ongoing challenge. Violence in the Middle East might be one source of displacement, though the potential impacts of climate change on migration patterns are likely to be significantly larger. Most of those crossing the Mediterranean are Africans, driven by violence, poor governance or inadequate employment opportunities.

Considering the violence which is prevalent in parts of the Middle East reminds us that many people are being forcibly displaced. Many such people are able to stay within their own country, since conflict is affecting part, but not all, of their nation; but the economic effects of forcible displacement are still profound, although we must remember that there are positive developments in some places within countries experiencing violent conflict; it is rare that conflicts engulf the whole of a country.

A religious element to displacement has been all too evident in a number of places. A slogan which was seen early in the Syrian crisis translates as, "The Christians to Beirut and the Alawites to the grave," encapsulating the dynamic that the religious groups who experienced the most brutality can be described as being those who were 'Muslims of the wrong type'. In places such as Mosul in Iraq, Christians, Yezidis and others were subjected to either forced displacement or oppression, sometimes severe. Yet their Shi'ite Muslim neighbours were all too often murdered on the spot by members of Daesh as well; the self-proclaimed 'Islamic State' was, it was clear, for certain Muslims only.

The nature of the Church (a word used here as a collective term meaning 'the followers of Jesus Christ') has changed over time. The earliest Church was mostly from a Jewish background. Gentiles began to join in significant numbers within a few years. Church history records that the Church came predominantly from a Gentile background within a few centuries, with the element of the Church who had a Jewish background having largely died out.

The Church of today in the Middle East is undergoing a profound change. The demographics of Christian communities have been changing for decades, indicated most notably by statistics from the West Bank, where Christians have gone from being 12% of the population in 1967 to just over 1% in 2016. Whenever academic studies of the religious demographics of a specific location are undertaken, they typically reveal that the percentage of Christians is lower than that generally cited. This documents the trend of decades that some Christians emigrate from the region and also that, in most places, Christian families typically have fewer children than members of other religious groups do. For most Christian communities, the fact of continuing systemic discrimination and marginalisation has been a greater *push* factor causing migration than sporadic violent attacks have been. All too often it is the brightest, and those with the most resources, who leave; the brain drain has affected Middle Eastern societies of which Christian communities are an historic component. Church leaders regularly, persistently and sensitively ask that people stay and remain part of the Christian community. Equally, they recognise the reasons why some choose to leave; the *push* and *pull* factors are widely recognised. Nevertheless, leaving should be the option of last resort for all.

Christian leaders throughout the Middle East consistently ask that fellow Christians in other parts of the world focus on enabling Christians to stay in the region in order to continue their life and witness where they were born, contributing to peace building, to good governance, and to the recognition that diverse communities and countries are more likely to be prosperous and peaceful than segregated ones.

Yet to say, as some do, that the Middle East is being denuded of Christians is to overlook another trend: amidst the events of today people are choosing to become adherents of Christianity. This has also been the case for decades; the difference now is that greater numbers are actively converting from other faiths. Of these, some embrace the term *Christian* and participate in worship in church buildings. Others are more discreet, and in several locations the whole outward nature of the church has changed, moving from being officially identified as Christian, and meeting in legally recognised church buildings, to being made up of people from non-Christian backgrounds meeting in homes.

Of those who convert to Christianity, many experience some form of rejection and persecution by family, friends, society and state. Most are able to adapt and remain where they are. A number do move, but not too far. For a few, and it is only a few, the only viable option for survival is to leave the region. Determining who genuinely has no other viable option is rarely easy. The considered opinion of Christian leaders in the Middle East is an essential element in determining who are genuine converts whose situation necessitates that they leave. Iran is an exception to this pattern: the number of converts who are obliged to leave is higher.

Relocating outside the Middle East for religious reasons is rarely easy to do, and becoming well established in a different country in another part of the world is a process that frequently takes several years. A significant amount of support is required, crucially listening, engaging with people's experience, and providing informed counsel. The decision to leave the region – or to attempt to leave – should never be made lightly; it is the option of last resort because of the significant cost in personal, social, legal and financial terms that is involved.

Furthermore, wherever it is required, an attempt should be made to acquire study or work visas, due to the serious risk of death, loss of liberty or the loss of custody of children. In some cases the only realistic option for migration is to use refugee or asylum systems, accepting the timescales and inherent risks of using such systems for religiously motivated cases. These systems should be treated as the option of last resort within the option of last resort.

What must be kept in mind is that for converts to Christianity who leave their region because of persecution, descriptive studies suggest that up to 90% of them stop practising their Christian faith within ten years of arriving in a Western country. Iranians are thought to be an exception to this; the 'stop practising' rate is thought to be lower amongst this community; but it is still not zero. Christians who help to extract the persecuted from the Middle East should recognise that providing physical safety might come at the cost of spiritual practice. Yet there are cases where leaving the region is the only viable option. Pastoral sensitivity is required, and discernment of the truly genuine cases is frequently anything but simple.

Amidst the violence in cities such as Aleppo (since 2011) and Mosul (since 2014), a few Christians have chosen to remain, motivated by the desire to serve those who were unable or unwilling to leave. In situations of large-scale displacement, some people are physically unable to move – typically the elderly, the infirm or the very young. Those who choose to stay do so to continue caring for relatives or, in the case of priests, nuns and other church staff, to continue serving those communities of which they are an integral part.

In recipient locations, both in the Middle East and elsewhere, the opportunity beckons for Christians to set the culture and create a climate of welcome, respect, and embrace of those arriving. Likewise, when people are able to return there will be a great need for reconstruction, not just of buildings, but more significantly of communal harmony. There will be a great need for forgiveness and reconciliation, which will not be easy given the tendency of all too many people to hold grudges and seek revenge. The need to embrace pluralistic attitudes and to establish a culture of mutual respect will not be easily achieved. If this does not happen, further conflict is extremely likely. The Christian presence in the Middle East has been recognised and acknowledged by several political leaders in the Middle East as a crucial component of achieving communal harmony. Enabling Christians to remain is of critical importance to the future of the Middle East. The alternative to their remaining is that all people of goodwill who seek a better future for their families will be obliged to leave. As one analyst remarked, "A Middle East without the presence of recognised Christian communities should be a frightening prospect for all." The result of such a situation would be likely to make the migrant flows of 2015 and 2016 look small.

In supporting the displaced, we need to be aware that being well-meaning is necessary but not sufficient. Working amongst and alongside the forcibly displaced requires a degree of awareness about what these fellow human beings have experienced. Good preparation is essential and (fortunately) is increasingly widely provided by competent organisations.

These pages have included powerful examples of what some people will do *for* and *to* others; sacrifice and service have contrasted with cruelty and oppression. Good news can be found amidst the bad, although one often needs to search for it. More people need to consciously seek good news and not simply dwell on the bad. We need to be 'good news' people.

Appendix 1
RLP Policy statement – Relocation as a Response to Persecution

Adopted by the Religious Liberty Partnership in March 2011; modified and reaffirmed in March 2013; and modified and reaffirmed again in April 2017.

Context

- Christians in many parts of the world face continuing or increasing persecution – whether by State authorities, extremist groups, communities or families.

- In Scripture we see three main responses to pressure and persecution: to accept and endure (e.g. 2 Timothy 3:10-13), to challenge or resist (e.g. Acts 22:25-29), and to flee (e.g. Acts 9:23-25).

- Especially within the Middle East, those facing religious persecution, and those supporting them, are often quick to assume that relocation (i.e. fleeing or extraction) is the only viable option, or that it is the most appropriate response.

- Amongst church leaders across the Middle East there is a strong consensus that indigenous Christians should stay in their countries wherever possible, and where that is not possible, that they should stay within the region. Alongside their passionate pleas is the expressed desire to not be judgemental of those who choose to leave the region.

- Based on the testimony of Christians who have relocated from the Middle East, and on our experience of supporting those facing persecution, it is our firm conviction that hasty relocation outside of the region can be problematic both for the individual(s), families and communities concerned as well as for the wider church.

- As members of the **Religious Liberty Partnership** (RLP), we recognise the need to work collaboratively to meet the many support needs of those Christians persecuted because of their religious belief or practices and to nurture the continued presence and witness of the church where it is enduring persecution. We seek to follow the RLP Best Practices for Ministry to and with the Persecuted Church.[128]

Policy

We advise and assist Christians under persecution to relocate out of their country/region <u>only as a matter of last resort</u>, where no other viable options are available.

Commitment

In considering relocation as a response to religious persecution:

- We seek to understand and verify the nature of the situation before determining a response.
- We give due consideration to the advice of local church and ministry leaders and respond, where possible, with their authorisation.
- We acknowledge that some situations arise where people are obliged to make decisions on relocation in very short time frames; we will provide support as soon as we are able.
- We take account of medium- and long-term implications – both for the individuals, families

---

[128] Available on the RLP's website (www.rlpartnership.org).

and communities involved and for the church – as far as we are able.

- We consider in-country and in-region relocation options before pursuing out-of-region options.
- We collaborate with others to meet the many support needs of those facing persecution, whether they remain within their communities or are forced to relocate.
- We will contribute to the management of expectations regarding relocation by promoting a realistic understanding of the challenges involved so that those considering fleeing, together with those providing support, can make well-informed decisions.
- We will participate in analysis of the underlying causes of religious persecution and work with local Church leaders to identify and implement actions to mitigate the effects in the short term and address the causes in the longer term.

Rationale

Supporting healthy churches. We seek to support and foster the building up, not the depletion, of national churches in the Middle East – whether historical/recognised churches or the more recent church movements. In many countries in which the church is facing persecution, national church leaders have urged their Christian compatriots to remain in the country and not to emigrate. They recognise that, whenever possible, indigenous Christians should remain so that the church will continue as a witness to Christ and as a recognised part of a diverse society. The challenge to remain is especially great for the emerging communities of believers from non-Christian backgrounds who lack official recognition. The cycle of conversion-persecution-relocation must be broken if these communities are to flourish. The hasty relocation of Christians without realistic expectations or adequate planning also places a strain on the receiving church communities.

Promoting biblical perspectives. We seek to maintain and foster biblical perspectives on suffering and persecution within the worldwide church – including those supporting persecuted Christians. We may need to rethink our theology, recognising that being faithful followers of Jesus is not about avoiding persecution. We need to understand the different Biblical responses to persecution and depend on the Holy Spirit as we seek to discern the appropriate response in each situation.

Maintaining local witness. For some who face persecution, there may be appropriate ways in which they can manage relationships and adapt behaviour, work or patterns of religious meetings so that they can maintain a faithful witness while remaining in their location. Families and friends of those from non-Christian backgrounds are unlikely to be convinced of the relevance of a faith that divides and alienates family members.

Avoiding unintentional messages. By too readily or too hastily advising/assisting persecuted Christians to relocate to "the West," we can inadvertently send a signal that "the West" is in some way superior. This is an unhelpful attitude within the global church, and is sometimes promoted by those who have successfully settled in the West as well as by Westerners. We can also encourage spurious claims of religious persecution among those who may primarily be attracted by the lure of opportunity and material benefit they perceive elsewhere.

Prioritising local options. For those forced to flee because of threats to life or family, local (in-country or in-region) relocation options, where available, are typically more straightforward logistically, can be implemented more rapidly, are less costly financially, and involve less cultural adjustment than out-of-region relocation. It needs to be acknowledged that in-region options may be challenging to sustain in the longer term.

Advocating freedom of religion and belief. We believe that Christians together with all other religious communities should be afforded religious freedom. Such rights are described in the international covenants derived from the Universal Declaration of Human Rights (1948). We summarise religious freedom as the right to practice a religion of one's choosing alone or with others in private or public. Religious freedom should apply equally in communities of refugees and IDPs. We acknowledge that similar rights apply to adherents of non-religious belief systems and that such freedoms are derived from a number of basic rights including those of conscience, belief and assembly. We commit to advocating for freedom of religion and belief for all.

Promoting pluralistic societies. We recognise that the presence of indigenous Christian communities is part of the rich heritage of Middle Eastern countries. We believe that the creative dynamism that is typical of multi-ethnic and multi-religious societies enriches communities and nations. We acknowledge that some senior political leaders in the Middle East have recognised this, implicitly if not explicitly. For example, on 24th September 2014 King Abdullah of Jordan in an address to the UN General Assembly stated: "Let me say once again: Arab Christians are an integral part of my region's past, the present, and future."[129] President Sisi of Egypt has articulated his support for Egyptian Christians and demonstrated it by attending a service on 6th January 2015, Christmas Eve for Egyptian Christians. Such leaders are acknowledging that indigenous Christians enrich and promote cohesion within the societies of which they are a part. Some Middle Eastern writers have made similar statements.[130]

Supporting through partnering. Through partnership and cooperation, in-country or in-region alternatives can often be found, for example through short-stay, employment or study visas. If in-country or in-region options are not available, there may be viable options outside the region. Sometimes these

---

[129] King Abdullah's English language website; 24th September 2014; http://kingabdullah.jo/index.php/en_US/speeches/view/id/546/videoDisplay/0.html (accessed 5th August 2015)

[130] One example is Marwan Muasher's book *The Second Arab Awakening and The Battle for Pluralism* (2014, Yale University Press)

may not be long-term options (e.g. studying at a seminary or other theological institution) – but they leave more open the possibility of return (see below).

Meeting the range of support needs. In any case of relocation, it is vital that adequate attention be given to the wide range of support needs that arise for the individuals and their families – including spiritual, emotional/psychological, financial, medical, logistical, educational, occupational, etc. Through partnership and cooperation many of these needs can be met locally or in-region – sometimes more fully or adequately than out-of-region.

Recognising immigration challenges. Visa, immigration and asylum rules mean that out-of-region relocation is often time-consuming and challenging, with significant rates of non-acceptance, though work or study visas may be available for those with suitable qualifications. In particular, asylum/refugee systems and procedures are typically time-consuming (sometimes taking years), challenging (in terms of the necessary burden of proof), restrictive (for example, with limitations on movement or employment while awaiting determination of refugee status), and uncertain (there is a high rejection rate, with those rejected often then facing more severe pressure). For those who convert to Christianity we acknowledge that identifying genuine converts can be problematic for the authorities. We will assist wherever possible, providing honest assessments of their claims to have converted and what difficulties they may face if they were to return to their own country.

Recognising the scale of refugee movements. We acknowledge that many refugee systems have faced overwhelming demands and that the international community's long-standing failure to implement effective burden sharing mechanisms has strained the resources of those countries in the Middle East and elsewhere hosting large numbers of refugees. Consequently, we undertake to continuing pressing for local and international action to address the causes and effects of forced migration. We remain supportive of all efforts to resolve armed conflicts. We will continue to press for humanitarian support to be provided to all in need and to be supportive of the efforts of Christians throughout the Middle East actively engaged in such activities.

Acknowledging challenges for those who leave the region. Those who relocate outside their region often face significant challenges in adjusting – for example, to a new climate, language, culture and society, new temptations and even new church environments. Experience shows that there can be increased risk of some individuals falling away from Christian faith. For example, anecdotal evidence suggests that a majority of Middle Eastern Christians from non-Christian backgrounds who flee from persecution by relocating to "the West" end up losing their faith in their new location.

Maintaining the possibility of return. Relocation outside the region, especially if through asylum or refugee systems, is usually a long-term or permanent move. Even though some express a desire to return to their countries when the security situation allows, or are encouraged to do so, experience shows that very few in fact do so. Typically, viable in-country or in-region options leave more open the possibility of return. By leaving open the possibility of return for as long as possible, we also leave open to persecuted Christians the possibility for forgiveness and reconciliation with perpetrators, for the encouragement and strengthening of the local church, and for positive impact within their societies and nations through the presence and witness of the Church.

Relocating outside the region as a last resort. Although we advocate in-country or in-region relocation when it is necessary for Christians to flee, we recognise and affirm that it is sometimes appropriate and necessary for Christians to relocate outside their country or region, including through asylum/refugee systems. However, we affirm that out-of-region relocation should be the option of last resort. For those who have no option but to resort to asylum/refugee systems, these systems remain vital. We acknowledge that 'Western' countries have traditionally been the most generous in offering refugee resettlement and the best equipped to do so. We recognise that some countries in Asia, Africa and Latin America are involved in resettlement programmes. We commit to supporting those obliged to use asylum/refugee systems, and to seeking improvements to these systems.

Appendix 2
Do not prioritise Christians in refugee/asylum systems!

At various times since 2003 I have seen calls for Christians from certain countries in the Middle East to be helped to leave by giving them priority within refugee and asylum systems. In this appendix we look at where and why such calls emerge, what motivates them, and how they are heard across the Middle East.

What needs to be noted immediately is that such calls violate the Refugee Convention's injunction that eligibility and priority should be based on vulnerability. Discrimination on religious or other grounds violates Article 3 of the Convention. We might note that if a religious group is especially vulnerable, then members of that group may be given priority on vulnerability grounds, not on religious grounds *per se*.

Applying the rule in this way would mean assessing whether Christians were especially vulnerable. In areas affected by Daesh we have noted that the Shi'a would be the most vulnerable group, and I have heard of no calls to prioritise their resettlement in the West.

We have noted at several points that the consistent request of Christians leaders across the Middle East is that Christians should be enabled to remain, not helped to leave. Such calls often include considerations of pastoral sensitivity towards those Christians from the Middle East that have, or do choose, to leave.

The underlying agenda of Christians from the region needs to be heard carefully. There are a number of aspects to this.

One is that Christians from the region desire the clear rule of law to be applied equally to all, without discrimination on religious or other grounds. Such an undertaking is included in the constitution of most states, yet the practice is that there is discrimination.

The second is Christians from the region do not like use of the terms *majority* and *minority* in relation to religious demographics. In the Middle East, these terms set a context for conflict, for those who think they are a majority to oppress and exploit those who are different.

Thirdly, Christians from the region endeavour to keep in mind that Christianity originated in the Middle East. It is not a Western implant but an innate, long-standing part of the history, culture and society of the region. They desire to remain an integral part of societies, making their countries pluralistic for the benefit of all.

Finally, in the Syria section of Chapter 6, we quoted the Chaldean Bishop of Aleppo, who explained why calls for discrimination on religious grounds, from anyone, act to exacerbate the challenges faced by Christians in the Middle East.

Given the clear and consistent view of Christian leaders across the Middle East, why is it that some in the West call for the exact opposite?

Within Christian circles in the West one fears that all too many people have an inbuilt reaction along the lines of "poor them, let them come here," or more directly, "get them out of there." This overlooks the inevitable struggle that those who do migrate face in adjusting to Western societies which are very different to those in which they grew up. More significantly, that response overlooks an inherent characteristic of Christianity, which is that the faith is founded on following a suffering saviour who told his followers:

"I have told you these things, so that in me you may have peace. In this world you will have trouble. But take heart! I have overcome the world."[131]

This is not 'peace' in the sense of the absence of conflict. No; it is the deeper, fuller sense of knowing that one is loved and accepted by God and has a secure, eternal future with him.

I have heard one suggestion rooted in religious demographics which has been applied to France and other countries whose ethnically Arab residents are mostly from North Africa. These groups are overwhelmingly Muslim, and the countries in question would welcome some Arab Christians to adjust (enrich?) the demographic profile, a position which overlooks the fact that Arabs of different nationalities can have profound cultural differences.

Another argument concerns the integration of those who are accepted for resettlement in the West. This argument holds that Christians will integrate to the West better than Muslims. This is debatable, and needs much more sociological study, as both

---

[131] John 16:33

Christians and Muslims have faith communities that they can integrate into in most Western countries. Underlying this argument are concerns about Islamic radicalisation; but we have seen from the Syrian crisis that the greater risk of radicalisation is from nationals returning – as we also saw with the example of Tunisia in Chapter 8 – rather than from migrants entering the country.

We noted in Chapter 7 the UK's approach of accepting Syrians directly from camps in countries which neighbour Syria. One observation is that few Syrian Christians live in such camps. Consequently, the UK's policy might have a subtle bias against Christians; but I welcome this, since it is consistent with the requests of Syrian church leaders. As we noted in Chapter 7, the policy selects the most vulnerable people, and militates against people attempting hazardous and arduous journeys to and through Europe.

One aspect of the call from Christian leaders throughout the Middle East is for efforts to be focused on the causes of conflict, not solely on the resulting humanitarian needs. The latter will be never-ending if the former are neglected. How many citizens of the Middle East, of all faiths, do we want to become obliged to leave? How many are we willing to accommodate? What methods are we willing to permit our governments to employ, or to assist others in using, to stop irregular migrants reaching our communities?

In summary, Christian leaders across the Middle East are firmly opposed to prioritising Christians. The practice does not help the Church, exacerbates the discrimination they face, and deepens the pluralism deficit that is a key contributory cause of the Middle East's struggles.

For those whose primary agenda is to support the medium and long-term wellbeing of people and communities throughout the Middle East, the suggestion of prioritising Christians must be emphatically rejected. The same applies to any other community which is defined on religious grounds.

Appendix 3
A safe haven for Iraqi Christians on the Nineveh Plain?

In the Iraq section of Chapter 6 we remarked on the suggestion that an autonomous region for Christians might be created. Is this a viable possibility? What are the motivations behind such a suggestion? What practical considerations are relevant? What would such a region do for the culture and dynamism of Iraq?

Calls for the creation of an autonomous area for Christians have been made since the turmoil that followed the 2003 invasion. Prior to 2011, almost all such calls were made by Iraqis living abroad. In April 2011 more calls were made by Christians in Iraq, some of whom were members of parliament.[132] They wanted to create a safe area within the predominantly Arabic-speaking part of Iraq. The usual location mentioned in these suggestions is called the Nineveh Plain, part of Nineveh Province, to the north and east of the city of Mosul and bordering the provinces of

---

[132] Al-Arabiya; *Iraqi Christians demand an autonomous region*; 5th April 2011; www.alarabiya.net/articles/2011/04/05/144308.html (accessed on 8th December 2016)

Dohuk and Arbil, which are part of the Kurdistan Regional Government-administered area. Iraq's 2005 constitution includes provisions for the creation of autonomous zones, which would have similar status to the KRG region within the federal political structure of Iraq.

A modified proposal emerged during 2017, when a number of political parties presented a joint request to the KRG that the Nineveh Plain be granted administrative autonomy under the protection of the KRG's security services. This possibility emerges from the KRG's control of the area, which was achieved in its confrontations with Daesh. The status of such a development is debatable, since the KRG's control of the area arises from military conflict, not from due political and legal process. The proposal appears to be a pragmatic request that those displaced from the area should be given authority to rebuild their communities,[133] and such an initiative should be welcomed.

[133] Fides News Service; *Christian political parties insist: administrative autonomy for the Nineveh Plain*; 4th April 2017; www.fides.org/en/news/62063-ASIA_IRAQ_Christian_political_parties_insist_administrative_autonomy_for_the_Nineveh_Plain (accessed 5th May 2017)

This request applies for all residents of the Nineveh Plain; it is not limited to a call for special treatment for one religious group. Many Christians live in this area, as do Yezidis and adherents of several strands of Islam. Some of these people are ethnically Arabs, while others are Kurds or Turkmen. As such, the call for an autonomous Nineveh Plain is a call for good, clear administration of a multi-religious and multi-ethnic area. Such an area has the potential to model good governance of a pluralistic society. We saw a similar development in northeast Syria in Chapter 6, and it is an opportunity to create another part of the Middle East that functions for the benefit of diverse communities, modelling what is achievable elsewhere in the region.

It is clear that local authorities need to be able to determine the legitimate ownership of land, and administer planning permission for the construction of private property and public infrastructure. They need access to appropriate public funding and the mechanisms through which they can demonstrate good stewardship of the resources provided. Crucially, they need security services to ensure protection from attack, and the clear rule of law applied equally to all. At present these are being provided by the KRG, and the request is that this continues.

The previous suggestions of an autonomous area specifically for Christians need to be rejected, primarily because they are rooted in in the principle of segregation on religious lines. My previous book, *Identity Crisis*, argues that such segregation is one of the fundamental reasons why Middle Eastern societies are the way they are. Creating a region which is for Christians alone accepts and reinforces this narrative, and as such it cannot be part of the long-term solution to the social, economic and political issues of Iraq, or any other country in the Middle East.

Other reasons for rejecting the suggestion are that it could be construed as obliging all Iraqi Christians to move to the designated area, including those who have long been resident in Baghdad. They would need to sell their homes and businesses and relocate within Iraq. Such relocation would require the creation or improvement of infrastructure, including education facilities and public services to support those moving into the area. Conversely, what would become of the non-Christians living in the designated area? Would they be forced to leave, or allowed to remain? What rights would be given to those who remain? Would they be treated equally, or have a lower status than Christians in some senses? If they remain, in what sense would the area be 'Christian'? Furthermore, it is unclear what form of internal governance the area would have, how strong its law enforcement services would be, or how strong its relationships would be with the surrounding provinces and the national government in Baghdad. Finally, some are concerned that concentrating Christians in one geographical area would make them an easier target for anyone whose aim is to wipe out the Christian presence in Iraq.

What Iraq requires, post-Daesh, is good local governance that works for all residents of each area irrespective of the ethnic and religious identities of those present. Each area needs to provide a sense of security and of being part of a shared future. These local and regional arrangements need to be respected within a federal system. Providing such services, and making them widely trusted, is unlikely to be an easy task. Failure to achieve this is likely to lead to the emergence of some other group to seize control of those parts of Iraq that believe they are not being treated fairly by the central government.

One objective of the post-Daesh era must be to encourage those who have been displaced within and from Iraq to return. To do so, most will want to see military and law enforcement services that give assurance of safety from attack, and the clear rule of law applied equally to all. In April 2017 these services were being provided on the Nineveh Plain by the KRG, and the proposal was that this arrangement continued. The current arrangement is likely to be trusted by some, but not by all.

Within the wider context, something which is critical for the Kurds is the status of the city of Kirkuk, which many Kurds regard as their ancestral capital, and which has come under their protection since summer 2014. Consequently, the KRG is unlikely to agree to any changes to their recognised boundaries which do not include Kirkuk. The central government in Baghdad and the KRG have struggled to agree a process for addressing the status of Kirkuk or making any other changes to the KRG's area of jurisdiction.

Appendix 4
Deportation – why not just send people home?

In Western countries it is often asked why asylum seekers whose applications are rejected are not simply sent home. This appendix explains some of the factors that make sending people home both complex and problematic.

We will start with the story of someone who was 'sent home' or, more accurately, was 'taken home' but ended up where she started. As you read the following, keep in mind what it cost.

A European country decided to deport a failed asylum seeker, a convert from Islam to Christianity. Two officials flew with Sara (not her real name) back to her country. She had been absent for several years. She was denied entry, since her documents were out of date. The European officials escorting Sara took her to a neighbouring country, where they went to her country's embassy. That embassy was unable to provide the necessary documentation. The European officials took Sara back to their country. Sara was pleased to be back, but had been seriously stressed by the process.

This study illustrates a number of the complexities in the process of sending people home. Firstly, the problem of incomplete or out-of-date documents. Some desperate people deliberately destroy documents in order to complicate and delay their deportation; others have acquired false documentation – for example, Iraqis (and others) with fake Syrian passports, as we saw in Chapter 7.

Such considerations lead to the next potential pitfall: the home country may refuse to admit those who have been returned. Knowing where people are from is one thing; being able to demonstrate it beyond reasonable doubt is a greater challenge, and is essential for deportation.

One aspect of the EU's agreements with Turkey and Afghanistan is that they simplify the process of returning people. The EU's commitment is that it will only send people who it is sure are nationals; Turkey and Afghanistan have undertaken to accept the EU's decisions on this. The EU is endeavouring to establish similar arrangements with several African countries, as we discussed in Chapter 9.

So, in Sara's case, what were the costs? There is the human cost for Sara. There is also the human cost for the two officials who accompanied her, who were away from their homes and families. Then there are the financial costs for travel and accommodation while travelling, as well as food and drink for the three travellers. The flight costs may have been considerable.

We need to realise that deportations can be complex, time-consuming, expensive, and not always successful.

By contrast, I was at a European airport one evening taking a flight to Egypt. Two police officers arrived at the departure gate escorting two men. The men were shown onto the aircraft, and their passports handed to the chief cabin steward. The men were being deported. The existence of a direct flight simplified the process, and consequently the cost, of this.

There is a further reason why returning people to their own country is not always effective in the long term. I was told the story of a Sudanese man who was deported from Yemen. Six months later, his friends in Yemen were surprised to see him again. He explained that he had repeated his previous journey, by land to the Somali coast and then via sea crossing in a small boat. His desire to make a better life somewhere in the Arabian Peninsula was strong enough to motivate him to make the hazardous journey a second time.

For countries which are hosting failed asylum seekers, deportation is usually the option of last resort. Voluntary departures are much preferred, and a number of countries have offered incentives to migrants choosing this option: one example is France (see Chapter 7), while another is Israel's offer of incentives to Sudanese migrants.

Countries close to the source of forcibly displaced people are in some cases in an easier position when deporting people. They are much closer to the migrants' place of origin, making the transportation costs much lower. There is also the option of using mass transportation, which reduces the cost per person returned.

Alas, this proximity also creates opportunities to act in unscrupulous ways. I have heard two stories of situations involving Iran's treatment of some Afghans, and Jordan's treatment of some Iraqis. In Chapter 2 we noted that Iran hosted an estimated three and a half million Afghans, of whom one million had no official status. On occasions, some of these people were deported by being forcibly transported across the border into Afghanistan, apparently without the use of official crossings.

We noted in Chapter 6 that Jordan has hosted Iraqis since 2003. A small number of these were forcibly returned to Iraq, including some who had been granted refugee status by the UNHCR before the Jordanian authorities detained them during the evening and transported them to and across the border during the night. Those who were affected tried contacting the UNHCR, leaving messages on the answer phones. By the time the relevant offices opened the next day, those who had called were on the other side of the border.

Both examples are blatant violations of international norms. One hopes that they were isolated incidents, though there are undoubtedly similar stories of brutality by officials of other countries. One trusts that better management of the forcibly displaced, and increased burden sharing, will reduce the motivation for countries to act in such brutal and unjust ways. One also trusts that investigative journalists and NGOs active in supporting the displaced will continue to highlight abuses of power. We saw an example of this in Chapter 7 in Human Rights Watch's reports of attacks on boats between Turkey and Greece.

Abbreviations

AQIM	Al-Qaeda in the Islamic Maghreb
AU	African Union
EU	European Union
FBO	Faith Based Organisation
FoRB	Freedom of Religion or Belief
GCC	Gulf Cooperation Council
IDP	Internally Displaced Person
IDPs	Internally Displaced Persons
IOM	International Organisation for Migration
KRG	Kurdish Regional Government (Iraq)
NGO	Non-Governmental Organisation
RLP	Religious Liberty Partnership
UAE	United Arab Emirates
UK	United Kingdom
UN	United Nations
UNHCR	United Nations High Commission for Refugees
UNRWA	United Nations Relief and Works Agency for Palestine Refugees in the Near East
USA	United States of America
VEO	Violent Extremist Organisation

Glossary

Agnostic: someone who is undecided about the existence of God in the sense of a supreme personal being who has made himself known, to some extent, to mankind.

Alawite: a religious, and ethnic, group located in Lebanon, Turkey and Syria; some regard it as a branch of Shi'a Islam, others as a distinct religion.

Apostate: someone who has left Islam; whether they have become an adherent of another faith, an atheist or agnostic is irrelevant.

Arab League: a supra-national organisation whose membership includes the countries of the Arab world (see below) and a few closely related countries, including Djibouti and Somalia.

Arab Spring: a socio-political phenomenon that arose in 2011 affecting most countries in the Middle East, North Africa and the Arabian Peninsula, which was typified by protests which called for reform of governance structures, greater opportunity for all, and recognition of the dignity and worth of all citizens, and included calls for a reduction in – if not an end to – nepotism and corruption; subsequently referred to as the 'Arab Awakening' and the 'Arab Revolutions' by various commentators.

Arab world: those countries located in the Middle East, North Africa and the Arabian Peninsula where Arabic is a national language (and the mother tongue of many citizens); namely Algeria, Bahrain, Egypt, Iraq, Jordan, Kuwait, Lebanon, Libya, Mauritania, Morocco, Oman, Qatar, Palestine, Saudi Arabia, Sudan, Syria, Tunisia, United Arab Emirates (UAE) and Yemen; many citizens of these countries are not ethnically Arabic, e.g. the Kurds (see below), Druze and the various Berber peoples across North Africa; the term can suggest uniformity when the reality is diversity amongst these 19 states.

Armenian genocide: term used by some to describe events in 1914 and 1915 in which many Armenian people were murdered, forcibly displaced or died while fleeing from the Ottoman authorities.

Ash-Shabaab: an armed group that emerged in southern Somalia around 2006; predominantly Somali, although there are reports of foreign members, notably Pakistanis; has conducted operations in parts of Kenya; often referred to as al-Shabaab, although this violates the rules of Arabic grammar; literally, 'the youth'.

Asylum seeker: someone who applies to be allowed to remain in the country they are in because they are fearful of returning to their own country; many countries operate asylum systems; the UN operates a refugee system in countries which do not have an asylum system.

Atheist: someone who believes that there is no God in the sense of a supreme personal being.

Baha'i: a distinct religion that emerged out of Islam in the nineteenth century; its international headquarters are in Haifa, Israel.

Black market: economic activity outside normal accounting, audit and taxation systems; includes work performed by those who have no legal authority to work in the country where they are.

Black September: September 1970 in Jordan, when the Jordanian government used its army to force a large number of Palestinians to leave the country; most of the displaced moved through Syria to Lebanon, although some stayed in Syria; not to be confused with the Black September Organisation, an armed group of the same name active from September 1970 to September 1973.

Brain drain: the tendency for the brightest, most well educated and most well qualified people in a country to emigrate.

Camp: a place where a group of forcibly displaced people are living; some become de facto towns.

Camp David Accords: agreement between Egypt and Israel, negotiated in 1978 and formally signed in March 1979; key elements included the return of the Sinai Peninsula to Egypt, with the area being de-militarised.

Christian: a follower of Jesus Christ; an adherent to Christianity, taken to mean someone who would give assent to the Nicene Creed of 352; some such people do not use the term Christian to describe themselves (see Chapter 10).

Closed camp: a camp (see above) in which all residents are obliged to be officially registered and require a permit to leave the camp for any reason.

Daesh: an armed group that arose in Iraq before re-emerging in Syria; the group's original official title was The Islamic State of Iraq and ash-Sham; it is referred to as The Islamic State in Iraq and Syria (ISIS) and The Islamic State in Iraq and the Levant (ISIL) in some sources because the Arabic phrase Belad As-Sham can refer to Syria and also the entire Levant; the group re-titled itself The Islamic State in July 2014, while the term Daesh is used by many in the Middle East and is derived from an approximate acronym of the group's name in Arabic, *Dawleh al-Islamiya fi l'Iraq w'ash-Sham*.

Darfur: the western three provinces of Sudan, namely Northern Darfur, Western Darfur and Southern Darfur; literally, the land of the Fur people/tribe.

Deism: philosophical position asserting that a God does not interfere in creation.

Deportation: the process of removing someone from a country, usually by transporting them to a country in which they have nationality.

Diaspora: collective term for nationals of a country living in other countries.

Disputed territory: a geographic area whose sovereignty the UN regards as contested by two or more parties – either recognised states or bodies seeking recognition of statehood.

Displaced persons: asylum seekers, refugees and IDPs; people who have left their homes to seek shelter and safety elsewhere; sometimes more explicitly referred to as forcibly displaced persons.

Dublin Principle: within the EU, enacts the principle that people must apply for asylum status in the first member country that they enter.

Ecclesiology: part of Christian theology addressing the nature and understanding of Church, meaning being God's people; includes both being gathered together for worship and scattered amongst society.

Economic migrant: a person who has moved to a country of which they are not a citizen in search of work; upon securing employment they would be termed a migrant worker (see below); likewise should they establish themselves with self-employed status.

Expulsion: the removal from a country of a non-citizen who holds residency status; often those being expelled are given a defined short period in which to leave; sometimes implemented by denying re-entry to an expatriate resident who is returning from a period of time elsewhere.

Family reunification: concept that a migrant with residency in one country should be able to sponsor family members to join them; usually includes criteria to ensure that the resident has the financial means to support their relatives after reunification.

Fatah: political party in the West Bank and (to a lesser extent) the Gaza Strip; has an armed wing commonly referred to as the al-Aqsa Martyrs Brigade.

FBO: Faith Based Organisation, a type of NGO (see below) whose motivation and organisational and operational principles are rooted in a religious belief; many have charitable status; vary in size from individual local places of worship – churches, mosques, synagogues, etc. – to national and international organisations.

Female-headed household: a family unit comprising a woman and one or more children with no man present or able to provide for the family; often occurs due to the man having been killed; includes cases where a husband or father has left and is unable or unwilling to send financial support to his wife and children.

FoRB: Freedom of Religion or Belief; combines freedom of religion and freedom of conscience; recognises that proponents of belief systems such as humanism and secularism and adherents of religions utilise very similar aspects of international human rights, including rights to freedom of thought, belief, association and the press.

Forcibly displaced: a person who has migrated due to force of circumstances; includes those fleeing violent conflict and natural disasters.

GCC: Gulf Cooperation Council; a supra-national body comprising Bahrain, Kuwait, Oman, Qatar, Saudi Arabia and the United Arab Emirates (UAE).

Genocide: a crime defined in international law which covers the deliberate attempt to destroy in whole or in part a national, ethnic, racial or religious group; can be by murder, serious bodily harm, preventing births, forcibly transferring children to another group, or imposing conditions designed to bring about the destruction of the group.

Gentile: someone who is not a Jew.

Gulf States: the small countries of the Arabian Peninsula, usually taken to mean Kuwait, Bahrain, Qatar and the UAE; in some contexts it includes Oman; the term GCC (see above) would be used to include Saudi Arabia.

Hamas: a group in the West Bank and the Gaza Strip with political, social and military wings; founded in 1988; led by Khaled Mashal who lives in Qatar; Ismail Haniya, resident in the Gaza Strip, became leader of the political wing in May 2017.

Hezbollah: an organisation based in Lebanon with political, social service and military departments; most members are Shi'a (see below); led by Sheikh Hassan Nasrallah; literally, 'the party of God'; formed following Israel's invasion of Lebanon in 1982.

House church: a group of people who meet regularly in a home for worship, prayer, teaching and mutual encouragement; often indicates that there is no officially recognised place of worship in which they can meet; also referred to as a 'house fellowship'.

IDP: Internally Displaced Person; someone who has felt obliged to leave their home but remains within their own country.

Injil: name given by Muslims to what Christians call the New Testament

Inward investment: in economics, money from abroad which is used to start or expand commercial enterprises.

IOM: International Organisation for Migration, founded in 1951 to assist in resettlement programmes; it became a Partner Organisation of the UN during 2016.

Irregular migration: a term used to describe the movement of those who cross borders without using legally recognised points of entry or passport and visa systems; often applicable to the forcibly displaced; a deliberately gentler term than 'illegal migration'; includes those who formally register for refugee status and those who do not.

Isa: name of Jesus in the Injil (see above), and amongst many Muslims.

Jizya: financial system within Islam; it is a tax paid by non-Muslims only to the authorities in recognition that they are being provided protection and are not permitted to join the armed forces; spelt jizyah in some sources.

JCPOA: Joint Comprehensive Plan of Action; an agreement between Iran and the 'P5+1' group of nations (China,

France, Germany, Russia, the UK and the USA), signed in January 2016 under which Iran accepted greater monitoring and restrictions on its nuclear programme in exchange for economic sanctions being eased and international trade facilitated.

Kafala: system used in some countries under which employers sponsor the residency permits of their staff; one effect of this is to tie the employee to one employer, which reduces the rights of the employee; it often enables challenging poor working conditions and problematic treatment.

Kurd: member of an ethnic group with significant numbers in Iran, Iraq, Syria and Turkey; they are commonly regarded as the largest ethnic group in the world without a state; there are seven distinct dialects in the Kurdish language.

Kurdish Regional Government: a duly constituted body that governs three of Iraq's 18 provinces as an autonomous region within Iraq's federal structure; the provinces are Arbil, Dohuk and Suliamaniyah.

Levant: literally, the lands around Damascus; typically understood to mean modern day Iraq, Jordan, Lebanon and Syria; some usages include Israel, the West Bank and the Gaza Strip.

Migrant: someone who moves to another country in search of work and a better life; some migrants enter other countries legally as tourists or students, or due to visa-free travel. (Many countries have visa-free travel for certain other countries, e.g. Turkey and Iran, the USA and Canada; the EU is the largest grouping of countries with such a system).

Migrant worker: a person working in a country other than their own; includes those with employment and those who are self-employed.

Mizrahim: ethnically Jewish Israeli citizens whose families lived in predominantly Arab countries prior to emigrating to Israel.

Nahr al-Bared: one of 12 Palestinian camps in Lebanon, located near to Tripoli; scene of violent clashes involving the army and members of an armed group, May to September 2007.

Nakba: Arabic term used by Palestinians to describe the forced displacement of Palestinians in 1947 and 1948 during the creation of the state of Israel; literally, *catastrophe.*

New York Declaration: issued on 19th September 2016 at the conclusion of a UN summit on migration; it covers regular and irregular migration.

NGO: Non-Governmental Organisation, usually a charity or not-for-profit organisation; such entities are independent of any government control, although they do have to ensure due legal compliance with the laws of the country in which they are registered, and all countries in which they are operating.

Nineveh Plain: geographic area of Iraq close to the city of Mosul and bordering the provinces of Arbil and Dohuk, which are administered by the Kurdish Regional Government.

Palestinian: an ethnic group, part of the Arab peoples; the name is derived from the Philistines, although the people are not their descendants, since the Palestinians are a Semitic people and the Philistines were not.

Patron: one who provides resources and opportunities in return for loyalty; see the Saudi Arabia section of Chapter 4.

Patronage: system in which people are dependent on the services of a patron for social and economic advancement and security.

People smuggler: someone who assists another person to cross one or more international borders illegally, for financial or other material gain.

People trafficker: someone who takes another person from one location to another without their consent; can apply within country as well as to those who cross national borders; applies to anyone escorting minors who does not have the consent of their legal guardian(s).

Pluralism: (a) the view that diverse groups can live well together in society by acknowledging and celebrating their ethnic, linguistic, religious and other differences; (b) belief in the validity of a diversity of views and practices, demonstrated by a conscious effort to understand each other's point of view. The former is corporate and generally passive, the latter is personal and active.

Pluralism deficit: the absence, in part or whole, of pluralism; often characterised by the suppression of those who are different from the norm either ethnically or religiously; common indicators of a pluralism deficit are the existence of discrimination in education, public sector employment, public services, and planning permission (both in general and specifically for places of worship) – these indicators can occur within legal frameworks; a pluralism deficit can also occur in the attitudes and actions of local officials, sometimes in violation of the law.

Polisario: a movement seeking independence for Western Sahara, an area between Morocco and Mauritania that the UN regards as a disputed territory.

Protected status: recognition that a refugee/asylum seeker cannot safely return at this time, but that it is expected that they will be able to do so at some point in the foreseeable future.

Pull factor: circumstances that make a particular destination attractive to those considering migrating.

Push factor: circumstances that prompt people to consider leaving their present situation.

Refoulement: forcibly returning a person to a place where it is certain or likely that they will face threats to their life or liberty.

Refugee: someone whose application for refugee status has been accepted by the UN; at this point they become eligible for resettlement (see below).

Refugee Convention: the UN Refugee Convention of 1951, plus the additional Protocol of 1967 (see Chapter 9); of the members of the Arab League (see above), Algeria, Egypt, Israel, Mauritania, Morocco, Somalia, Sudan, Tunisia, and Yemen are state parties; whereas Bahrain, Iraq, Jordan, Kuwait, Lebanon, Libya, Oman, Qatar, Saudi Arabia Syria and UAE are not state parties; Iran and Turkey are state parties.

Refugee seeker: someone who has applied to the UN for protection because they believe they cannot go home; the criteria for acceptance to refugee status are: (i) fear of loss of life or liberty; (ii) evidence to support such a fear; and (iii) that their own government is unable or unwilling to protect them.

Regular migration: a term used to describe those who cross borders using legally recognised points of entry, and passport and visa systems; it contrasts with *irregular migration* (see above); includes tourists and migrant workers.

Religious registration: system in which all citizens are registered as belonging to one of a defined set of religious communities; determines which religiously-based legal system is applicable for marriage and other matters of family status.

Remittances: money sent to family members by those working abroad.

Resettlement: the process of finding for a refugee (see above) a country that is willing to accept them with a view to granting them citizenship.

Salafi: a puritanical form of Sunni Islam; has several distinct forms – see Jonathan Andrews' *Identity Crisis* (2016, Gilead Books Publishing), Appendix 3.

Saudi-isation: policies and programmes of the government of Saudi Arabia aimed at boosting employment of nationals and reducing the number of migrant workers in the country; became a little more formalised as Vision 2030 in April 2016.

Schengen Area: European countries with no controls over their common borders; an EU mechanism that includes many but not all EU member states, plus some non-member countries – for example, Norway and Switzerland are within the Schengen Area but are not EU members, whilst Cyprus, Ireland and (at the time of writing) the UK are EU members, but not part of the Schengen Area.

Shi'a: a strand within Islam; the adjective form is Shi'ite.

Six Day War: a conflict which lasted from 5th to 10th June 1967, involving Israel and an alliance of Egypt, Jordan and Syria; it ended with Israel having taken control of the Sinai Peninsula (which was returned to Egypt under the Camp David Accords), the Gaza Strip, the West Bank including East Jerusalem, and approximately 70% of the Golan Heights.

Smuggler: see people smuggler, above.

Stateless: a person who is not a national of any state.

State party: a country that has formally endorsed a UN convention (in this book, the Refugee Convention); states must formally endorse each UN covenant or convention on a particular area of human rights.

Sunni: a strand within Islam.

Sunni Awakening: an initiative in Iraq in 2006 which significantly reduced sectarian violence in Sunni-majority areas of western Iraq by encouraging improved relationships between local communities and the central government in Baghdad.

Trafficker: see people trafficker, above.

Transit country: a country crossed by a migrant on their journey in which they have no intention to remain any longer than necessary.

Urbanisation: the movement of population from living in rural to urban settings; it has strong links to modernisation and industrialisation; it has major implications for economics, and for public planning and public services such as education and health care.

UNHCR: United Nations High Commission for Refugees, the body that operates the international refugee system; also referred to as the UN Refugee Agency; founded in 1950, replacing several predecessor bodies; the head of the UNHCR is sometimes referred to as the United Nations High Commissioner for Refugees, which also abbreviates to UNHCR.

UNRWA: United Nations Relief and Works Agency for Palestine Refugees in the Near East; provides education, health care and social services to Palestinians displaced by events surrounding the creation of the state of Israel in 1948 and their descendants; founded in 1949; mandate renewed every three years by the UN General Assembly.

UN Refugee Agency: see UNHCR.

VEO: violent extremist organisation, also referred to as an armed group or (in some circles) 'terrorist group'.

Voluntary return: returning to one's country of origin; it automatically invalidates any refugee or asylum application or status.

West: or The West, a geopolitical term meaning Europe, North America and Australasia.

World Refugee Year: June 1959 to June 1960; designated by the UN to draw particular attention to refugees in Europe, the Middle East, and China, and encourage more UN members to ratify the 1951 UN Refugee Convention.

Yezidi: a Kurdish community whose distinct monotheistic religious beliefs are derived from Zoroastrianism and ancient Mesopotamian religions; most are located in northern Iraq, with small numbers in Syria and amongst Kurdish diasporas................

For Further Reading

Albright (2006): Madeleine Albright; *The Mighty and the Almighty*; MacMillan

Andrew and Janssen (2007): Brother Andrew and Al Janssen; *Secret Believers*; Hodder & Stoughton

Andrews (2016): Jonathan Andrews; *Identity Crisis – Religious Registration in the Middle East*; Gilead Books Publishing

Axworthy (2008): Michael Axworthy; *Iran, Empire of the Mind*; Penguin

Boyd-MacMillan (2006): Ron Boyd-MacMillan; *Faith that Endures*; Sovereign World

Chapman (2015): Colin Chapman; *Whose Promised Land?* (fifth edition); Lion Hudson

Fisk (2001): Robert Fisk; *Pity the Nation* (third edition); Oxford University Press

Hampton (2016): Anna Hampton; *Facing Danger: A Guide Through Risk*; Zendagi Press

Hurst (2010): David Hurst; *Beware of Small States – Lebanon, Battleground of the Middle East*; Faber and Faber

Kendal (2016): Elizabeth Kendal; *After Saturday Comes Sunday*; Resource Publications

Micklethwait and Wooldridge (2009): John Micklethwait and Adrian Wooldridge; *God is Back*; Penguin

Muasher (2014): Marwan Muasher; *The Second Arab Awakening and The Battle for Pluralism*; Yale University Press

Naylor (2015): Chris Naylor; *Postcards from the Middle East*; Lion Hudson

Newton (2015): John Newton; *Religious Freedom Today – The Catholic View*; Catholic Truth Society

Parker (2001): Russ Parker; *Healing Wounded History*; D.L.T.; republished in 2012 by SPCK Publishing

Phillips (2016): Christopher Phillips; *The Battle for Syria: International Rivalry in the New Middle East*; Yale University Press

Pinnock (2001): Clark Pinnock; *Most Moved Mover*; Paternoster

Ripken (2013): Nik Ripken; *The Insanity of God*; B&H Publishing Group

Rostampour and Amirizadeh (2013): Maryam Rostampour and Marziyeh Amirizadeh; *Captive in Iran*; Tyndale

Rogan (2012): Eugene Rogan; *The Arabs: A History, Second Edition*; Penguin Books

Smith (2016): Dave Smith; *Refugee Stories – seven personal journeys behind the headlines*; Instant Apostle

Sookhdeo (2014): Patrick Sookhdeo (editor); *The Essential Guide for Helping Refugees*; Isaac Publishing

Spencer (2004): Nick Spencer; *Asylum and Immigration*; Paternoster

Tinti and Reitano (2016): Peter Tinti and Tuesday Reitano; *Migrant, Refugee, Smuggler, Saviour*; Hurst Publishers

Verwer (2015): George Verwer; *More Drops – Mystery, Mercy, Messiology*; CWR